Mothering and Blogging

The Radical Act of the Mommyblog

Demeter Press
726 Atkinson College, York University
4700 Keele Street
Toronto, Ontario M3J 1P3
Telephone: (416) 736-2100 x 60366
Email: arm@yorku.ca Web site: www.yorku.ca/arm

Demeter Press logo based on Skulptur "Demeter" by Maria-Luise Bodirsky <www.keramik-atelier.bodirsky.edu>

Cover Art: Tiffany Ard, "Blue egg, view from my cave," watercolour, 5" x 7", 2008.

Cover Design/Interior Design: Luciana Ricciutelli

Printed and Bound in Canada

Library and Archives Canada Cataloguing in Publication

Mothering and blogging : the radical act of the mommyblog / edited by May Friedman and Shana L. Calixte.

Includes bibliographical references.
ISBN 978-1-55014-488-8

1. Motherhood—Blogs—Social aspects. 2. Parenting—Blogs—Social aspects. 3. Blogs—Social aspects. I. Friedman, May, 1975- II. Calixte, Shana L., 1976-

HQ759.M8835 2009   306.874'3028567   C2009-901685-0

Mothering and Blogging

The Radical Act of the Mommyblog

Edited by
May Friedman and Shana L. Calixte

DEMETER PRESS
TORONTO, CANADA

Table of Contents

Acknowledgements

We began our exploration of the topic of mothering and blogging the way collaborators sometimes do—over endless cups of tea and exclamations of shared experiences. As we grew closer as friends and colleagues, we also grew literally, over burgeoning bellies as we progressed through simultaneous pregnancies. We held "book meetings" while breastfeeding, discussed content while shushing babies, and pushed the book into the world while doing the very tangible work of mothering.

This book has been a real labour of love for us, with many fantastic doulas and midwives along the way. In particular, we would like to thank Andrea O'Reilly, head of the Association for Research on Mothering (ARM) and Editor-in-Chief of Demeter Press, for allowing us the opportunity to explore this exciting topic. We appreciate the tireless patience of Renée Knapp (ARM goddess extraordinaire) with our endless enquiries, and want to thank Luciana Ricciutelli for her contributions to the book's design. Tiffany Ard, an exceptional mommyblogger in her own regard, took our half-formed ideas and turned them into a wonderful cover for this book.

Without the exceptional people we have encountered online, there would be no book. Our participation in the mamasphere has enriched both our lives. In particular, Shana would like to thank the various lesbian/queer folks online who provided support for five years as she charted, inseminated, got pregnant, gave birth, and reared children, while May appreciates the honesty and candidness of the many mommybloggers who have allowed her to timidly lurk around their lives.

Lastly, we want to acknowledge the contributions (and interruptions!) of our families: Dan, Noah and Molly; and Jen and Leandré. Without you this book would have gotten finished a whole lot faster, but we would have had a lot less to say.

Foreword

Small World: Maternal Blogging, Virtual Friendship, and the Computer-Mediated Self

JUDITH STADTMAN TUCKER

> Yay! I am finally blogging ... I have been stalking other blogs and am riveted by the writers ... their honesty, their friendships, their camaraderie ... all of it. Now, it is my turn to join the club ... OK, this blog may be simple—but it is mine and I really hope someone reads it and maybe even reads it again and maybe someday some-body new will stalk my blog.... (*BlogHer*, "One Really Happy Hen..." August 29, 2007)

Initially dismissed as the "inconsequential chatter" of an unorthodox clique of techno-geeks, today the "blogging revolution" is hailed as a mainstream trend (*CNN.com*, "Blogging goes mainstream," March 10, 2003; *Wired.com*, "The Blogging Revolution," May 2002). In light of the actual penetration of blogging into contemporary life—as I write this, only ten percent of Internet users in the United States read weblogs on a daily basis, and one in five do not know what a "blog" is[1]—reports that the explosive growth of the blogosphere has transformed popular and political culture may be exaggerated. In reality, the eruption of blogging as a mass medium is so new that popular spellchecking programs flag the word "blogger" (*Boston.com*, "E-male," August 10, 2007). Nevertheless, millions of North Americans would agree with the *BusinessWeek.com* reporter who observed, "It's hard to imagine the world without blogs" ("The Future of the Blog," February 24, 2006).

Although blogging is celebrated as a new breed of upstart journal-ism, the massive stream of computer-mediated communication (CMC) known as the "blogosphere" is principally a repository for tens of mil-lions of first-person monologues on the subject of everyday life. While major media highlight the activities of top-ranking political bloggers, only eleven percent of U.S. bloggers write about public issues as a main topic. According to the Pew Internet and American Life Research Center, one-half of all bloggers write mostly for their own enjoyment, not to attract an audience. The majority (77 percent) use blogging as an outlet for creative self-expression and to share personal stories. A minority of U.S. bloggers—just 13 percent—say blogging is an important part of their lives. [2]

Blogging's reputation as an avant-garde and potentially disruptive medium is due partly to its accessibility—in under an hour, anyone with the inclination and an Internet connection can create a weblog for all the wired world to see—but also reflects a fascination with the bewildering diversity of online subcultures the blogging craze has spawned. Given the ease and appeal of blogging as a means of developing—or reclaiming—a unique, subjective voice as inspiration and time allow, it's not surprising that thousands (perhaps even tens of thousands)[3] of North American mothers are adding their perspectives on motherhood, mothering, and domestic life to the virtual mix.

Why mothers blog is not a very provocative question. Like most personal bloggers, mothers blog because they can, and because they hope to gain something from it. That "something" could include connecting with like-minded mothers in the digital sphere, carving out a virtual room of one's own, or experiencing the liberating sensation of letting it all hang out, online—to list just a few possibilities. Moreover, well-educated, professional-class mothers—whose voices tend to dominate the maternal blogosphere—are accustomed to full participation in cultural life, and blogging may fortify or restore a sense of visibility (Stadtman Tucker 2001).

A more interesting area of inquiry is *how mothers experience blogging* as a creative and social practice. As with other public and private aspects of motherhood, the practice and experience of maternal blogging is shaped by preexisting structures and cultural norms as well as mothers' intentions and fantasies. With that in mind, we might ask: What factors influence mothers' expectations and experience of blogging as a rewarding practice? How do mother-bloggers replicate and resist the received culture of the blogosphere? How does blogging technology create new opportunities for, and impose limits on, maternal narrative and self-presentation? Are the technical and social conventions of blogging consistent with its idealization as an emancipatory or subversive practice? How do real world barriers to inclusion based on race, class, ethnicity, ability, and sexual identity intersect with blogging as a maternal activity? To answer these questions, let's begin at the beginning.

The Evolution of Blogging Culture, 1.0: The Primordial Soup

*No single metaphor completely conveys the nature of cyberspace.
Virtual communities are places where people meet, and they are
also tools.*
　　　　　　　　　　　　　—Howard Rheingold (45)

The idiosyncratic culture of the blogosphere is rooted in the technical, commercial, and social evolution of the Internet itself. Originally designed to prevent an interruption of defense communications during a catastrophic nuclear attack, the Internet gradually emerged as a site of social interaction as members of the technology community tweaked or developed programs to enhance user-to-user communication. Although non-institutional users could access networked communication services as early as the mid-1980s, Internet adoption remained low: as late as 1989, only nine percent of U.S. adults reported using a computer outside of school or work, and fewer than six percent of home users sent email or visited online bulletin boards (U.S. Census Bureau 1991).

Although mainly the province of a small population of technically-adept users (affectionately known as "freaks and geeks"), a variety of online communication forums were available in the 1980s and early 1990s, including electronic bulletin boards (BBS), real-time chat (IRC), networked discussion groups (Usenet), and interactive, text-based virtual worlds known as MUDs ("Multi-User Domains") and MOOs (a version of MUD). Concurrent with this activity was the intellectual construction of "cyberspace" as a new, untamed frontier—an unregulated expanse where reality is infinitely flexible and fluid rules of self-presentation allow net-goers to shed the dreary trappings of their embodied, "meat world" identities.

Articulations of cyberspace as a site of emancipation were informed by poststructural theories that captivated the techno-intelligentsia of the day. As Stephen Doheny-Farina writes in *The Wired Neighborhood*, "The net is often characterized as the proving ground of the postmodern self: a self that is fragmented, every changing, ambiguous, and perhaps even liberated.... Individuals are disembodied, and, in theory, unbound by the body's constraints" (65). However, early scholarship on Internet culture recognized that at a utilitarian level, "Internet itself is part of everyday life; it is part of the most banal aspects of social interaction" (Argyle and Shields 58), and acknowledged that relationships forged in virtual communities have embodied, and sometimes painful, emotional consequences (Argyle 139-140). Of all the theory and folklore surrounding the emergence of cyberculture, the image of the online social sphere as "a unique place that allows for the transgression of cultural rules, the breaking of taboos, the freedom to express what you need to, when you need to" (Argyle 137) had the strongest sticking power in the public mind.

Spurred by a convergence of technological breakthroughs and regulatory changes—including the development of the electronic transfer protocol for the World Wide Web (1990-1993), the release of the first web browser with a graphic user interface (1993), and lifting of restrictions on commercial use of the Internet (1995)—online activity by non-institutional users rose rapidly in the late 1990s. In 1997, 56.4 million U.S. adults (41 percent) owned home computers, and 44 percent used the Internet (U.S. Census Bureau 1999). By 2007, 71 percent of U.S. adults were spending time online.[4] Lee Rainie and John Horrigan of the Pew Internet project report that the Internet—and more explicitly, web access[5]—has fundamentally transformed civic and private life in the industrialized world: "The Internet has reached into—and, in some cases, reshaped—just about every important realm of modern life. It has changed the way we inform ourselves, amuse ourselves, care for ourselves, educate ourselves, work, shop, bank, pray and stay in touch" ("A decade of adoption," January 25, 2005).

The web's defining feature—the ability to insert hypertext links pointing to external references into user-created content—also presented new possibilities for forming online social networks. "I saw the Web as not just a many-to-many multimedia broadcasting medium, but as a social medium," writes Internet pioneer Howard Rheingold. "The first time I saw the Web, I wanted to create communities there" (334).

The Evolution of Blogging Culture, 2.0: The Fossil Record

> My "You Blogroll Me and I'll Blogroll You" blogroll seemed like a good idea at the time.... But now? I'm buried.... AND I don't want to hurt anyone's feelings by removing them from my (immensely-growing) blogroll. Because I'm sensitive like that, ya' know. (*In the Trenches of Mommyhood*, "Blogroll Blabber," August 28, 2007)

Like the culture and practices of the CMC forums that predated it, the rise of the weblog—and the development of blogging technology—were driven by the intellectual culture and social imaginary[6] of a wired elite comprised of university students, academics, and professionals in the emerging technology industry.

Personal websites featuring an eclectic combination of news, opinion, practical advice, and the owner's random reflections on the absurdity of life have been around since 1994, but blogging aficionados date the birth of the proto-blogosphere—which consisted of fewer than 100 hand-crafted weblogs—between 1996 and early 1999 (Blood 8). The adoption of the classic weblog format was partly a response to the sudden influx of online content—including a profusion of bland commercial fare and folksy personal home pages—that inundated the World Wide Web in the late 1990s. In the years leading up to the introduction of efficient search engine technology, a subset of high-frequency Internet users resorted to trolling the web for exceptionally relevant, weirdly amusing, or one-of-a-kind resources, creating no-frills web pages, or "microportals," to save and share their finds. "The weblog," wrote Julian Dibbel in 2001, "reflects our own attempts to assimilate the glut of immaterial data loosed upon us by the 'discovery' of the networked world" (73).

A typical weblog entry provided one or more links to external sites with a short description or comment about the source. New additions appeared at the top of the page; older entries were preserved as an archive. Separate entries were usually identified by date, or the blog owner might add a title and insert idle musings, arcane insights, or waggish observations about current events and daily life. Digital technology and tech culture were popular topics of discussion—people who published weblogs during this period were employed almost exclusively in the Internet industry, although a few were journalists and technology writers who picked up coding skills. Most were men, but a handful of women also produced well-respected blogs.

Since dynamic applications for adding reader comments did not yet exist, early bloggers conducted cross-blog conversations by writing a response, question, or comment on their own home page with a link back to another blogger's post. Originally an adaptation to the limitations of web technology, the tradition of "blogrolling" and spreading "linky love"—insider slang for reciprocal linking—is now considered a basic and indispensable practice of blogging. Pioneering bloggers used cross-referencing and reciprocal linking to demonstrate goodwill or snub other bloggers (Mead 49-50), a practice that continues today.

In the second half of 1999, several developers released commercial web applications empowering web surfers with no technical expertise to create online diaries or simple blogs—one popular version, Blogger, advertised its product as "Push Button Publishing for the People." At the end of 1999, there were an estimated 400 blogs (Rhodes 102); by October 2004, there were four million (*Sifry's Alerts*, "State of the

Blogosphere," October 10, 2004). Even before blogging started to attract a mass audience, the blogging community sorted into its characteristic status hierarchy of superstars, insiders, outsiders, and nobodies (most bloggers today, and nearly all personal journal-style bloggers, occupy the last category).

"The myth, of course, holds that all bloggers are equal, because we can all set out our wares on the great egalitarian Internet, where the best ideas bubble to the surface," wrote blogger Joe Clark in 2002. "...The reality is rather different" (60). Denouncing the "unbearable incestuousness" of early blogosphere, Clark complained that

> The nominal purpose of Weblogs is to point out links of inter-
> est.... But since so many leading Weblogs are written by folks
> in the Internet biz, their entire lives are online. You can write up
> what you did with your real-life friend yesterday, but you can't
> link to that experience. You ... link to what your online friend
> blogged yesterday. (59)

Stress on the importance of cultivating an original, unfiltered voice encouraged the formation of status hierarchies and cults of personality in the early blogosphere. Although bloggers debated whether form or content were more determinative of "what makes a blog a blog," voice and personality were considered paramount. Dave Winer, credited as the author of one of the earliest blogs, concluded, "It wasn't so much the form, although most blogs seem to follow a similar form, nor was it the content, rather it was the voice.... If it was one voice, unedited, not determined by group-think—then it was a blog, no matter what form it took" (*Scripting News*, "The unedited voice of a person," January 1, 2007). Other bloggers defined blogs as "an interactive extension of who you are" (*CamWorld*, "More About Weblogs," May 11, 1999), or "a form of exteriorized psychology ... a part of you, or of your psyche" (Clark 68). Seasoned bloggers advised newcomers to "post unique original stuff and people will notice you," but cautioned, "If you are doing this for reasons other than personal satisfaction, chances are you will be disappointed" (Metascene 150).

Blogging as a Form: Medium Versus Message

> Over the years, mommybloggers have been accused of being
> everything from being boring and fluffy—lacking substance—to
> narcissistic and self-absorbed. Actually, I find that to be the excep-

tion rather than the rule. I read many, many mommyblogs every week. Rarely—if ever—do I leave a blog without a story. A story about a family, a person, a child or a life that has been changed. (*Blogher*, "Mommybloggers—and More," April 30, 2007)

As a form of personal writing, blogging has been compared to diary-keeping, letter-writing, pamphleteering, talk radio, and memoir. But unlike the writing and broadcast genres that prefigure it, blogging—as a practice and medium—is unique in its digital dependency. When the first weblogging tools were developed, functionality followed form—applications such as Blogger were designed to automate what bloggers were already doing through a more laborious process. Although the founding bloggerati actively discussed the nature and value of blogging, there was less deliberation about the potential limitations of the format itself, particularly whether an embedded emphasis on the new, the ephemeral, and the episodic conflicts with the defense of blogs as socially significant texts (as opposed to navel-gazing or pointless blather).

Nor was attention given to the possibility that the social and intellectual homogeneity of the proto-blogging community would give rise to standards—including a preference for brevity, the centrality of cross-linking, the reduction of navigation cues, and the fixed display of text in reverse chronological order—which, once encoded into the blogging format, might variously inspire, frustrate, or dictate the self-presentation of non-technical users as they re-purposed the blogging template to meet their needs. The unspoken premise of blogging is that depth and context are expendable, because everyone understands what you're talking about and why it matters. In this paradigm, authority is derived from presentation, and substance is optional.

The primacy of voice over context—and obstacles to sustained storytelling created by the reverse chronological ordering of entries—is especially germane for bloggers who try to refashion blogging as an outlet for maternal narrative. Unlike conventional websites which can be adapted to mimic print genres associated with formal narrative writing, the blog template obligates readers to start at the end of the story every time they visit a blog. The blog writer, on the other hand, may envision her project as a coherent (if perpetually unfinished) self-portrait that tracks to a clear storyline. For better or worse, weblog structure—as well as received elements of blogging culture—favor the representation of maternal experience as a series of casual, disjointed events, rather than as a connected, complex whole. The requirement that new readers should be instantly familiar with—and ideally, sympathetic to—the context of the mother blogger's unfurling narrative facilitates the transfer of mainstream metaphors and representations of motherhood into the culture of the "mamasphere," and results in a preponderance of similar voices among top mom blogs.

The effect of imposed norms on the practice and content of motherhood blogs may explain the discrepancy between passionate accounts of maternal blogging as an empowering and even transformative endeavor, and reactions of uninitiated observers (meaning, everyone who's not an active writer or consumer of mother-made blogs) who disparage "mommyblogs" as plodding and self-indulgent. "Mother blogs are real, raw and authentic," writes blogger Ann Douglas. "Their content isn't sliced, diced, homogenized and filtered through the mainstream parenting media.... They reflect the reality—and the messiness—of real life, with kids. Hearing about the experiences of other parents can be tremendously affirming and empowering" (*The Mother of All Blogs*, "Mothering in the Age of the Blog," October 28, 2006).

David Hochman, reporting for the *New York Times*, is less enthused: "The world's most thankless occupation, parenthood, has never inspired so much copy. For the generation that begat reality television it seems that there is not a tale from the crib (no matter how mundane or scatological) that is unworthy of narration."

It's a suitably postmodern quandary that both appraisals may be equally true. For those immersed in the mamasphere, writes Andrea Buchanan, motherhood blogs are a rich source of affirming, authentic stories and invigorating social interactions (*Mothers Movement Online*, "The Secret Lives of Mothers," February 2006). To the rest of the world, motherhood blogs—and personal blogs in general—may seem insipid, irrelevant, and not worth seeking out. "The Internet was hyped for years as the tool that would put mass communication back in the hands of the common man," blogs a writer on the technoculture site, *KuroShin*. "Unfortunately, it turned out that the common man really had nothing to say.... Nobody wants to know about what kind of toothpaste you use, what your mood icon looks like at the moment, or how sorry you are for not updating your site regularly" ("Web Logs Suck," April 21, 2001).

Blogging as Community: "I Wish I Was There to Help You and Hold Your Hand"

> I can be a friend to someone on the Internet ... but I can't take them a casserole when they're sick. I can't drive her to a medical appointment. I can't watch her kids for a few hours so she can go

spend some time wandering in a bookstore. I can't do anything practical to make the things that hurt in her life any better. I can read. I can respond ... in words. That's all. *(BlogRhet,* "How to measure the utility function of the Internet," August 31, 2007)

I think I became too accustomed to the Internet having my back, as you'd say, and when there was no comment in over 24h I was devastated ... I felt like all the people who once read and helped keep me afloat were no longer around and would soon forget, I felt no one cared anymore ... it's not like I ever had that many comments - but I became used to a certain amount of them, to certain people, and once they started dwindling I felt like I was talking to myself ... If someone had told me years ago that I'd be sad bcs my computer doesn't seem to talk back to me anymore I'd have laughed in your face. *(Kvetch,* "I have just disabled my comments..." August 24, 2007)

An often-cited bonus of maternal blogging is the sense of community created by casual cross-talk between mother-bloggers and their core audience (which, given the significant overlap between blog-readers and blog writers, is mainly comprised of other mother-bloggers). Loyal readers also offer support—usually of the emotional variety, but sometimes extending into the real-world—when mothers blog about difficult transitions or personal crises.

Typically, readers respond with words of sympathy, sometimes adding an expressed desire for embodied connection. When the author of *IzzyMom* blogged about her husband's email affair with an ex-girlfriend, readers offered an outpouring of support and advice ("Betrayed," August 30, 2007). "I am available to you on so many levels including beyond these bytes and into meatspace," writes a reader who identifies herself as an "admiring fan and friend." "If you need to come out to California to chill, our home is big, in the woods and near the beach ... you'll get your own bedroom, robe, a new toothbrush and we'll go for spa treatments." Another reader responds, "I wish I was there to help you and hold your hand...." It's worth noting that in the middle of this emotionally-charged exchange (the "Betrayed" post received 178 comments), a novice blogger left a comment asking *IzzyMom* to link to her blog.

Although a relatively recent addition to the basic arsenal of blogging tools, the comment feature—a dynamic application that lets readers add a personal response to the end of a particular blog entry—is considered essential to promoting social interaction in the blogosphere. As with other blogging standards and practices, the comment feature is a mixed blessing. Posting comments allows readers to feel engaged with their favorite bloggers, and bloggers can hold a conversation with readers by participating in a comment thread. In the best-case scenario, frequent, thoughtful, and well-articulated posts from the comment community add to a blog's character and content depth.

Leaving comments on popular motherhood blogs is also recommended as a way for lesser-known bloggers to raise their profile and blog rank, creating a perverse incentive for superfluous or superficial commentary. "I do believe that if you comment, they will come. Meaning, if you read and comment all over the Internets, bloggers being a friendly and cyber-savvy bunch will return the favor and visit your blog," writes the author of *Kvetch*, who notes that commentating-as-self-promotion has a downside: "If you're reading blogs and commenting as a marketing mechanism, then do you become a loyal reader, a member of each blogger's inner circle, or do you read and comment remaining on the fringe—not really caring what came before or what comes next?" ("There's a Blogster in the Closet," August 24, 2007). In worst-case examples, the comment function can be used to conduct hostile attacks. In an informal online survey of more than 70 mother-bloggers, nearly half reported receiving reader comments they considered "deliberately offensive, hurtful or hateful." On the other hand, nine out of ten said they had formed positive personal relationships with people they met through their blogs.[7]

To the extent that blogs are a both a broadcast and participatory medium, motherhood blogging is unquestionably a social practice. But is blogging a *relational* practice? I contend that *it is not*, even though the practice of blogging can lead to the formation of genuine and important friendships, on- and off-line. Although bloggers and their devout readers may develop an emotional connection they describe as "knowing" each other, the relational practices necessary for establishing intimate ties require a degree of mutuality that is inconsistent with the blogging paradigm.

The Power Dynamics of Blogging and the Computer-Mediated Self

Don't get me wrong. I love all of you. I say that in all seriousness. I feel embraced, part of a sisterhood (and in some cases, a brotherhood) in a way that I never have before ... But were we to meet on the street, I don't think you'd really like me.... This is a one-dimensional medium, and we all pick and choose what we reveal about ourselves, consciously or unconsciously.

Face-to-face, our small ticks and quirks are too visceral— they can't be subverted.... But in the blogosphere, we can be the best and brightest versions of our selves. All the time. (*BlogRhet*, "Persona," June 21, 2007)

As Susan C. Herring and her co-authors explain in an analysis of weblogs as a communication genre, predictions that blogging will transform society are based on the popular misconception that weblogs are an entirely original form. They point out that rather than evolving from an untried technology or medium, blogs are a fusion of two established "content management systems"—the "one-to-many" communication model of static web pages, and the "many-to-many" model of online message boards. Herring explains that this hybridization structures the dynamics of power and self-presentation in a specific way:

> Author and reader roles in web pages are highly asymmetrical, in contrast with the fully symmetrical give and take of unmoderated discussion forums; blogs allow limited exchanges (in the form of comments), while according blog author and readers asymmetrical communication rights—the author retains ultimate control over the blog's content. (Herring, Scheidt, Bonus and Wright 10)

Herring suggests the "intermediate" characteristics of blogs "allow authors to experience social interaction while giving them control over the communication space." The protective field offered by asymmetrical power (which can be enhanced by blogging under a pseudonym) frees "ordinary people to self-express publicly" (11). It also makes blogging an attractive option for mothers who crave visibility but wish to control the intensity of the public gaze. Blogging is, quiet literally, an empowering practice—but mainly within the boundaries of the blogger's blog.

The asymmetry of communication rights and content control in blog-based social interaction raises important questions about the nature and meaning of blog-dependent bonds. The emotional content of relationships made in the maternal blogosphere is undeniably real, but the point of connection is largely imaginary—that is, the mother-blogger, who leads the dance, imagines she will attract readers who understand what she's talking about and why it matters, and readers imagine they can get to know the mother-blogger through her abbreviated, episodic narrative and voice.

Unlike the improvisational free-for-all of online message boards, which—even when moderated—give equal weight to participants' presence, blogs create a natural performance space where the break between the author's entry and the comment area functions as a proscenium and defines the relationship between the narrator and her interactive audience. Rather than offering readers a raw, unexpurgated chronicle of one mother's life, maternal blogging can be construed as a performance of the self, a practice through which the mother recreates the setting and substance of her life through a few well-crafted lines of text. As the author of *Her Bad Mother* explains in "I'm Not Really Bad, I Just Blog That Way" *(May 2, 2007)*, "Her Bad Mother is not me. That is, she is not entirely me.... She's a character. A true character, but still: a *character*, of a sort."

> I perform as Her Bad Mother. I interrogate myself as Her Bad Mother. Her Bad Mother is me, splashed on canvas, edited on film, choreographed on the stage, plotted on paper, spread out on the analyst's couch, telling my tale, the True and Amazing Adventures of Me As I Choose To See Me, Much Of The Time, And How I Want You To See Me, All Of The Time.

Relationships situated exclusively in the maternal blogosphere are also a kind of performance—a performance of friendship based on the perception of shared experiences and values, genuine goodwill, and caring intentions. The paradox of virtual relationships is that they are largely symbolic, and—on an emotional level—completely real.

Diversity and Inclusion in the Maternal Blogosphere

> ...Let me confirm it for you: the mommyblogging community is white. And I am not ... I have made an effort to find blogs (specifically, [motherhood blogs]) by minorities. And they're out there, but not as many as I wish there were, and certainly not in numbers that would drive the point home that we're here and living and loving and have just as much to offer as anyone else ... there is a void of comments and conversation from women (and mothers) from the perspective of a minority voice. (*BlogRhet*, "Am I In, or Am I Out," July 16, 2007)

As noted in the preceding discussion, the concept and evolution of blogging technology and culture was directed by the needs and intellectual sensibilities of a homogenous subset of high-immersion Internet users—a provenance that continues to influence which bloggers gain entry into the mainstream of a given blogging community, and who is prone to exclusion. Rather than rendering the social dimensions of race, class, gender, age, ability, and sexual identity invisible and irrelevant—as was promised by early articulations of digital communities as emancipatory social spaces—the undeniable relationship between economic status, cultural capital, and inclusion in online social networks highlights the lack of diversity in blogosphere.

The predominance of white, professional-class voices in the maternal blogosphere reflects the demographic composition of the blogosphere as a whole. According to a recent survey, bloggers are less likely to be white than Internet users as a group, but the majority of American bloggers—60 percent—self-identify as white, while eleven percent are African American and nineteen percent are Latino. Thirty-seven percent of U.S. bloggers have a college degree, compared to 27 percent of American adults overall. Most tellingly, U.S. bloggers are three times more likely to be "knowledge-based professional workers" than men and women in the general population (Lenhart and Fox 30-31).

Although blogging is often extolled as a democratizing force, there are both material and social preconditions for participation in the blogosphere, including literacy, English literacy (the majority of blogs are written in English), regular access to a private or public Internet connection, basic computer skills and familiarity with the web browser environment, baseline knowledge of how to locate blogs that match one's personal interests and values, and enough free time to read, contribute to, or create a blog—impediments which are statistically more likely to affect low-income, non-urban, and non-white populations. Mother bloggers (and bloggers in general) exacerbate obstacles to inclusion by referencing running jokes or using blog-specific jargon that may be incomprehensible to entry-level users (such as widespread use of the terms "hack" and "meme") to signal their status as insiders. While "anyone" can join the "blogging mom clique" (*Mothers Movement Online*, "The Blogging Mom Clique," February 2006), the self-selected exclusivity of the blogosphere is one of its defining characteristics—and potentially, one of its great attractions.

Yet mothering in the digital age also provides new forums for mothers to find connection in common cultural experiences and shared identities. One multiracial mother blogger writes, "I think that one of the great developments in the blogosphere over the past few years has been the emergence of sites people of color come together to share their experiences in a safe place for discussion and consideration" (*BlogRhet*, "Race and Collaborative Blogging," August 15, 2007). Even so, the reproduction of "real life" parenting norms grounded in white, professional-class privilege—frequently conveyed through narratives of how mother bloggers resist or resent the dominant script of "intensive" motherhood, and through cues related to career status, homeownership, and other social markers—create robust barriers to the perception of "likeness" and inclusion for mothers who self-identify, or are easily appraised, as different.

Given the rapidly changing nature of the maternal blogosphere and the expanding universe of mothers who populate it, it's impossible—and irresponsible—to make broad projections about how mother bloggers negotiate the dimensions of race, ethnicity, ability, heteronormativity, and social privilege through self-presentation and friendship formation in blogging communities. At the time of writing, a cursory review of author-assigned tags applied to thousands of "mommy and family blogs" listed by the *BlogHer.com* directory suggests that relatively few mother bloggers tackle "race, ethnicity, and culture" as a regular topic. But given the unpredictable ebb and flow of subject matter on personal blogs, even evidence of voluntary classification may be misleading.

A more constructive line of inquiry for mother bloggers and scholars inspired by their activities might be: What would the maternal blogosphere look and feel like if it were genuinely inclusive? And, how can we measure progress toward that goal? The mamasphere—and the real world—will have to undergo a major evolution (and possibly a revolution) before the voices and experiences of a representative cross-section of North American mothers are equally validated by the dominant culture. Until that fine day, it's fanciful to imagine that the structure and subculture of the blogosphere are inherently favorable to diversity and inclusion.

Blogging as a Meaning-Making Practice

I woke up yesterday (Saturday) morning and decided I didn't want to blog anymore. It is partially because I am overwhelmed by it. I hate to do anything half assed and I am lacking the energy to go any further ... The other part of it is that I really love writing but I recently realized that I need a subject and focus ... I was wasting time writing stuff that didn't [give] me the satisfaction that I am looking for ... (*Plain Jane Mom*, "Why I stopped blogging," August 19, 2007)

"You want to make it big doing this, don't you?" asked Piper ... I didn't really know what to say to that. What does that even mean in the blog world? Ad revenue? Recognition? A publisher? I don't

know. There are thousands and thousands of blogs out there ...
So where is this going? I started out doing this for myself, and
because friends said "you should write this down somewhere" ...
I liked the idea of being able to see my words "in print."(@*Home
in The World*, "Blog Ambition," August 22, 2007)

I'm not a habitual blog-reader, but in preparation for this book I spent
several weeks randomly visiting mother-made blogs and following links
to other mother-made blogs, reading entries and related comments as I
surfed along. In a disconcerting moment of self-awareness, I realized that
with the exception of bloggers I knew through personal correspondence
or in real life, I felt strangely detached from the authors. Rather than
relating to each mom blogger as a real woman, raising real children, in
a real, uncertain, and complicated world, I imagined the narrators as
fictional characters—I was concerned for their hardships and fates in the
same way I felt concern for Jane Eyre or Harry Potter. The renditions of
maternal life I discovered in the mamasphere were vibrant and completely
recognizable to me—and among the most engaging blogs, the blogger's
personality came through loud and clear. But did I "connect?" No. To
be perfectly honest, I felt like an interloper.

Blogging enthusiasts will protest that "lurking" dilutes the quality
of the blog experience. I enjoyed my brief immersion into the world of
motherhood blogs, nonetheless—many are skillfully written, thoughtful, touching, amusing, and enlightening. But I didn't connect—and that
disturbed me, because I want to see the lives of other mothers as real
and full of meaning.

Perhaps the problem is that I'm a "macro" person. I tend to think about
the big picture, and the majority of the motherhood blogs I sampled
were resolutely "micro"—a collection of ruminations on the fleeting and
incidental, a paean to the subtle pleasures and predictable irritations that
texture the surface of everyday life. Mom-blogs document all the trivial,
quirky, messy, familiar, funny, beautiful stuff that would otherwise go
unnoticed, the ephemeral moments which are remarkable only because
they matter to you, the blogger.

Which, of course, is exactly what blogs are good for—*if you are blogging for reasons other than personal satisfaction, chances are you will
be disappointed.* Or, as first-generation blogger Brigitte Eaton remarked,
"weblogs are wonderful," but "they're not changing the world with their
content, they're not going to make anyone huge amounts of money, but
they are a form of self-expression and community which others enjoy
reading" (Rhodes 103).

Rather than romanticizing motherhood blogging for its potential to transform mothering as we know it, let's love it for what it is—a private, meaning-making ritual which is open to public view. And while any mother can theoretically opt into the blogging mom club, the easy camaraderie of mamasphere and the value of blogging as a self-validating practice are partly derived from the fact that the mother-blogger community is currently small and relatively homogenous. The mamasphere can—and should—be more inclusive and diverse. But as it expands to amplify a wider range of voices, it will become a different kind of place.

As an outsider in the mother blogging community—an interloper—I realize my credibility with the in-crowd hovers around zero. But looking at the big picture, I offer this humble proposal for a *real* blogging mom revolution: Rise up, mamas, and break with the stale traditions of the blogosphere! Instead of courting reciprocal links or fretting about search engine optimization, maternal blogging can be practiced to optimize the *experience* of the mother-blogger and the inclusion of her readers. This might mean abandoning common practices that encourage insincerity or place additional time burdens on the blogger. It could include reorganizing or re-labeling archived content so that new readers can easily find and read from the beginning of the story. It may require a voluntary ban on phony techno-jargon and insider jokes. And rather than approaching blogging as an open-ended project, every new blog should be launched with the understanding that it has a finite life-span which ends when it outlives its usefulness as a tool for self-expression.[8] Motherhood blogs may not have the power to change the world—but mothers do have the power to change the way we blog.

[1]According to the Pew Internet & American Life research project, 12 percent of U.S. Internet users have created an online journal or weblog, but only 3 percent manage or create blog content on a daily basis ("Internet Activities," July 22, 2008 [table] and "Daily Internet Activities," January 2009 [table], Retrieved January 31, 2009, www.pewInternet.org). An August 2007 industry survey conducted by Synovate Marketing found that 80 percent of survey respondents knew what a blog was, with survey-takers between the ages of 25-24 more likely to be knowledgeable about blogs than older Americans. The Synovate eNation survey also found that while 50 percent of survey respondents had visited a blog, the majority of blog-readers (39 percent) visited blogs less than once a month, and only 20 percent reported visiting blogs at least once a day ("New Study Shows American's Blogging Behavior," August 30, 2007,

Retrieved 31 January, 2009, www.synovate.com).

[2]A 2006 study by the Pew Internet & American Life Project describes bloggers as "the Internet's new storytellers," finding that most U.S. bloggers are not highly immersed in the blogosphere, with 60 percent devoting around two hours a week to blogging and one quarter dedicating between three and five hours a week. However, a relatively high number of blogger—43 percent—maintain more than one blog. Half of U.S. bloggers report that they blog for themselves (52 percent), while one-third blog mostly to engage or entertain an audience (Lenhart and Fox, *Bloggers,* July 2006).

[3]It is impossible to accurately estimate the number of individual mothers who contribute to the blogoshpere. A search of the blog tracking website *Technorati* (www.technorati.com) returns a list of just over 3,200 blogs related to motherhood, but other sources put the number closer to10,000. Higher figures are deceptive, however, because nearly half of all bloggers maintain more than one blog, and 26 percent author three or more (Lenhart and Fox 10). At the time of writing, *BlogHer,* a directory of women-authored blogs (www.blogher.org), listed approximately 4,600 blogs using the tag "mommy and family." It seems likely that there are fewer than 5,000 active mommybloggers—and possibly closer to 2,500—but there may be as many as 50,000. By any estimate, motherhood bloggers continue to represent a tiny subset of mothers using the Internet.

[4]Based on information from the 2005 Canadian Internet Use Survey, adults in Canada and the U.S. have comparable levels of Internet use and comparable demographic characteristics, with Internet use concentrated among younger adults, individuals with higher levels of education, and higher-earning households (Statistics Canada, *The Daily*, August 15, 2006). Internet use is slightly lower among households in the UK than in North America (National Statistics (UK): Internet Access 2007).

[5]The term "Internet" is often used interchangeably with the term "web" (World Wide Web), since the web is what most people see and use when they go online to access services, search for information, or participate in social networking. Web protocols, and the development of compatible applications to enhance the functionality of the web environment, have transformed personal computers into full-featured, interactive multimedia devices. Internet protocols continue to drive core operations of computer-mediated communication, including the ability of home users to connect to the global network.

[6]Charles Taylor describes the "social imaginary" as "the ways people imagine their social existence" and "the common understanding that makes possible common practices and a widely shared sense of legitimacy." "It

often happens," Taylor writes, "that what start off as theories held by a few people come to infiltrate the social imaginary, first of elites, perhaps, and then of the whole society" (23-24).

[7]In preparation for writing this essay, I designed an informal online survey using the SurveyMonkey web application and announced it on several popular group blogs and the *Mothers Movement Online*. Seventy-three mother-bloggers volunteered to take the survey between August 15 and September 15, 2007. The survey was not intended to be scientifically rigorous or attract a representative sample, but results support my intuition that the practices and motivations of mother-bloggers are similar to those of U.S. bloggers overall. For example, six out of ten mothers who took the survey said their primary reason for blogging was self-expression, sharing personal stories, and keeping in touch with friends and family. Only one responder classified her blog as "citizen journalism."

[8]Sadly, the first, buoyant blog entry of the writer quoted at the opening of this essay ("One Really Happy Hen … ") was also her last. The post received no comments. Of the bloggers cited in this essay, several have moved on to new projects or discontinued posting to their motherhood blogs.

Works Cited

@Home in The World. Retrieved September 7, 2007. <homeintheworld. typepad.com>.

Argyle, Katie and Rob Shields. "Is there a Body in the Net?" Ed. Rob Shields. *Cultures of Internet*. London: Sage Publications, 1996. 58-69.

Argyle, Katie. "Life after Death." *Cultures of Internet*. Ed. Rob Shields. London: Sage Publications, 1996. 133-141.

BlogHer. Retrieved September, 2007-January 2009. <www.blogher. com>.

BlogRhet. Retrieved September 2007-February 2008. <blogrhet.blogspot. com>.

Blood, Rebecca. "Weblogs: A History and Perspective." *We've Got Blog*. Ed. John Rodzvilla. Cambridge, MA: Perseus Publishing, 2002. 7-16.

Boston.com. "E-male" by Ellen Goodman. Retrieved September 7, 2007. <www.boston.com>.

Buchanan, Andrea. "The Secret Lives of Mothers." *Mothers Movement Online*. Retrieved Sept. 15, 2007. <www.mothersmovement.org>.

Business Week.com. Retrieved September 7, 2007. <www.businessweek. com>.

CamWorld. Retrieved September 9, 2007. <www.camworld.com>.

Clark, Joe. "Deconstructing 'You've Got Blog'." *We've Got Blog*. Ed. John Rodzvilla. Cambridge, MA: Perseus Publishing, 2002. 57-68.

CNN.com. Retrieved September 6, 2007. <www.cnn.com>.

Dibbel, Julian. "Portrait of the Blogger as a Young Man." *We've Got Blog*. Ed. John Rodzvilla. Cambridge, MA: Perseus Publishing, 2002. 69-77.

Doheny-Farina, Stephen. *The Wired Neighborhood*. New Haven, CT: Yale University Press, 1996.

Dornfest, Asha. "The Blogging Mom Clique: Anyone Can Join." *Mothers Movement Online*. Retrieved February 16, 2008. <www.mothersmovement.org>.

Her Bad Mother. Retrieved September 14, 2007. <badladies.blogspot. com>.

Herring, Susan C., Lois Ann Scheidt, Sabrina Bonus, and Elijah Wright. "Bridging the Gap: A Genre Analysis of Weblogs." *Proceedings of the 37th Hawaii International Conference on System Science HICSS04*. January 5-8, 2004. Retrieved August 30, 2007. <www.ics.uci.edu>.

Hochman, David. "Mommy (and me)." *New York Times* 30 Jan. 2005: Sunday Styles 1-6.

In the Trenches of Mommyhood. Retrieved September 6, 2007. <sarahviz. blogspot.com>.

IzzyMom. Retrieved September 4, 2007. <izzymom.com>.

Kuro5hin. Retrieved September 14, 2007. <www.kuro5hin.org>.

Kvetch Blog. Retrieved September 6, 2007. <orthoticcontessa.com>.

Lenhart, Amanda and Susannah Fox. *Bloggers: A portrait of the Internet's new storytellers*. Pew Internet and American Life Project. July 2006. Retrieved September 7, 2007. <www.pewInternet.org>.

Mead, Rebecca. "You've Got Blog." *We've Got Blog*. Ed. John Rodzvilla. Cambridge, MA: Perseus Publishing, 2002. 47-56.

Metascene. "Ten Tips for Building a Bionic Weblog." *We've Got Blog*. Ed. John Rodzvilla. Cambridge, MA: Perseus Publishing, 2002. 150-165.

Plain Jane Mom. Retrieved September 6, 2007. <plainjanemom.com>.

Rainie, Lee and John Horrigan. "A decade of adoption: How the Internet has woven itself into American life." Pew Internet & American Life Project. January 25, 2005. Retrieved September 9, 2007. <www. pewInternet.org>.

Rheingold, Howard. *The Virtual Community*. Second Edition. Cambridge,

MA: MIT Press, 2000.

Rhodes, John S. "In the Trenches with a Weblog Pioneer: An Interview with the Force Behind EatonWeb, Brigitte F. Eaton." *We've Got Blog*. Ed. John Rodzvilla. Cambridge, MA: Perseus Publishing, 2002. 99-103.

Scripting News. Retrieved September 6, 2007. <www.scripting.com>.

Sifry's Alerts. Retrieved September 9, 2007. <www.sifry.com>>

Stadtman Tucker, Judith. "Mothering in the Digital Age." *Mothering in the Third Wave* Ed. Amber Kinser. Toronto: Demeter Press, 2008. 199-212.

Sullivan, Andrew. "The Blogging Revolution." *Wired*. Retrieved September 6, 2007. <www.wired.com>.

Taylor, Charles. *Modern Social Imaginaries*. Durham, NC: Duke University Press, 2004.

The Mother of All Blogs. Retrieved November 7, 2006. <www.parentinglibrary.com>.

U.S. Census Bureau. "Purpose and Frequency of Computer Use at Home by Persons 18 Years and Older: October 1989." *Computer Use in the United States: October 1989* (P23-171). Issued February 1991. Table 5.

U.S. Census Bureau. "Purpose of Computer Use at Home by People 18 Years and Over: October 1997." *Computer Use in the United States: October 1997 (P20-522)*. Issued October 1999. Table 7.

Introduction

MAY FRIEDMAN AND SHANA L. CALIXTE

The aim of going around the room in a meeting to hear each woman's testimony, a common—and exciting—practice in consciousness-raising, is to help stay focused on a point, to bring the discussion back to the main subject after exploring a tangent, to get the experience of as many people as possible in the common pool of knowledge. The purpose of hearing from everyone was never to be nice or tolerant or to develop speaking skill or the "ability to listen." It was to get closer to the truth. Knowledge and information would make it possible for people to be "able" to speak. The purpose of hearing people's feelings and experience was not therapy, was not to give someone a chance to get something off her chest ... that is something for a friendship. It was to hear what she had to say. The importance of listening to a woman's feelings was collectively to analyze the situation of women, not to analyze *her*. The idea was not to change women, was not to make "internal changes" except in the sense of knowing more. It was and is the conditions women face, it's male supremacy, we want to change. (Sarachild 144-50)

Mothering has always been a daunting and consuming enterprise. Mothering at the dawn of the twenty-first century, for certain women, has emerged as an especially peculiar dialogue between expectations and realities, between lives lived and the responses to those lives. For women who participate in the parenting world of the blogosphere, the nature of that call and response has had a dynamic and altering effect, both on individual mothers and on the institution of motherhood as a whole.

The mommyblog is the perfect cyborg artefact of mothering: here we sit with our leaking contracting bodies while telling our robots about our feelings and using totally unembodied technology to represent ourselves in these bits and bytes of representation of pushing and hollering and being vomited on and sweating in the night. Mommyblogs are, on the one hand, very potent and real and also very sanitized by their very nature as virtual; the multisensory experience of motherhood reduced down to letters and words on a screen and distilled into a neat and tidy box, as though one could mail a dear friend motherhood, and she would open her door and it would be in her mailbox. Yet what makes mommyblogging such an exceptional pursuit, and what has fuelled the analysis put forth in this volume is the extent to which mommyblogs are totally unsanitized. On the one hand, motherhood is reduced, yet for many fans of the genre, mommyblogs put forth a version of motherhood more honest and raw than any representation of motherhood found elsewhere.

We came to this topic as editors, as mothers and as Internet-literate habitués of the mamasphere. Our lives, and those of the majority of the authors within this volume, have unquestioningly been changed as a result of parenting in an Internet era. A brief exploration of our personal orientation to the topic opens the door to our exultation and anxiety about the dynamic world of the mommyblog.

May:

> For the last week, I've noticed faces in the grocery stores that I might have glanced past before and wondered more actively about what kind of extraordinary experiences they might be willing to share, what secrets they possess and if they might be one of the remarkable women I may one day happen upon on the Internet. (*Tiny Mantras*, "Who are you and what are we doing here together?" October 27, 2007.)

My son was born in 2003 and is therefore approximately the same age as the mamasphere. The proto-mommyblogs that existed at that time were viewed as notoriously narcissistic at best, and abusive of the children they chronicled at worst. Yet for me, as a new mother, I found something exceptionally nourishing in the stories I could access online. Housebound and alienated, the ability to "get the experience of as many people as possible in the common pool of knowledge" (Sarachild, 146) set my course as a mother. When I felt apart from parents in my community, I could find a mother online who shared my values. Regardless of the parenting concerns I experienced (and like any new parent, my worries ranged from the sublime to the ridiculous), I could find solace, advice and creative expression. I could also find frustration, post-partum depression and flat out rage. Nowhere in the sanitized parenting world I inhabited "in real life" was there any discussion of the dreariness of new motherhood, its frustrations, its toll on partnerships and the ways that feminism was potentially being threatened by the siren-song of an increasingly child-centred society. Ripe for the guilt trip of assuming I was the only mother who occasionally found her darling blessing somewhat *dull*, I stumbled over to my computer and there found salvation. Yet to this day I have never typed a word on any blog of my own. For me, the joy of blogging comes solely as a spectator; yet there is no question that my parenting practice, and indeed, my *view of myself as a mother within the world* have been irreparably altered by the privilege of parenting in a blogging age.

Shana:

> First of all, you will not like me. That is not necessary i do this with a vengeance, not so that i can be feared and/or vilified. this is an act of love … not for any individual popular bloggers feeding off cults of personality. No. this is an act of solidarity with things political in the hope that what we understand as politics on the "left" will one day be fused with a well developed sense of ethics and emotional intelligence. (*one tenacious baby mama*, "CNN, Fox and emotional button-pushing through media … the amerikkkan way," April 19, 2007.)

Before my little one was born, I decided to start a blog to capture my experiences as a black, queer, butch identified lesbian, trying to get pregnant. My intent was to keep a journal to keep myself sane (as anyone who is trying to get pregnant with a lack of sperm can surely understand) and to also seek out a community around those issues that had me theorizing about my future parenting—issues of race, sexuality and gender. It was 2005, and my earlier ventures into the blogosphere had not even touched upon parenting or mommyblogs (I had an earlier blog from 1999-2002 which I had abandoned). As a result, I was amazed to find a small but growing community of lesbian/bi/queer folks creating families. These families had a similar need to talk about the messiness that was involved in parenting, specifically as parents with fewer social and legal protections than most.

I never really did see myself as a "mommyblogger" in the time when I was most actively blogging. I saw myself as a political activist, urging those online to rethink their own biases around the institution of motherhood, but also to critique the very exclusive frames of reference many have around what it means to be queer, black and a mom. Blogging for me was cathartic, but it was also highly political. I enjoyed blogging about my ideas around motherhood, and seeing how other people negotiated these very intense issues around racism, homophobia, classism and general oppression. It was my solace to find others who were at one time checking their fertile mucus, negotiating donor relationships and wondering who would be mama or mommy. Yet it was even more critical for me to theorize just a bit more about what kinds of possibilities there are for mamas who are queering the very definition of family, and how these "queeruptions" intersect with other axes of identity and oppression.

Even though I believe I have a lot of knowledge around these things, I knew I didn't have all the answers. Even though I have been and continue to be highly critical of the topics that are not given much airtime in the mamasphere (as we will touch on below, and as many of the authors in this volume discuss at length), I was still relieved that at least some folks were attempting to take on the hard topics. In my experience, the blogosphere has been different than say, the folks I would meet at parenting drop ins who quickly ran away from me when I started making noise around sexuality or class or race. At least in the mamasphere, I can keep poking. It sometimes turns ugly, and that is something that is a downside to this type of community building. However, you know you've been able to say what you wanted to say and folks can't pretend you didn't say it. That is why I am so invested in the mamasphere and mommyblogging—I see the potential for a radical change in the way we think about mothering and parenting, and how our queer families are challenging the status quo, one blog at a time.

Mommyblog: Why We Embrace the Term

> ...[T]he term "mommyblogger" has come to more broadly be used to simply signify bad writing. i've lately seen the term thrown out as a kind of comprehensive put-down, aimed at blogs not even vaguely about parenting or children, written by people who don't even have kids. obviously the singling-out of "mommybloggers" as a catch-all condemnation has a lot to do with the status of women in society and, more specifi-

cally, societal attitudes about motherhood. (*MommyBloggers*, "Mommybloggers dish with Tracey Goughran-Perez," January 9, 2006.)

Motherhood has become big business. Quite distinct from the marketing directed at mothers on behalf of their children (for example, toys, "sippy" cups, steroid-free organic lunch meats), mothers are now the recipients of vast media attention as a market of their own. In the world of sound bites, most of this attention focuses on the words "mom" or "mommy," with all of its nauseating overtones: the "momoir," "mommylit," and, of course, mommyblogs. Moms and mommies conjure up images of doting apron-clad sycophants smilingly paying homage to their tiny sovereigns. Why, as feminist academics, then, do we insist on referring to the authors of the parenting blogosphere as mommybloggers?

First and foremost, the extent to which the term has organically emerged as the *de facto* terminology of reference cannot be underestimated. A quick Google search for "mother bloggers" yields fewer than two thousand hits, while a search for "mommybloggers" brings up over eighty thousand hits. To refer to this genre by any other name, then, is potentially disingenuous, and, in an era so overwhelmingly powered by the search engine, may result in the burying of blogs who seek to rescue this medium from the taint of patriarchal motherhood. Beyond simple logistics, however, a powerful reclamation of the term has been mounting, a reclamation that we seek to participate in and fuel.

Our motivation for using the word is two-fold. On the one hand, we are speaking ironically to signify the incredulity we feel when multidimensional women are so easily reduced to such limited terminology. Our second motivation, however, is the reclamation of words that we feel can be used to signify the extraordinary power that is being harnessed by women on the web. If this book adequately begins to convey the complexity of women's lives, then perhaps in the future calling someone a mommyblogger will be a choice compliment rather than a damning epithet. As mothers all over the web—dynamic, diverse mothers—reclaim this term, they lay claim to cyberspace through the medium of the blog, and they likewise resist the typecasting of themselves as the stereotypical "mommies" discussed above. This reclamation manifests in anger, in argument, but overwhelming in humour. Tracey Goughran-Perez, aka Sweetney, is the mommyblogger quoted above. She created a T-shirt that perhaps sums up the ironic tone taken by many women who have been pegged by this term. The T-shirt reads "I'm a fucking mommyblogger (bite me)." Mommybloggers are having a profound impact, then, on the social construction of both blogging and motherhood.

A Radical Act

> I for one like the idea that the mommy-blogosphere is one place where, in years to come, people will turn to see *what women were up to at the turn of the 21st century,* and not the manicured profiles of women in mainstream magazines. (*BlogRhet,* "How much of this is about redefining 'mommy'?" February 12, 2007.)

It was the binky drop that echoed around the mamasphere.

In 2005, David Hochman penned a piece called "Mommy and Me," which appeared in the Style section of the *New York Times.* Profiling a number of big names in the mamasphere, the experiences of *dooce's* Heather Armstrong, *Dot Moms'* Julia M. Moos and *finslippy's* Alice Bradley were all included, as they shared their own experiences of mothering and blogging.

However, most who read the piece (including many of our contributors) saw only one theme emerge from the story: mommybloggers were portrayed as a bunch of navel gazers, and their self-centered obsession with the lint within needed to be called out for what it really was—narcissism. One particular quote from Hochman that troubled many stated:

> Today's parents—older, more established and socialized to voicing their emotion—may be uniquely equipped to document their children's lives, but what they seem most likely to complain and marvel about is their own. The baby blog in many cases is an online shrine to parental self-absorption.

Although directed at "parents" the text was riddled with snippets that read to many as just another example of mother blame. Hochman had taken the words of mommybloggers, and had found within them a concerning selfishness. Not only were mothers spending too much time blogging about the minutiae of childrearing, they were, in essence, fostering a potentially child-harming culture of motherhood. Hochman provocatively asked, "…the question is, at who's expense? How will the bloggee feel, say, 16 years from now, when her prom date Googles her entire existence?" (Hochman, 2005). Many in the mamasphere were quick to reply. Eden Marriott Kennedy stated:

Good morning, I'm humorless and resentful, as are many moms who blog. We overscrutinize our children's every excretion and whore out adorable anecdotes about them just to get attention for ourselves! (*Fussy,* "Good morning," January 31, 2005.)

Others saw the ongoing faulting of mothers, and the impossibility of change. As Melissa Summers notes,

In the end what this article shows me, once again, is that we can't win no matter what we do. If we aren't worried about our kids, we're neglectful. If we think (and write) about the things our kids do we're called hand wringing obsessives. Hooray New York Times for capturing the essence of mothering! (*Suburban Bliss,* "A near miss," January 30, 2005)

Why mothering had been singled out was also of concern for mommybloggers. Jen Lawrence (who tackles other problems within the mamasphere in chapter eight of this volume) noted,

For me, the question is not whether blogging about parenting is self-absorbed but why blogging about parenting is considered more self absorbed than writing about, say, one's trip to the North Pole by dogsled? (*Mothered Up Beyond All Recognition,* "The politics of blogging," January 29, 2005)

Although it has been nearly four years since the piece was penned, the words of Hochman continue to echo in the minds of mamas online, especially when new critiques arise. In May 2008, Kathy Lee Gifford interviewed *dooce*'s Heather Armstrong on the Today Show. Seemingly without doing much research, Gifford spent most of the interview trivializing the experiences of moms online, specifically those who had found themselves in better situations financially (like Armstrong) as well as showcasing "The Story Of How Kathy Lee Gifford Is Afraid Of Her Computer" (*BlogHer,* "The Business of MommyBlogging on the Today Show." May 7, 2008).

Mommybloggers had strong words for Ms. Gifford, and expressed once again, their disappointment with the lack of understanding from the news media around the real usefulness and importance of mothers who blog.

Perhaps more troubling than the condemnation of mommybloggers by news reporters has been the general lack of respect from elsewhere within the blogosphere. In 2005, three hundred women came together for the first conference specifically aimed at women who blog. BlogHer (now a 700-plus person, multi-day conference in its fourth year) was born to answer the question "where are the women who blog? At the first such conference, however, mothers who predominantly blogged about their children, families and/or domestic concerns were marginalized and targeted as fulfilling the stereotype of women bloggers as solely capable of documenting cute stories about their kids. As the conference drew to a close, one participant made the following claim: "If you women stopped blogging about [your]selves [you] could change the world" (*BlogHer*, "BlogHer '06 Session Discussion: MommyBlogging is a Radical Act! May 20, 2006). Notable mommyblogger Alice Bradley of *finslippy* responded succinctly: "MommyBlogging *is* a radical act." With the benefit of hindsight, Bradley qualified her remarks thusly:

> We readers and authors of parenting blogs are looking for a representation of authentic experience that we're not getting elsewhere. We sure as hell aren't getting it from the parenting magazines. If you want to find out how to make nutritious muffins that look like kitty cats, you can read those. But a parenting magazine will never help you feel less alone, less stupid, less ridiculous. This is the service I think parenting blogs provide- we share our lopsided, slightly hysterical, often exaggerated but more or less authentic experiences. (Ibid)

The authors in this collection follow on Bradley's claim, maintaining that while the mamasphere is certainly both problematic and limited, for some mothers it is a powerful step toward unmasking motherhood (Maushart, 1997). Such an analysis, however, must not overstate the influence and scope of the mamasphere: while Bradley drew attention to the ghettoization of mothers within the blogosphere, a similar marginalization occurs between mothers as women with non-normative social locations are relegated to the margins of this emergent field.

Limitations of the Genre: Ghettoization within the Blogosphere

> Is this just me? Do any minorities who read [mommyblogs] ever feel like, "WTF? I so can't relate?" Does anyone else feel sometimes that the mommyblog world is a microcosm of the United States, where white voices lead and prevail and there

seems little room for minorities? And where these white voices seemingly have little to no experiences beyond their white world? (*BlogRhet*, "Am I In Or Am I Out?" July 16, 2007.)

This collection of work on the mamasphere does not shy away from looking at some of the harder questions around exclusion and marginality. The mamasphere continues to reproduce oppressive hierarchies, where the voices of the white, the able, the middle class and the heterosexual are often heard first and most often.

At the 2007 BlogHer conference, Mocha Momma, a well-known blogger of colour, pointed out the very real concern that moms of colour were not being included in the seemingly ever growing net of marketers hitting up mommybloggers for ad space and other promotional items. At this conference, Mocha Momma asked her fellow blogging mothers to not only engage with her concerns, but to back her up when the marketers (and audience) ignored the question, or simply told others that they had "no idea what to do with [women of colour]" (*CityMama* 2007). Unfortunately, the silence that surrounded her concerns is indicative of the worries that many have about the exclusivity of the mamasphere.

Issues of sexuality, class, ability, race, gender identity and many other axes of oppression are often shielded by a larger set of voices that speak from positions of normality. To that end, when one thinks of a "mommyblogger" and what she might write about, many would be shocked to see the experiences of racism or homophobia entering the discussion. And even though these topics are not solely for those most affected by them, the mamasphere continues to both evade the hard topics and to avoid, for the most part, taking a hard look at itself. Why is it that the most popular mommybloggers are, or are assumed to be, white? Why do issues of whiteness, ablebodiedness, heteronormativity, and class privilege never seem to be at the top of our discussions? Do these concerns not affect our parenting and choices for mothering?

When issues of power and oppression are raised as concerns for some in the mamasphere, the questions keeps coming up. Do race and ethnicity matter? Do we really need to talk about sexuality? How does class affect who gets to be online to do the blogging that moms are doing? In the end, mommybloggers who occupy positions of marginalization believe it does matter. As most mommybloggers would state, their personal experiences with motherhood translates into a political creation of community. The incorporation of an anti-oppression politics of parenting is an important and critical change required to create a functional and radical mamasphere.

The general question seems to be: does race matter in the blogo-sphere?... For me, for this Cubanita, it does matter. I want you to know me as I am, as I see myself. I want you to expand your horizons and get to know people who are different, even as you make your way through the delicate topics of race and culture. I want to be part of a larger parenting/blogging community without feeling like my ethnicity is ignored or unimportant simply because the majority doesn't quite know how to address it. (*BlogRhet*, "Race and Ethnicity: It Matters." August 6, 2007)

The analysis above lends credence to the fact that the mamasphere is both limited and potentially deleterious in its impact on the institution of motherhood. Specifically, mommyblogging in the present day may go a far way toward unmasking motherhood for very particular mothers, while simultaneously constructing new strictures for mothers who parent on the margins of normative society. Given that the genre is growing astro-nomically (as Judith Stadtman Tuckers' foreword to this volume amply demonstrates), how can mommyblogging be redeemed? What steps can be taken—if any—to ensure that the reclamation of the term mommyblog goes beyond pat assurances of powerful sisterhood and strong mamas? Can mommyblogging, as a method, create systemic change?

As a methodology, the effect of a chorus of voices is exceptionally powerful. Mommybloggers are creating a mosaic of modern motherhood. Like any mosaic, certain colours dominate the landscape, yet, despite this limitation, the overall effect is still of multiplicity rather than of a dominant narrative. The fact that thousands upon thousands of women have created their own narrative—despite the obvious threads of the master narrative which underpin each maternal account—has shifted the terrain of twenty-first century motherhood and will continue to do so. While in no way downplaying the digital divide, mommyblog-ging is a self-publishing technique that is available to a huge group of people—women—who would otherwise not be able to reach out nearly as effectively. Although we are not naive enough to suggest that the Inter-net is a zone where talent is the only arbiter (i.e., where all good writers get read equally), mommyblogs nonetheless allow an ability to find like minds, and to push through the burden of isolation that is synonymous with modern day motherhood.

Yet the multiplicity that renders the blogosphere so fascinating and rich might also highlight the limits of this genre. It is tempting to see the mamasphere as the best, richest instance of consciousness raising imaginable—allowing for (albeit limited) diversity, not constrained by geographical boundaries or time-bound limitations such as child care and free time. In the absence of a defining motivation such as that articulated in the consciousness raising literature that began this introduction, however, the mamasphere might yet lack the capacity to thoroughly refute critiques focusing on solipsism and self-absorption. A truly radical mamasphere would allow mothers to collectively analyze the sources of discomfort, joy, boredom and enlightenment, resulting in a focus that would highlight the situation of mothers broadly, that would "analyze the situation of women," rather than simply maintaining anecdotes of thousands of singular lives. We are optimistic that this version of the mamasphere is already emerging. The presence of group blogs that tackle heady issues (for example, *LesbianFamily; BlogRhet;* and *KimchiMamas*, to name but a few) herald a move beyond blogging as an individualistic pursuit, beyond the community that has been created within the mamasphere, and further yet toward the creation of a truly radical force toward reclaiming motherhood as a complicated, messy and ultimately extraordinary terrain.

In this Collection

This anthology begins with Judith Stadtman Tucker's superb foreword. Stadtman Tucker provides an excellent orientation to the blogosphere, considering a range of motivations and concerns that have contributed to this emergent genre. By setting the stage, Stadtman Tucker provides the context for further chapters that use a combination of personal experience and theoretical analysis to peer more closely at the highlights and sore spots of the mamasphere.

The ability to create nontraditional connections is at the heart of Dawn Friedman's chapter, "Someone Else's Shoes: How On-Blog Discourse Changed a Real Life Adoption." Friedman, a mommyblogger since before the phrase was coined, discusses the process through which her blog, initially a place to record her thoughts and concerns, evolved into a complex and ongoing dialogue with her readers. As a mother with both biological and adopted children, Friedman documented her experiences with infertility and adoption, using the blog as a way to process her experiences and feelings. Friedman chronicles the ways that her real life experiences were enriched and altered as a result of dialogue on her blog. In particular, Friedman's experience of being challenged by birth mothers who found her website—but who were not involved in her daughter's adoption—forced her to re-consider her assumptions and concerns regarding her daughter and her daughter's first mother. Friedman pays tribute to the way in which the blogosphere thus allows for dialogue among potentially strange bedfellows, people who might unite over shared circumstances (in this case adoption) but who are nonetheless often set apart from one another in the world offline.

Julie Palmer's chapter, "Blogging Pregnancy: Ultrasonography, Connectivity and Identity Construction" provides a critical look at the Canadian-born UK blogger Lisa Durbin, and her use of ultrasound pictures in the creation of identity. Palmer's piece critically engages the ways in which this technology (both ultrasound and blogging) complicates and re-imagines the process of pregnancy, birth and motherhood and therefore contributes a very complex reading of the mamasphere as an embodied experience.

Jennifer Gilbert joins this collection from the other side of the nursery. In "I Kid You Not," Gilbert chronicles the ways that the mamasphere actively dissuaded her from motherhood. In scrolling through the mamasphere, Gilbert was exposed to motherhood unmasked, a sharp contrast from the sanitized and saccharine representations she saw all around her offline. Her view of motherhood, with all its flaws and challenges, led Gilbert and her partner to opt against any attempt to conceive biological children. Gilbert's irreverent piece, however, does not simply posit the Internet as a sinister form of birth control, but instead makes a powerful case for choice: both choice in viewing motherhood as optional rather than simply "the next stage" for many young women living normative lives, but also for the possibility of motherhood to be radically re-imagined. Gilbert's conclusions regarding the future of her own family provide a solid claim for the ways that access to information and individual stories can broaden the possibilities for mothering practice in ways that have both personal and political outcomes.

Lisa Ferris's chapter, "Kindred Keyboard Connections," speaks to the isolation commonly faced by new mothers in relating her own personal experience as the mother of twin boys. In her chapter, Ferris speaks to the ability of the mamasphere to specifically assist families who might struggle with communication off-line. As a mother with disabilities, Ferris found that the Internet was an invaluable tool in allowing her to connect with other mothers in ways that were genuine and thorough, that did not require an initial dance of politeness and withheld information before the day-to-day challenges of parenting were revealed and discussed. Although Ferris' piece speaks most explicitly to the ways that the blogosphere assisted her communication around the axis of her disabilities, her chapter is most provocative as it takes up other issues of identity, speaking to the myriad ways that her situation is unique and compelling—as the mother of multiples, as a feminist mother, as a parent with a unique situation regarding conception and co-parenting. Ferris' chapter echoes her blog in framing her life as complicated and multifarious—in short, the life of any mother—rather than reducing her to "that disabled mom."

Challenging the exclusivity of the mamasphere, Shana Calixte and Jillian Johnson share an instant messenger chat about their realities as queer black mamas online in "Marginality in the Mamasphere: Queers Racializing the Family Tree." Highlighting their own experiences, these two mothers discuss the very complex terrain of racism, homophobia, classism and ageism online and within the mamasphere, and the challenges their presence makes to a seemingly uniform experience of mothering online. Their chapter provides an important critique of the ways race and sexuality are (or are not) taken up in the mamasphere, and ask all mommybloggers to pay critical attention to the spaces of exclusion created online.

In "*Meter Politikon*: On the "Politics" of Mommyblogging," Catherine Connors mounts a passionate defense of the mamasphere. Connors rejects notions of the mamasphere as inherently political, arguing instead that the world of mommybloggers is a supple, dynamic community that, like all communities, struggles with notions of identity and popularity. In contrast to other authors within this collection, Connors' maintains that the mamasphere has risen to the challenge of negotiating the difficult terrain of commercial interest and identity-driven content. Her chapter argues that mommybloggers are nourished by the increased monetism of the blogosphere and that the mamasphere engages with the politics of identity on a sophisticated and thoughtful level.

Ann Douglas looks at the evolution of the mamasphere, considering the ways that the pressures of marketing and financial incentives, coupled with more old-fashioned problems such as mother-blame and defensive judgments, have resulted in a mamasphere that may not work in aid of mothers. In "Web 2.0, Meet the MommyBlogger," Douglas examines how market forces manipulate the need for popularity and consensus within mommyblogs, arguing that the result is a very potent form of bullying that may result in mothers being exposed to greater judgement than ever before.

Jen Lawrence writes in dialogue with Catherine Connors' *Meter Politikon*, arguing that mommyblogs have become big business. In her chapter, "Blog for Rent: How Marketing is Changing our Mothering Conversations," Lawrence shares her own journey into the monetizing of mommyblogs and the benefits and pitfalls that come with the inclusion of marketers in the mamasphere. Her chapter asks the hard question: can mommybloggers make money off of their words without losing their credibility or compromising their ethics? Lawrence discusses how the truly radical act of sharing stories of mothering online changes when the commercial is included in the mamasphere.

After searching for others online and coming up with only a few hits with the words, "pregnant" and "lesbian," Liza Barry-Kessler decided to create an online space for lesbian moms who are trying to conceive, are pregnant and/or are raising kids. In "LesbianFamily.org," Barry-Kessler responds to the marginalization of lesbians in the mamasphere, and brings to light the needs of a community that is parenting, often without legal protections and outside of social norms. In her chapter, she discusses the creation of the site, the various ways it has changed throughout its existence, and the important ways it has connected lesbian women throughout the mamasphere. Her chapter highlights how a space for community building and change can be created. Barry-Kessler challenges those in the mamasphere who have ignored the realities of lesbian families, and lesbian mamas online.

Melissa Camara Wilkins might just be one those moms Hochman would see as "self-absorbed." In her chapter, "Beyond Cute: A Mom, a Blog and a Question of Content," Wilkins challenges this generalization by sharing her personal journey as a mother who uses her blog as a way to tell her own stories, which do not necessarily include the everyday goings on of her children. As she states, she is looking to "subvert the cultural norms of motherhood," and she reveals how blogging has been critical for opening up spaces of communication and sharing for many mothers online. She speaks to the contradictions of presenting a unified online mothering community, as well as an essential mothering identity. Her chapter reveals how the very use of the medium for mothers, and the words, whether political, personal or a mix of both, create a community for those searching for the same.

Following on Wilkins' piece, Oana Petrica provides a fruitful analysis of the internationalization of mommyblogging. In looking at the specifics of Romanian mommyblogger and media personality Ada Demirgian, Petrica argues that motherhood is simultaneously subverted—through the medium of public storytelling—and reaffirmed, through the patriarchal story that is told. Petrica argues that it is Demirgian's specific location as a post-communist mother that contributes to her social location and her affirmation of traditional motherhood.

May Friedman, in "Schadenfreude for Mittelschmerz? Or, Why I Read Infertility Blogs," asks us to consider why we find the mamasphere so compelling. Using the lens of her own fascination with infertility blogs, Friedman considers the variety of motivators that make the genre of the mommyblog, and its ugly step-sister, the infertility blog, such hot topics. By examining the ways that motherhood and femininity are viewed as synonymous, Friedman examines the ways that infertility narratives may challenge both maternal privilege and traditional notions of womanhood.

Closing the collection, Elizabeth Podnieks turns the lens of the blogosphere outward, chronicling the ways that celebrity mothering practice has become a specific sub-genre of star-gazing. Podnieks' analysis looks at blogs created in order to discuss and share the details of celebrity mothers and their offspring. Podnieks situates her analysis within the broader sociology of fan culture, considering the ways that some bloggers aim to both create connection with famous mothers (a radical re-invention of "sisterhood is powerful" through the medium of motherhood), while others instead see celebrity motherhood as an example of excess, focusing on motherhood as a focal point for a broader criticism of star culture.

The chapters of this collection deliberately resist the notion that only traditional scholarly knowledge is valid. In this vein, we allow contributors from a range of different backgrounds to consider both anecdotal and other knowledge as relevant for study. The foregrounding of personal voices is consistent with the type of feminist scholarship that we both create, and wish we saw more of. The contributors of this collection not only relay their experiences, but open that experience to scrutiny and analysis, resulting in a nuanced and critical reading of mommyblogs.

We hope that the final product allows you, our reader, to consider the incredible messiness and complexity of the mamasphere—the ways we can't live without it and the ways we can't live with it as it is right now. Above all else, we hope that this collection creates dialogue, allows for as many new questions as it answers, and begins to legitimize this incredible new field of study.

Works Cited

BlogHer. Retrieved May 16, 2008. <www.blogher.com>.
BlogRhet. Retrieved Nov. 2007-present. <http://blogrhet.blogspot.com>.
CaféPress. Sweetney.com Store. Retrieved July 2, 2008. http://www.cafepress.com/sweetney
CityMama. "Putting the PR people on notice." July 27, 2007. <www.citymama.typepad.com>.

CityMama. Retrieved June 29, 2008. <www. citymama.typepad.com>.

Fussy. Retrieved May 2006 to present. <www.fussy.org>.

Hochman, David. "Mommy and Me." *New York Times,* 30 January 2005, Style. Retrieved from <http://www.nytimes.com/2005/01/30/fashion/30moms.html>.

Maushart, Susan. *The Mask of Motherhood: How Becoming a Mother Changes Our Lives and Why We Never Talk About It.* New York: New Press, 1997.

MommyBloggers. Retrieved May 22, 2008.<www.mommybloggers.com>.

Mothered Up Beyond All Recognition (MUBAR). Retrieved June 23, 2008. <http://tomama.blogs.com/mubar>.

one tenacious baby mama. Retrieved July, 2007. <http://darkdaughta.blogspot.com>.

Sarachild, Kathie. "Consciousness-Raising: A Radical Weapon." *Feminist Revolution.* New York: Random House, 1978. 144-150.

Suburban Bliss. Retrieved June 27, 2008. <www.suburbanbliss.net>.

Tiny Mantras. Retrieved June 23, 2008. <http://tzt.blogspot.com>.

Chapter One

Someone Else's Shoes

How On-Blog Discourse Changed a Real Life Adoption

DAWN FRIEDMAN

[W]e become the autobiographical narratives by which we tell about our lives. (Bruner 691)

I began blogging as a writing experiment. I was inspired to try it after stumbling on a group of intensely personal journals written by a group of third-wave feminists. The blog that interested me most was by a woman named Phoenix Amon, who I first "met" through an email list for women with pregnancies due in February 1997. When the list disbanded I went looking for her online and found her web design business and then her journal. The now defunct journal, *One Hand Clapping*, was an intimate rumination on her daily life and it surprised me because it was so revealing. Phoenix didn't have comments and I felt too shy to email and tell her I was reading but I visited her site every day (actually several times a day when I logged on to check email) looking for updates. I was so intrigued by Phoenix's journal that I thought about trying online journaling for myself, mostly as a writing practice. While I'd been writing (and journaling) since learning how to hold a pen properly, my son's arrival put a severe crimp in my creative output and I was feeling rusty. I hoped having an audience would hold me accountable to keep the journal up and—most importantly—to move forward in my thoughts instead of indulging in repetitive ruminations. Finally I thought that an open (but personal) journal would be a little bit like performance art because it would be an organic entity—growing in a virtual world, changing with every entry and being shaped by its public place in the environment.

So in January of 2001, I began hand-coding my blog at the web site that came free with my email account. Across the top I gave myself the title "*this woman's work*" based on the Kate Bush song of the same name.

At the end of each entry I would place an email link, "write me" and that was my very primitive way—a testament to my lack of technological skill—of adding comments. Having an email link instead of comments allowed me to keep my discussions private, which felt safer to me. If someone had an issue with something I wrote, I could deal with the complaint in private and never have to defend myself in front of what I worried would be a judgmental audience.

At the start I was writing about parenting my then preschool-aged son and the ins and outs of our days. I also wrote about our family's decision to convert my son and myself to Judaism, which garnered some critical emails and made me even more leery about adding comments:

> Writing in a blog is somehow more cathartic than writing in a "real" journal because of the whole audience aspect. I may be limited in what I feel comfortable saying but knowing that other people are reading it is a good thing, too. On the other hand, I don't feel like rigging up a comments feature because I don't necessarily need this to be a two-way writing extravaganza. I don't mind it when folks email me but if I had a comments feature, I'd probably be checking it a lot and then starting dialogues with people I don't know. That can get a person in trouble, which is why so many of us have sworn off online boards and listserves. I told my therapist about the criticism I got from some online people about my conversion and she pointed out that I didn't need to engage with those people. True, but I always feel like I have an obligation to give people another point of view. I have a delusion that even close-minded people could turn open-minded if you give them a pretty little turn of phrase. So far it hasn't happened. (*This Woman's Work*, December 31, 2001)

What I wasn't saying—but what I was feeling—was that I was scared that comments would influence my blog *too* much. I wasn't keen on inviting people to actually participate in my space. (I willfully ignored the fact that, as a reader, I was frustrated that Phoenix' blog didn't have comments.) Having the email link gave me an out—let me look welcoming—but actually created a hurdle not every reader was willing to leap (because once they sent an email they effectively opened their email box up to me, too).

As blogging became more popular and blogging software became easier to manage (and as my tech skills increased enough to figure out how to install a system), I had trouble justifying my one-way street journal.

Visitors expected to be able to comment and several people emailed to say they wanted to be able to talk back to me on-blog. So I took a deep breath and made the leap. In fall of 2002 I began blogging under my own domain (www.thiswomanswork.com) and I added comments. My fourth wall was officially torn down—my blog was now truly open to my visitors.

As it turned out, my fears were unjustified; comments improved my blog. Allowing public discourse gave my journal depth as well as breadth. Giving more control to my readers promoted them to co-creators as they helped direct my narrative. Their comments have become part of my archives, stretching the conversation out in the discussions that run below entries. Their words are there juxtaposed against *my* words, asking more of me, and asking explicitly (in their questions and criticisms) and obscurely (in their encouragement and appreciation). Much-commented posts have often inspired me to write again on the same topic.

Adding comments also cemented my place in the larger virtual community. When a commenter links they have the opportunity to leave their own blog address. Because comments made it easier to carry a conversation back and forth from my blog to another and vice versa, "this woman's work" became part of the community quilt of blogging.

After struggling to have another baby for three years (and blogging about our struggle) my husband and I began discussing adoption in earnest in 2003—and of course I blogged that, too. By then updating my blog was part of my morning routine. I'd pour a cup of coffee, set my then six-year-old son to play nearby and blog. I brought my readers along as we sent away for brochures, debated our options and finally settled in with an agency specializing in domestic infant adoptions. I blogged about writing the profile (the letter given to expectant mothers who were considering adoption), about going to the trainings and about our home-study. I blogged about my whole-hearted excitement about open adoption—an adoption with letters, pictures and even visits between our family and the child's birth family—and my husband's more cautious acceptance that openness would benefit our prospective child.

I also blogged about our decision to become a transracial family. My husband, son and I are white and we decided to use our agency's African American program, meaning that the child we would eventually adopt would be of African descent.

Aimee had been reading and commenting on my blog for some time but the first time she presented herself to me as a birth mom was in a comment on an entry written in October 2003. At that time, we were in the process of being "matched" with a pregnant woman named Tanisha whom I referred to on-blog as "T." Matching, in adoption parlance, meant that Tanisha had chosen our profile and was thinking about placing her yet-to-be-born son with us. I was cautiously excited but realistic about what this meant. Our agency social worker, Denise, told us that there was a 50/50 chance of any adoption "match" failing and explained that most women contacting the agency were exploring adoption—not necessarily committing to it. As it turned out, Tanisha didn't place. She decided to parent her child before we had the opportunity to meet her. Still the situation gave me opportunity to further explore my feelings about our adoption and the role the woman who would choose us would play in our family.

Aimee responded to a post I wrote in mid-November 2003 called, "Entitlement Revisited." In the entry I lamented the tendency of some hopeful parents who wrote scathingly about women they "matched" with and who, like Tanisha, ultimately changed their minds and decided to parent.

"Grief I can understand," I wrote. "Loss, sorrow, anger, frustration—yes, I can totally appreciate having those feelings in general but when it's targeted at the birth-mom, I don't get that. After all, it is her baby and as much as I want T. to place her baby with me, I am always aware that I can't know the path that their relationship is meant to take." (*This Woman's Work*, "Entitlement Revisited," November 16, 2003)

Aimee responded, in part,

> Being a birth mother is the single most lonely, sad, difficult thing of my life.... I normally avoid places where adoption is discussed [but] I really appreciate the thoughtfulness, kindness, compassion, that you express for ... birth mothers ... your writing about it has really helped me calm down a bit and think about things from a place other than my own pain. (Ibid)

With that comment, Aimee changed my blog.

In traditional adoption communities there's a chasm between adoptive parents and birth parents. Our local adoption support group is made up entirely of adoptive families and our agency's training included one scant hour with a birth mother. (Our group's inexperience with birth parenthood was apparent—we stared at her like she was a celebrity. That young woman, only about six months post-partum at our training, suffered yearning gazes with dignity and answered our questions with tired patience.)

Aimee's comment bridged the chasm in which I was writing in two ways. One, she made me remember that there are birth parents among us; she effectively un-othered the other. Two, she reminded me that birth parents have a context—have an existence—outside of adoption. I knew Aimee first as a fellow mom who responded to my posts about home-schooling and using baking soda to wash my hair instead of shampoo. By disclosing her birth motherhood she reminded me that every woman who places a child shouldn't be defined by that singular role.

When I read her post, (when I realized she was a birth mother), I was startled. I felt ashamed, as if I had been caught out talking about someone behind her back. I read back through my archives and wondered what she saw in them. I felt my perspective shift—almost with an audible "thunk"—as Aimee slid into focus as a whole, rounded person who was also a birth mother. I had no idea if she was the only birth parent reading me but from there on out I decided to presume that in any group—in real life or online—any person in front of me might know what it is to place a child for adoption.

But there was more to the way she changed my narrative (and changed me). In that unexpected comment, Aimee told me that I was thoughtful, kind and compassionate. I felt charged with responsibility; I had something to live up to. Without necessarily intending to, her virtual presence in my blog audience would hold me to my promises.

About two months after Aimee's comment, we were "matched" with another woman, named Jessica. This time the adoption plan remained in place and at the end of March 2004 her daughter was born. Then, three days later, she became our daughter. Madison's birthday and the day she came home received more visitors and more comments than my blog had ever had. In the midst of well wishes, Aimee's comment moved me the most, "Oh Dawn, she's just beautiful. Congratulations. Best wishes to you (and Brett and Noah and Madison!) and many prayers for J" (*This Woman's Work*, "She's here!" April 2, 2004).

After Madison's arrival, I grappled with depression brought on in part by bearing witness to Jessica's profound grief. Ours was the kind of fully open adoption I hoped for right from the start with regular phone calls and visits. These were an ongoing reminder of how much Jessica was hurting. It didn't matter how much she reassured me that she felt she'd made the right decision; her grief scared me in its intensity. I already cared deeply for Jessica as a woman—not just as a mother to my daughter. She mattered so much to me and I didn't know how to make sense of our adoption. How could our family's joy justify the depth of Jessica's heartache? I blogged about it a great deal and for the first year post-place-ment, between the baby book entries about Madison's achievements and pictures of her dimpled and drooling self, I wrote long and hard about adoption—about ours in particular and others in general.

Within the safe confines of my blog—within my personal virtual space—I confessed things to my readers that I wasn't ready to tackle in my relationship with Jessica. "I still don't understand why we get to be Madison's parents and why Jessica has to carry the hurt," I blogged in October 2004, when Madison was six months old. "I don't mean that I can't understand why Jessica chose adoption; I'm saying that I can't wrap my head around a universe where such a choice is necessary" (*This Woman's Work,* "Misty water-colored memories," October 12, 2004).

By then there were two other birth mothers regularly reading and commenting on my blog. Laurel blogs (www.magicpointeshoe.com) and has three children, the oldest of whom she placed in a closed adoption. She responded to the above entry with:

> Is it sadness or pity? I'm really not meaning to be snarky. It's just that anytime I've ever mentioned being a birthmother people get that look on their face.... Becoming a birthmother is just as a complex emotional roller coaster of conflicting ideas as you were going through when you adopted Madison. (Ibid)

And I blogged back:

> I think that what I hadn't recognized and which Magicpointe-shoe is helping me to see is that my sad feelings were all about me.... I was projecting. I'm still projecting. But I also think that if the world was more fair, if there was no racism or classism or sexism, that Jessica might have been able to parent. I still think that in a broad way, in a great big overarching philosophical way, her decision was coerced. (*This Woman's Work,*"A Good Question", October 13, 2004)

Katie E., a birth mother in a fully open adoption who does not have a blog, commented:

> I do certainly agree that racism and classism can play a major role in some women's decision to pursue adoption for their children, but in reading these posts I also feel somewhat insulted because it leaves out a huge number of birth moms, myself included. (Ibid)

That exchange, which went on across several entries, reminded me that our adoption could be and should be interpreted and experienced personally as well as politically. To my feminist sensibilities there were several big picture issues that led to Jessica's decision to place Madison with us. If we lived in a world where the work of motherhood was valued, there would be programs to help her practically and financially. If we lived in a world where we didn't have rigid views of what it meant to be a "good" mother, women like Jessica would have emotional support. I felt undone by the impossible injustice of Jessica's loss and my gain.

Katie E.'s response helped me appreciate that Jessica's decision—while made in a particular cultural context—was not invalid because of that context. By focusing on the theoretical issues, I realized, I was ignoring Jessica's right to make decisions within her personal experience. And that gave me the encouragement I needed to go to Jessica directly to ask my questions. Our relationship deepened because I had other women to turn to first.

Through my blog and with the help of my commenters, I was able to write my way through a dialogue that demanded that I see Jessica as her own person, author of her own story, and as someone who was experiencing our adoption in ways I couldn't predict or control.

Looking back, I imagine that if I had never blogged, if I had never added comments to my blog, Aimee likely would not have written me. I don't know if Laurel and Katie E. would have felt welcome to argue with me without one another's presence. I do know that the conversations wouldn't have—couldn't have—happened in the same way.

There were other commenters who positively impacted our adoption—Lisa V., an adoptive mother in a fully-open adoption; Shannon, who was then waiting to adopt and asked hard questions; Maria, whose negative open adoption experience made me even more determined to build a strong relationship with Jessica. But the conversations I had with women who placed a child were those that most influenced—and continue to influence—my feelings about Jessica, about Madison and about myself in my role in the adoption.

Jessica is not the token birth mother in our lives. While she and I often talk about adoption philosophies and theories, she is not my only birth mom resource. I am less inclined to generalize our own story than I might be if she were the only birth mother I had to talk to. At the same time I am able to ask her to speak only for herself in large part because I am privy to a wider conversation.

I write to discover how I really feel and what I really believe. Blogging opens up this process and invites my readers to help me understand myself. When I sit down and click to my blog ready to start an entry, I don't always know what I'll say but I do know how to start. I let myself think "out loud" with my fingers on the keyboard and I count on the responses of my readers to help me to figure out where to go next.

Works Cited

Bruner, J. S. "Life as Narrative." *Social Research* 54 (1987): 1-17.
Friedman, Dawn. *This Woman's Work.* <http://www.thiswomanswork. com>.

Chapter Two

Blogging Pregnancy

Ultrasonography, Connectivity and Identity Construction

JULIE PALMER

Mainstream fetal images tend to represent the fetus as an autonomous individual, appearing to exist separately from the maternal body and in a vacuum, away from the social and political context of pregnancy. This perspective makes it possible to see women and their fetuses as competing subjects whose rights are in conflict. All that is social about pregnancy (kinship, identity, naming, reciprocity, interdependence, etc.) is erased and replaced with the biological (Franklin). These themes have been developed by a number of feminist authors including Carole Stabile and Rosalind Petchesky.

Inspired by Lisa Durbin's, *blog from: a baby*, I want to explore the potential of online sonograms for re-thinking the ways in which visualised fetuses are connected (and disconnected) from the embodied biological and social context of childbearing. Attention to the technology of blogging, hypertext, might suggest new ways of thinking about the issues. I am thinking of hypertext both literally—as the materialisation of a link between items online—and metaphorically—as a metaphor for particular kinds of connections. The motivation for this approach is my observation that, in contrast to mainstream texts, bloggers make tangible connections between fetal scan pictures, the embodied experience of pregnancy, and social aspects of childbearing.

Rebecca Blood describes blogging as link-driven, characterised by in-built, now largely automated, connectivity made possible by hypertext: we click on some text and it takes us elsewhere. Emboldened by Donna Haraway's suggestion that "hypertext is an instrument for reconstructing common sense about relatedness" (125), I wonder whether hypertext is a tool which might be used to reconnect the visualised fetus with women's pregnant bodies and the wider social and political context.

Certainly, hypertext has its problems as a technology and metaphor of connection, most notably "the trope does not suggest which connections make sense for which purposes" (Haraway 127) but, nonetheless, it might enable new ways of thinking about the issues.

George Landow also suggests that hypertext might provide a "laboratory" for critical theorists to test their ideas, particularly ideas about democratisation and non-hierarchical ways of thinking and acting (2). The relevance of these technological models of connectivity to pregnancy emerges for me by comparing them with JaneMaree Maher's notion of the "placental body." Maher suggests that the placenta, as both matter and metaphor, might disrupt the mainstream visual representation of the fetus as separate and autonomous and offer new possibilities for thinking about subjectivity that emphasise interconnectedness, process, in-between-ness and liminality. While Maher reconstructs the connections between women and fetuses by drawing attention back to the placenta—the organic material that literally connects the developing fetus to the womb—perhaps hypertext can do some of the same work of making connections in the online context and beyond.

Introducing "blog from: a baby"

blog from: a baby (now renamed *You'll Take an Eye Out! Words from a Mother*) is written by Lisa, a Canadian from Toronto who has made her home in Britain. Lisa begins her blog in June 2004, when she decides with her male partner to try for a baby. She becomes pregnant soon after and announces the pregnancy online. There follows a witty and detailed account of her pregnancy through to the birth of her son. This account of pregnancy might be read as punctuated by ultrasound examinations and, even between appointments, ultrasound often influences this blogger's thoughts as she anticipates the next scan, or makes plans on the basis of the information that she received at the last scan. In the UK, women are routinely offered two ultrasound examinations as part of their National Health Service (NHS) antenatal care: the first at twelve weeks to date the pregnancy and a second at twenty weeks for purposes of prenatal testing. These two ultrasound examinations constitute important milestones in this account of pregnancy. Lisa summarises thus:

—the first few weeks: still not quite believing that I'm pregnant. Very nervous, super aware of every twinge and ache, and bursting to tell the world.

—after you spill the beans: worried that I've jinxed it. Feel slightly panicky until the first scan date, which takes flippin' forever.
—after the first scan: on cloud nine, still not entirely convinced that there's a baby in there, and feeling less panicky. Wait until the next scan, which takes flippin' forever.
—after the second scan: big relief, and joy at knowing the gender and letting the shopping commence. Once the baby's movements get stronger and I get an impressive bump, it's all so much more real...Super duper mega excited.
—waiting for the delivery: in progress...
(*You'll Take an Eye Out! Words from a Mother*, "Home Stretch," December 2, 2004).

Lisa told me via email that her blog serves two purposes—it updates friends and family, but it is also a source of information for other pregnant women (Durbin 2005). Indeed she positions her account as a valuable alternative to published pregnancy guides that she has found unhelpful. Lisa continues to update the site until her baby boy is born in February and beyond, and she told me that many 'complete strangers' followed her entire pregnancy and continued to read after her son was born.

Lisa inevitably describes her pregnancy in ways that are shaped by her social and cultural context, both in terms of congruence and opposition, and I think we can suppose that a close reading tells us something about the transition to motherhood in contemporary culture. However if "[m]otherhood is...classed and raced" and if "much of the work of mothering involves negotiating, repeating and reciting gendered, classed and raced norms" (Byrne 106) then the blog is also shaped by aspects of the author's identity and is less generalizable. There is some evidence that people read those blogs that are written by others who are similar to them, in age, gender, race, location, and profession (Karlsson 143), and therefore what we know about Lisa might also tell us something about the likely wider audience that her blog reaches. Therefore the analysis presented here is limited by attention to a single case and theme and might be best understood as a node within a much larger networked understanding of pregnancy blogging.

I have selected a small number of posts between June 2004 and the birth of Lisa's first child in February 2005 that all relate to ultrasound scanning, and to Lisa's sense of the developing fetus and of herself as pregnant woman and mother. Lisa continues to write online about pregnancy and motherhood, and readers can find the URL of her blog in the works cited section.

Hypertext and the Placenta

Hypertext refers to a series of blocks of text connected by links which the reader can navigate to create different pathways through the network. The links may connect items within a work, as well as connecting to those external to it, and the effect is to "create a text that is experienced as nonlinear, or, more properly, as multilinear or multisequential" (Landow 4). Like hypertext, the placenta is a "liminal point of between that is always already within" and it marks a point of, and a tension between, distinction as well as connection (Maher 103, 101). As such, in models of connection, two connected objects are neither separate nor identical.

Both Landow and Maher work with ideas of mutable space and connections. For Maher the "space of the pregnant body is one that continually changes" and:

> If one can understand the relation between the maternal and foetal [sic] entities as fluid and processual, as placental, pregnancy ceases to represent a contest for full articulation between two subjects potentially in competition. Instead the possibility of an embodied subject that does not depend on the fixity of its edges emerges (100-101).

So here "placental" means a condition of relation that is fluid, mutable and intertextual.

However, the materiality of the links is different. While I think both hypertext and the placenta have the rhetorical potential to reconnect the visualised fetus with women and with pregnant bodies, perhaps a hypertext model can also offer re-connections with the non-biological context of pregnancy. The placenta, even as a metaphor, might refer to the organic body more easily than to the social.

Presenting Pip

As I read *You'll Take an Eye Out: Words from a Mother* (formerly *blog from: a baby*), I have a sense of interdependent identities in process: as Lisa constructs an identity for "Pip" (as she identifies the fetus) as "baby," she also constructs herself as a pregnant subject and as "mother," and encourages her readers to interact with these new subjects.

It is through the narrative of the twelve-week dating scan that "Pip" is first introduced to the social world:

Presenting Pip!

I promise you, that is actually a baby … Pip was very quiet for the entire scan, moving only when I was asked to cough…. The baby was snuggled into a little space in my womb, and taking after its mother, really couldn't bother to be entertaining at 8:20 in the morning. The lovely ultrasound lady first told us that there was only one baby in there, and then pointed out the heartbeat. That's when I burst into tears that didn't stop flowing for the duration of the scan. Pip has two arms and two legs, is measuring 13 weeks and 1 day … and was kind enough to give us a bit of a wave…. We're so relieved and it's really nice to finally be able to go "public." Now I think I can just enjoy being pregnant. Well done, little Pip (*You'll Take an Eye Out! Words from a Mother,* "our little star of the screen," August 13, 2004).

"Pip" is the name given to the baby when the expectant parents read that the embryo is the size of an apple pip, and the name sticks for the duration of the pregnancy. The twelve-week scan is the point at which Lisa feels able to "go public" with her pregnancy. The moment of "going public" is here mediated by ultrasound scanning as the technology that provides evidence of realness and viability—"Pip has two arms and two legs." For other parents, this landmark may be reached differently. For example, for women attempting to conceive using in-vitro fertilisation (IVF) or donor insemination, their relation with different technologies might necessitate going public earlier, in order to take time out of work or family commitments to go to appointments or meet donors.

The heading of this post—"Presenting Pip"—draws on the language of stage and screen and is evocative of a dramatic first appearance or unveiling. Although "Pip" has already been named (at least with a nickname) and spoken *about*, this is the first time we "see" little "Pip" and the first time "Pip" is addressed directly—"Well done, little Pip." Marilyn Strathern argues that the body is central to personhood: "Culturally speaking, we can see the person when the person appears as an individual, and we see an individual when we see a body" (50). A sonogram can testify to the presence of a body, of something from which sound waves rebound, and the visual presence of "Pip" is deeply significant, despite the lack of clarity of the scan, as evidence of the existence and wellbeing of the fetus. With the pregnancy dated and confirmed, "Pip" can be introduced to family and friends. "Pip" is no longer anonymous. The narrative begins to construct a personality for the fetus which is understood in relation to Lisa's—"Pip" takes after his mother. Lisa and "Pip" are connected and alike: genetically, physically and socially.

More information is later gleaned about "Pip." The sex of the fetus is revealed as part of a commercial ultrasound scan and further influences Lisa's description of the fetus as well as her own identity. Firstly, she suggests that "Pip" is of a shy disposition:

> He was a bit modest at first and wouldn't uncross his legs so the nice scan lady could get a peek. It might have had something to do with the fact that she was training two other women during my scan, so he may have been shy around 4 women.... (*You'll Take an Eye Out! Words from a Mother* "peekaboo," October 13, 2004)

Once "Pip" is gendered, the difficulty of visualising the genitals can be narrated as a tale of modesty in the face of (hetero)sexual difference. Newly-gendered "Pip" is also imaged in three-dimensions, in detailed, rounded pictures in sepia tones, in an upright, portrait-like pose. He is "smiling." A short time after the scan, Lisa reports using the words "our son" for the first time (*You'll Take an Eye Out! Words from a Mother,* "I like that one 'cos it's red," October 18, 2004). "Pip" becomes a more three-dimensional character, both literally and metaphorically, with this new information. "Pip" is somebody's "son": Lisa and her partner are "parents" of a little boy.

Lisa's reasoning for undertaking the 3D scan is to do with learning the sex of the baby and preparing for parenthood:

> it would allow us to know the gender earlier ... and get a few funky 3D images at the same time.... We wanted to do some baby-related shopping in the States, and it would be handy to know the sex of our baby while we're out there.... I really don't like yellow and don't care to inflict it on our child. (*You'll Take an Eye Out! Words from a Mother,* "sneak preview," August 19, 2004)

She books the scan and eagerly awaits another "peek at Pip" (*You'll Take an Eye Out! Words from a Mother,* "dream interpretation 101," September 1, 2004). This interesting trio of factors—an ultrasound scan picture, the sex identified, and shopping or consumption *on behalf of* the fetus—contribute to the construction of fetal personhood, and the imagining of a new little individual who needs (gender appropriate) material things which parents must provide: "Buying things for the fetus on some level amounts to recognizing it as an individual consumer, a baby, a person" (Taylor 2000: 401). Lisa's role as a mother can take on a new dimension once she feels free to shop for the new baby.

"Pip" and Lisa's identities evolve further with each subsequent scan. Lisa describes her second National Health Service (NHS) scan thus:

> After a bit of a stressful journey to the hospital (traffic was a nightmare), we had our big scan this morning. Very pleased to say that all is well and little Pip is doing splendidly. He weighed in at an estimated 451g. and measured 22 weeks (just under a week bigger), and all of his organs /face /skin /bones /extremities are normal. As the sonographer was measuring his femur, we could see that Pip is indeed a little boy.... He rolled around, waved his arms and legs at us, and gave us a few kicks. If the baby's activity inside the womb is any indication of what he'll be like on the outside, we'll definitely have our hands full.
>
> My placenta is high and posterior, and I think this is why I've felt Pip moving around for quite a few weeks now. His latest trick is tapdancing on my bladder. He's so very talented. (*You'll Take an Eye Out! Words from a Mother*, "happy and healthy," October 14, 2004)

More information about the body of the fetus is expressed, in the first instance, as medical measurements and pronouncements that "all is well." The information from the scan is relayed online and taken up to carry important social significance. He is active and healthy: he "tap dances" on his mother's bladder. "Pip" is pictured in a classic profile shot, easily recognisable to unskilled viewers as well as reminiscent of portraiture, setting the scene for describing this individual in terms of temperament and personality. Lisa imagines an interaction with her baby. He is moving around *for her*, in response to her. She anticipates that "Pip" will be an active baby, that his behaviour in the womb is indicative of his behaviour after birth. While "Pip's" movements are now mediated by the position of her placenta, a marker of their literal and anatomical connection, she also anticipates their later impact on her role as mother.

This sense of interconnection between Lisa and "Pip" is mirrored in other aspects of the blog too. For example, the 'bump' is carefully observed and documented. Lisa provides a series of "belly pics" at 13, 14, 24, 29, 33 and 39 weeks, digital photographs of her changing body. In one example, the photograph of the 'bump' is explicitly described as a photograph of "Pip" and Lisa *together* (*You'll Take an Eye Out! Words from a Mother*, "bumpity bump bump," August 20, 2004). Her swollen belly represents the presence of "Pip" but also her own progression towards motherhood. Lisa's assertion that this is a photograph of her *with* "Pip" evokes images of mother and child, and suggests a relational identity.

"Pip" is not only connected to Lisa. Lisa eagerly awaits a time when her male partner will be able to see or feel the movements in her uterus: "Although I've enjoyed this secret method of communication between "Pip" and myself for the past couple of months, I am really eager for Paul to get in on it now too" (*You'll Take an Eye Out! Words from a Mother*, "mind the bump," November 3, 2004). Whereas visualised fetal movements seen during a scan were perceived as an interaction, these examples suggest that fetal movement sensed in other ways is also valued as communication and as a connection between the baby and expectant parents. Lisa gets her wish and Paul finally feels the fetus move:

> Speaking of milestones, yet another exciting one occurred last night—Paul felt Pip squirm and kick for the very first time. Yay!... Paul put his hand on my tummy, and even though Pip did his usual 'ooh there's Daddy. I'm going to hide now' trick for a few seconds, he couldn't resist giving us a good wiggle that Paul could actually feel ... a round of applause for you my kicky boy. (*You'll Take an Eye Out! Words from a Mother*, "Oh, THERE you are!" November 25, 2004)

Again, an interaction is imagined, with the awkwardness of getting Paul to feel for movements at the right time described in terms of a playful baby who is deliberately avoiding sharing this 'secret communication' with any one else. "Pip," voiced by Lisa, addresses "Daddy" with these movements. They become a sign of the realness of the pregnancy and of "Pip," as well as a moment to imagine the triad of mother, father and child. The identity of mother, in this case, is constructed both in relation to a male father and a male child.

In her work on ultrasound, Janelle Taylor suggests a process of bonding through *spectatorship* which is associated with ultrasound and, if parents-to-be bond with the fetus during the examination through spectatorship, then these kinship bonds can be extended to other family members by showing them the sonogram. Of course, this is far from the only means of extending these bonds, and the analysis here rests on access to ultrasound technology (which is not universal) and a culturally specific understanding of that technology and the function it performs (see, for example, Mitchell and Georges for a comparison of Greek and Canadian understanding of ultrasound). However, in this case, sharing the image is important as a means of establishing or strengthening kinship links with the fetus (Taylor 1998: 32-33). The wider connection is with the "public" sphere, with an "audience" who is obliquely referenced in the account. This seems to refer not just to the couple and the sonographer but, once the sonogram is posted, pasted, recontextualised online, to those who read the blog, whether family members, friends, or passing strangers. In fact, Lisa seeks to share the sensations of fetal movement with a much wider audience when she makes a video file to show the movement of her belly and posts it to her blog (*You'll Take an Eye Out! Words from a Mother*, "now I've just got to resist the urge to stuff my face," December 21, 2004). Hypertext provides the technology with which to make this public, and a point of connection between the fetus and those who see or feel the movement. When the movement can be felt by Paul or seen by readers of the blog, connections are forged between the baby and a wider social circle. The opportunity to interact with this new subject, at least notionally and playfully, is provided by the comments feature of the blog.

Rethinking Interconnection

Whilst the construction of maternal body and fetus as "separated sites" (Maher 96) is problematic from a feminist perspective, my reading of Lisa's blog suggests that families do begin to construct the visualised fetus as a new family member and a semi-autonomous individual. If the use of hypertext links "simultaneously blurs borders and bridges gaps, yet draws attention to them" (Landow 20), writing online might resist dangerous (over)simplification of the pregnant subjectivity and fetal existence. Hypertext might be a way of reflecting blurred and porous boundaries between pregnant women, fetuses and the social world.

Perhaps simultaneously blurring boundaries and drawing attention to them is a way forward in our thinking about fetuses. It avoids the radical separation of the biological from the social aspects of pregnancy; it avoids simplifications that might suggest that the fetus is independent of the pregnant woman (untenable in terms of physiology) or that the fetus is indistinguishable from the pregnant woman (incongruous with many people's experience—we do begin to think of the fetus as a new baby as a pregnancy progresses).

In addition, the hypertext model potentially reconnects the fetus with all that is social about childbearing. Online, the sonogram is at least partially connected with stories of frustration about the traffic on the way to the hospital appointment, tales of morning-sickness and accounts of significant purchases both through narrative collage but also hypertext links that draw boundaries and make connections between different kinds of events and experiences over the course of a pregnancy. Readers can jump between posts, from the scan pictures to other landmarks: a positive pregnancy test, 'belly pics', first toy bought.

For Landow, hypertext has no fixed centre but is experienced by the readers as an "infinitely decenterable and recenterable system." So any text may have a central point, perhaps for a particular reader, but this centre will be mutable and transient (Derrida cited in Landow 37, 38). In principle, a sonogram may appear as part of a web of texts with no fixed central point. Lisa designates certain events "milestones," creating a click-able list of these key moments on the front page of the blog. The scan pictures are among these 'milestones', but their significance changes as the pregnancy progresses and other events take on similar or greater importance. Can a hypertextual understanding of pregnancy allow us to "recenter" the female body and pregnant women's subjectivity? If it could, this would also be a transient state. In this fluid model, both the fetus and the pregnant woman might move in and out of the centre depending on the context and on what is at stake. Other agents might move in and out of the centre, such as a non-birth mother, a father or other co-parent, and the centre would remain continuously temporary and mutable. Nonetheless, this kind of understanding might allow for a more nuanced and complicated view of the relationship between women and their fetuses and the social context of that relationship. Hypertext, as an imperfect model of connection, enables complex, networked interconnections, and provides a means of drawing boundaries and simultaneously blurring of them in ways that more closely resemble women's lived experiences of pregnancy.

My gratitude to Lisa Durbin for permission to cite from blog from: a baby. This chapter is based on my doctoral research which was funded by the Arts and Humanities Research Council (AHRC). Thanks also to Ann Kaloski for her continuing support and to Petra Nordqvist for comments on earlier drafts of this chapter.

Works Cited

Aarseth, Espen J. *Cybertext: Perspectives on Ergodic Literature.* Baltimore: John Hopkins Press, 1997.

Blood, Rebecca. "Weblogs: A History and Perspective." *Rebecca's pocket.* 7 September 2000. Retrieved July 2, 2005 <http://www.rebeccablood. net/essays/weblog_history.html>.

Byrne, Bridget. *White Lives: The Interplay of "Race," Class and Gender in Everyday Life.* Abingdon, Oxon: Routledge, 2006.

Durbin, Lisa. "Your blog." Email to Julie Palmer. 17 June 2005.

Franklin, Sarah. "Fetal Fascinations: New Dimensions of the Medical-Scientific Constructions of Fetal Personhood." *Off-Centre: Feminism and Cultural Studies.* Eds. Celia Lury and Jackie Stacey. London: HarperCollins Academic, 1991. 190-205.

Haraway, Donna. *Modest_Witness@Second_Millenium. Female Man©_ Meets_Oncomouse™.* New York: Routledge, 1997.

Karlsson, Lena. "Desperately Seeking Sameness: The Processes and Pleasures of Identification in Women's Diary Blog Reading." *Feminist Media Studies* 7 (2) (2007): 137-152.

Landow, George P. *Hypertext 2.0: The Convergence of Contemporary Critical Theory and Technology.* Baltimore: The John Hopkins University Press, 1997.

Maher, JaneMaree. "Visibly Pregnant: Toward a Placental Body." *Feminist Review* 72 (2002): 95-107.

Mitchell, Lisa and Eugenia Georges. "Cross-Cultural Cyborgs: Greek and Canadian Discourses on Fetal Ultrasound." *Feminist Studies* 23 (2) (1997): 373-401.

Petchesky, Rosalind Pollack. "Foetal Images: The Power of Visual Culture in the Politics of Reproduction." *Reproductive Technologies: Gender, Motherhood and Medicine.* Ed. Michelle Stanworth. Cambridge and Oxford: Polity Press in association with Basil Blackwell, 1987. 57-80.

Stabile, Carole A. *Feminism and the Technological Fix.* Manchester: Manchester University Press, 1994.

Strathern, Marilyn. *After Nature: English Kinship in the Late Twentieth Century.* Cambridge: Cambridge University Press, 1992.

Taylor, Janelle S. "Image of Contradiction: Obstetrical Ultrasound in American Culture." *Reproducing Reproduction: Kinship, Power and Technological Innovation.* Eds. Sarah Franklin and Helena Ragoné. Philadelphia: University of Pennsylvania Press, 1998. 15-45.

Taylor, Janelle S. "Of Sonograms and Baby Prams: Prenatal Diagnosis, Pregnancy, and Consumption." *Feminist Studies* 26 (2) (2000): 391-418.

Turkle, Sherry. *Life on the Screen: Identity in the Age of the Internet.* New York: Simon & Schuster, 1995.

You'll Take an Eye Out! Words from a Mother. Retrieved June 10, 2005. <http://www.wittydomainname.com/BlogJr.html>.

Chapter Three

I Kid You Not

How the Internet Talked Me Out of Traditional Mommyhood

JENNIFER GILBERT

[If you] do not have kids and have ever wondered what life would be like, just go turn on a blender and stick your face in it. That. —Heather Armstrong (*Dooce*, "Life without the nap," July 13, 2007)

On a December day when I was twenty-six years old, I sat in a waiting room and watched a parade of gray-faced men emerge from examination rooms and stagger by me, clutching packs of ice to their crotches and mumbling reassurances with woozy machismo. One particularly boisterous man came out, gave his wife a smile, and said, "That was no big deal!" Then he passed out.

As a swarm of nurses armed with orange juice descended upon this latest lawsuit risk, I kept my eyes trained on the door directly in front of me. My husband was in there.

How does a childless twenty-six-year-old end up in a generically upholstered chair, watching anxious wives bounce babies on their knees? What sort of influence motivates a small-town girl, under enormous cultural pressure to reproduce, to sit through an informational video starring a penis as the main character, pondering the odd audition that must have been involved? What prompted her to eagerly sign at least three separate waivers under the scrutiny of a dubious physician?

I'll tell you. It's called the mommyblog, and it changed my life.

Great Expectations

When I got married at the doddering age of twenty-two, a remarkable thing happened: the world went from begging me not to fornicate to begging me to enjoy the wonders of lovemaking as often as possible while the seeds of blessing took root in my womb. With the exchange of a few pieces of jewelry, what had been forbidden as a detestable, dirty act of unspeakable sin suddenly became the most promoted pastime this side of Gymboree. An enchanted era between compulsory abstinence and compulsory motherhood does exist, and the technical term for it is "a wedding reception." Make sure you enjoy it, because the very minute the clock turns midnight, your grandmother is allowed to publicly demand an heir.

Though I was startled to find myself fielding intensely personal questions regarding my gametes before my honeymoon jet lag had even worn off, I didn't mind the pressure. I wanted to be a mother. Who didn't? The booties were adorable, the showers were lavish, and the rewards were … well, I wasn't sure yet what the rewards were, but they had something to do with dimpled, chortling toddlers in footie pajamas. All I knew was that when I shoved a pillow under my stretchiest turtleneck sweater, I liked the grown-up, life-giving woman I saw in the mirror. I was going to be really cute pregnant, and everyone was going to look at me and buy me presents. When you're twenty-two, that's all the rationale you need for decisions that will drastically affect the rest of your living years. I shaped a few dim notions of crib mobiles and chubby baby cheeks into a conviction that I wanted to be a mother.

With my decision made, all I had to do was wait until it was time, financially speaking, for that first baby to be born. My husband and I bought a house, got a dog, and stood daydreaming in the small bedroom that would make a perfect nursery for any bundles of joy that might come along.

Thankfully, the mommyblog was conceived first.

The Bubble Bursts

I'll never forget the first time I visited a mommyblog. I'm not sure what I was expecting, but based on how eagerly parenting had been recommended to me, the first post I read should have gone something like this:

> Dear Internet,
>   Today the Hallmark card people came to photograph my life. I think the pictures came out pretty well, though little Spencer's Santa hat was a little crooked in the one where we're all celebrating his first Christmas with champagne toasts for the adults and hot chocolate for the little ones.

My husband, Preston, actually bought Spence his first little red trike—can you believe it? As if a nine-month-old has much use for that! I've told Preston that we're already spoiling Spence, but that man is just filled to bursting with pride, and there's no reasoning with him. (Secretly, I have to confess to you that Preston's excitement over our son makes me love my husband all the more, and I didn't even know that was possible.) I thought for sure that Spence would just stare at it in confusion, but instead he tugged the handlebar ribbons with one dimpled hand, then used his baby signs to say, "Thank you, Daddy. I love you!" We laughed and cried at the same time as our son reaffirmed what we already knew: parenting is all the goodness of chocolate pudding and fluffy kittens put together, but with none of the funny aftertaste. Happy holidays, everyone!

Instead (and if you will allow me to paraphrase), it went something like this:

OMG Internet,

Just when I thought nothing could possibly be left in there, Spencer's poop geyser erupted again. I ingested an unusual amount of it this time—that's the last time I speak while holding him. I think I'll feel better just as soon as I manage to brush my teeth. Of course, if I set Spence down, he'll scream until he chokes on his own vomit and turns a shade of blue that sends me into a hysterical panic, but my husband gets home at five, so the sweet relief of minty toothpaste is only six hours away. Well, provided my husband doesn't stop at the bar on the way home from work. Which, come to think of it, he's doing more and more these days. Sometimes I wish I were him, so I could just grab a bottle of whiskey and guzzle my way out of this mess. And I mean *all* the way out of this mess—as in, like, dead, because dying is the only way I'm ever going to get some sleep around here. Is it weird that I feel jealous every time I drive past a cemetery? They just seem so peaceful.

Ha, ha. Just kidding. What I mean to say is that being a mother is having your heart walk around outside your body and I can't imagine life without my son because I didn't know what love was until I looked into his eyes. Oh, crap, gotta go—Spence just yanked a clump of my hair out, the little imp, and my scalp is bleeding all over the keyboard.

I was, in a word, perturbed. The pride and love I had always imagined were there, for sure, but now these intensely positive emotions seemed sort of ... well, unjustifiable and deranged. These mothers weren't playing catch with their children in fields of daisies, like in the allergy medicine commercials. These mothers were mopping up puke at three in the morning, their sweatpants hiked up high enough that you could see the ringed bite marks on their calves. And if that commercial existed, I certainly hadn't seen it.

Everyone had always told me that parenting was terribly hard work, but "hard work" is a cliched, patronizing phrase that doesn't warrant much attention. To this day, I am sure that if my high school parenting class teacher had used the phrase "poop geyser," I could have better appreciated the urgency of contraception. As my wide eyes scanned one mommyblog after another, my education finally began. Never have the lessons of life as a parent been so cheaply and plentifully available to the public, and I took advantage.

A Virtual Chorus

During my months and years of mommyblog readership, my doubts grew from wee and niggling to enormous and crippling. Having children, I slowly realized, *would change everything*. Sure, people had told me this, but in my opinion they didn't deliver the information with the warranted intensity. At the very least, they could have grabbed my shoulders and shaken me until my teeth rattled while repeating the statement at top volume and punctuating their words with choked sobs.

Instead, they chuckled about it over tea cakes at baby showers, turning a lifetime of bone-weary servitude into a sip of Earl Grey and a rueful smile. Parents have a way of doing that, I've discovered. The indescribability of motherhood forces them into a mastery of understatement. I don't blame them for their glib remarks; motherhood is so large that writers are still trying to fit words around it. Millions of blogs later, people are still trying, but they get closer all the time.

The social contribution of the mommyblog has, at times, come into question. In 2005—the last year I spent shivering in the cold shadow of looming motherhood before fleeing entirely—*New York Times* reporter David Hochman wrote that in many cases, the mommyblog is "an online shrine to parental self-absorption." "For the generation that begat reality television," he wrote, "it seems that there is not a tale from the crib (no matter how mundane or scatological) that is unworthy of narration" ("Mommy (and Me)," January 30, 2005). But I saw nothing mundane in that virtual chorus of women who came tumbling through my computer screen and into my consciousness.

These women shared with me the incomparable joy of the first moment they laid eyes on their children; the proud heartbreak of the first day of school; and the helpless terror of a skyrocketing fever. With the perfunctory selflessness that I've come to associate almost exclusively with motherhood, these women diagrammed the anatomy of lives forever changed by mothering: expanded, stretched, and scarred, but more beautiful than ever. These bloggers have chronicled every episiotomic slice of the scalpel and every murmur of the overflowing heart, and they have done it with none of the tea-sipping coyness one might associate with croissant sandwiches from the local caterer.

Right after I established that mothering was a thankless, Sisyphean exercise that involved prying jellybeans and loose change out of a child's nose from sunup to sundown, I explored the emotional side of parenting. This tender underbelly of sentimentality, so often the very reason parents everywhere continue to get out of bed in the morning, appalled me even more. The last thing I wanted was to allow my heart to run around outside of my body. The pleasant connotation of this potentially disastrous proposition baffled me. What if my heart moved five states away, married someone I couldn't stand, and never ever called me except on Christmas and my birthday? I much preferred my heart right where it was, safely tethered to its aortic leash and then caged in bone for good measure.

As blogger after blogger echoed these themes of poignant sacrifice, my choice became clear. I backed off the procreation precipice, sold my house, and moved to the city. I traveled extensively, joined a roller derby league, and explored a different world in which tattoos would never have to be explained, inheritances could be spent, and alarm clocks had long been silenced. From the moment my hometown and its surrounding atmosphere of well-meaning expectation slid from my rearview mirror, a great weight was finally lifted. The relief was so intense that my husband and I promptly decided to seal the deal with two small incisions and a painkiller—proving that you can, in fact, be sterilized via wi-fi, though perhaps not quite as the alarmists might predict. With one early-morning appointment, I said goodbye to biological parenting.

Social Implications

By some accounts, a prophet said more than two thousand years ago that the truth will set you free. As a new millennium dawned centuries later, the Internet proved that the truth will set a lot of other people free as well, should you be so kind as to blog about it. It's not as if no book or magazine has ever covered the topic of motherhood, but the plenitude, breadth, and accessibility of the mommyblog changed everything.

According to demographics cited in *Advertising Age* magazine (Thompson 6), the average age of the mommyblog reader is 29 years old. One advertising survey of over thirteen thousand mommyblog readers noted that nearly half of them fell in the 22–30 age range (www.blogads.com, "2006 Mom Blogs Reader Survey"), and 805 of the survey respondents were even younger. Nearly half of all survey respondents answered that they read mommyblogs for their honesty. Participants weren't asked whether they had children themselves, but nearly a third noted that they didn't discuss parenting, babies, and children in their own lives on a weekly basis.

Meanwhile, it seems as if more women are waiting until their thirties or forties to have children. Now that women have both more time and more information to make a sound decision about their reproductive choices, I can only imagine how many fates have been changed by this new means of communication.

That sound decision could go either way, of course. The mommyblog didn't save me from an objectively unpleasant outcome. It merely equipped me with information. What I did with that information was up to me. Where so many would have shrugged and gone forward anyway—where so many would feel inspired to pay thousands of dollars for fertility treatments to go forward, if that turned out to be necessary—I chose another route. I chose it because I'm often too lazy even to feed myself, because I am impatient, because I adore sleep, and because I never, ever want a Tuesday night alone at the supermarket to feel like heaven. I chose it because this is who I am, and if I can't change that, I can at the very least avoid foisting it onto another human being.

Some would call my decision selfish. I call it responsible. In a more introspective world, no small percentage of parents would eventually acknowledge their unsuitability as caregivers. Thanks to the latest technology, I did it without ever giving birth in the first place. Welcome to the digital age.

It's a Small World After All

My life over the years since I loaded that first mommyblog doesn't resemble that of any mothers I know, but through it all, I've thought of them. When, during a typical trip with my husband (a commercial pilot), I soaked in a geothermally heated lagoon in Iceland, that awareness bobbed on the surface even as the steam rose and snow fell.

Whether I'm touring a marketplace in Tokyo or just contemplating my own bellybutton on my couch, one part of the view is the same: that other path, the one that winds away from a fork in the road created by a fifteen-minute outpatient surgery, is always there. I've never felt its grit under my feet, but that landscape is familiar to me nonetheless. The life within its borders (which are now cut and cauterized) will never be completely foreign to me. Blogs have thinned these boundaries, remapping society into a more intimate geography.

As warming as that idea might be, not everyone will find my story very inspirational, at least not thus far. I'm not sure it counts as a happy ending—my husband and I emerging from the door of that vasectomy clinic like butterflies from a very expensive cocoon, then taking flight toward a new adventure (one that, for my husband's sake, hopefully includes a few bags of frozen peas). Information is power, yes, but my choice to forgo the propagation of the species in favor of afternoon naps may not be considered a ringing endorsement for the mommyblog. Not everyone would consider this a tale of empowerment, but rather, one in which a self-absorbed medium begets an even more highly evolved version of egocentrism—one so concentrated and dense that it wobbles on the edge of collapsing into a black hole, rendering humanity extinct.

A richly informed choice can still be considered the wrong choice, especially if the priority system applied is one of those tiresome ones that does not value my personal happiness above all else. Allow me to redeem myself now, or at least nurture hope that I do not exist on this earth solely as a consumer whose travel belches pollution into the atmosphere and whose childfree dollars fund corporate sweatshops.

Once I decided not to have children, I was at a bit of a loss regarding my long-term plans. I didn't feel empty, or unfulfilled, but I did feel a certain sense of duty. If I wasn't going to have to stay up all night with a baby until I developed undereye bags of presidential proportions, the very least I could do was contribute to society in some other way. I paid attention when people spoke of volunteerism and charity work. I kept my well-rested eyes open, waiting for something to compel me.

I found answers, once again, in the mommyblog—the very medium that had steered me away from parenting in the first place.

The Erosion of Ignorance Continues

Allowing the culture around us to define parenting lends itself to an unnaturally narrow definition. According to my small-town upbringing, a mother was a woman who gave birth to a child. As I perused a wealth of adoption blogs, my mommyblog education quickly debunked this definition of motherhood as both ignorant and unimaginative.

Women who adopt children are mothers. Women who foster children are mothers. Women with stepchildren are mothers. Women who knit sweaters for their Chihuahuas and post pictures of the results online are ... not mothers in the technical sense, but nurturing in their own special way.

In retrospect, it seems so obvious that birthing and mothering are not the same thing, but one must never underestimate the ignorance of a young woman who lived along the same stretch of interstate until she was twenty-five years old. Before I abandoned my own more traditional dreams of motherhood, I had always assumed that adopting and fostering were what women did when they had no other choice. To me, such parenting options clearly fell into a column labeled "Plan B." As impossible as it might be to believe, it had never occurred to me that such a notion could be considered offensive. It probably needn't be explained that I didn't get out much back then.

Motherhood Reclaimed

I would imagine that most biological mothers cannot articulate exactly why they wanted children. Objectively speaking, no logical reason exists. Children don't bestow immortality. They aren't particularly likely to save the world or even do much besides replace their parents—who, in developed countries, are often unintentional over-consumers whose privileged existence does more harm than good, globally speaking. Children can never reciprocate the fierce brand of love they receive from their parents. Children are expensive, selfish, and exhausting.

Still, young women everywhere anticipate parenting with impatient excitement, and mothers everywhere find joy every day. Painstakingly scrapbooked albums are filled with photographs of birthday parties and trips to the beach, and wisps of hair are brushed back every night from small foreheads to make room for goodnight kisses. Somewhere past the edge of rationality lies wonder, and new parents discover it all the time.

The mommyblog removed my hopes of ever reaching that place, then renewed them all over again. With the same lack of logic that more typical parents-to-be exhibit all the time, I started to daydream about middle age, when I had seen the world and was ready to offer it something in return.

Some women knit booties or buy baby blankets; I researched foster care for teenagers and educated myself on attachment disorders. Some women ask their mothers for breastfeeding advice; I ran blog searches for foster and adoptive parents who described their difficulties and solutions in painstaking detail. The Internet offered me a vastly expanded horizon of family structures—biracial, same-sex, dual faith, and every other permutation of kinship under the sun—and suddenly, my interest in foster adoption didn't seem unusual. No two families are alike, and every family structure is valuable in its own way—and that's a sentiment the Internet has turned into a whopping understatement.

In some ways, these foster-adoption blogs painted an even less romantic portrait of motherhood: "I don't think that I can cure her, no matter how much I love her," wrote one blogger of her adopted daughter, who was exposed to drugs in utero (www.baggageandbug.com, 29 July 2007). Paradoxically, this version of motherhood was starker than the one that had scared me away. All the same, I had found my future once again ... but this time, my future and I started out together on brutally honest terms.

I don't know why I vastly prefer teenagers to toddlers. Objectively speaking, the differences (admittedly negligible during a tantrum) certainly don't always fall in the favor of the former. My heart would still be outside my body, after all—and worse, it would be sullen and moody and likely to storm off in a huff at the least provocation. Traditional biological parents want their hearts to crawl before they can walk; mine is likely to start off with a driver's license. Just like traditional motherhood, it should be terrifying ... but somehow, it just isn't, and in the illogical realm of parenting, an unjustifiable level of enthusiasm is all anyone really needs to get started.

Nowadays, my husband and I sound much like any recently married couple. "How many kids do you want?" I'll tease him. "Ten or twelve is okay, right?" The only difference is, we aren't talking about the near future (though we should probably start saving for college tuition just the same). We don't toss around baby names, but other than that, we have the same discussions as any other parents-to-be: what kind of house we want to live in, what our rules will be, and which one of us gets to stutter our way through the conversation about birth control.

I'm not sure exactly how my sons or daughters will turn out, and my expectations are perhaps more guarded than most. But, thanks to the mommyblog, I found the version of parental uncertainty that I could live with. I decided that even if my efforts resulted only in one additional person having somewhere to go for holidays and birthday dinners, I personally would feel more fulfilled than I ever would have as a traditional parent.

Somewhere in the future will stand a house full of people who were strangers not long ago. I can't tell you how often they will fight, how often tears will be shed, or how often everyone in question will ponder aloud whether heads should be examined. But I do have one hope. After raising my children, with their enormous emotional baggage and questionable odds and really unfortunate piercing decisions, I hope that I will still feel exactly as I do now about the digital medium: it informs, it empowers, and it helps us become exactly who we are.

And if I end up disenchanted with that medium instead ... well, perhaps I'll feel better after I blog about it.

Works Cited

Baggageandbug.com. "Blogathon 3 am." 29 July 2007. Accessed 2 Sept. 2007. [http://baggageandbug.com/2007/07/29/blogathon-3-am/]

BlogAds.com. "2006 Mom Blogs Reader Survey." 31 Mar. 2006. Pressflex LLC. Accessed 3 Sept. 2007. <http://www.blogads.com/survey/2006_mom_blogs_reader_survey.html>.

Dooce.com. "Life Without the Nap." 13 July 2007. Accessed 2 Sept. 2007. <http://www.dooce.com/archives/daily/07_13_2007.html>.

Hochman, David. "Mommy (and Me)." *The New York Times* 30 Jan. 2005.

Thompson, Stephanie. "Mommyblogs: A Marketer's Dream." *Advertising Age* 26 Feb. 2007: 6

Chapter Four

Kindred Keyboard Connections

How Blogging Helped a Deafblind Mother Find a Living, Breathing Community

LISA FERRIS

A few days ago, I took my two-and-a-half-year-old twin boys to a birthday party. This is likely a common occurrence for other moms, but for me it was unusual, and therefore especially significant. It was the first time they had ever been guests in another home; not including their father's apartment down the street.

I don't take personally that we aren't at the top of most people's invitation lists. We are a logistical nightmare, a demographic dilemma. We quite literally don't fit in. My co-parenting partner, Dwight, a man I have had a relationship with for thirteen years, is quadriplegic. His 500-pound power wheelchair can't make it into most people's homes. I am deafblind. I have some residual vision and hearing, but to go visiting requires that I take my toddlers on multiple buses and trains. And once I get to my destination, there is very little chance for me to be able to socialize. I can't hear most of the conversation, I can't easily see to perform the polite and expected etiquette of helping to prepare coffee or clear my own dishes—at least not easily while supervising twins. These are some of the logistical and physical barriers to our having a large social circle "in real life." But more difficult to define and overcome are the subtle attitudinal and lifestyle differences between us and many of our peers in our suburban, tract-housing community. Although both myself and my partner are well-educated—he has a degree in engineering and I have a Master's in Education—and both of us work part-time, we are at a significantly lower socioeconomic level than our neighbors. There are other significant differences. Dwight and I are not married because marriage would cause him to lose the medical insurance that provides for healthcare and equipment that his life depends on. We lived together in a small apartment before becoming parents, but the discovery of a double pregnancy and an offer from my father to rent, at cost, his wheelchair inaccessible house forced us to live apart. Although he can access the main floor of my small home via a homemade ramp through the garage, my partner now must live a few blocks away in his own apartment. To further complicate our story, our twins were conceived through third-party donor insemination due to fertility issues. Dwight is their legal adoptive parent, and so far their biology is not a huge aspect in our lives. But because wheelchair users are rather known to have fertility issues, and because having twins screams of fertility treatment, and because they simply don't look much like their father, we are an easy mark for judgment. People who have strong feelings about fertility treatments, unmarried parents and/or disabled parents have targeted us with nosy, rude and ill-informed comments and questions. Exchanges such as incorrect assumptions that we paid thousands of dollars for a "test-tube baby" while on "welfare" to calls to child protective services because my premature infants had some common eating issues at birth, or rude questions about whether our children are really "ours" have made us somewhat defensive about networking and socializing with people in our community.

I began blogging years ago. Blogs were strange, fringe, and geeky online diaries and I was a young career woman in my late twenties who was struggling to stay employed as my vision and hearing faded. I found writing online liberating for a number of reasons. It was a forum where I, a deafblind woman, could communicate on an equal footing. Communicating with people in real life is a constant struggle in which who I am—my thoughts, my intelligence, my grace and consideration, the essence of me—is lost in a physically exhausting struggle to simply keep track of what is going on around me. I sometimes feel like my personality is crushed by the failure of my vision and hearing to allow me to communicate in ways that people are familiar with. People who don't know me well seem to find me somewhere in a range between, at worst, mentally incompetent, or at best, quirky and discomforting. Online, by contrast, I found a small audience of intelligent peers who respected my opinions and engaged me in thoughtful discussions without regard to my disability. It was my nerdy secret social oasis.

During my pregnancy and after the birth of my children, I stopped blogging for about a year. After life calmed down and we were all sleeping through the night, I started a new blog, thinking that I would again have a little hobby to keep me sane through the exhaustive monotony of parenting two infants. Meanwhile, in my real life, I started to really worry about how our isolation would affect the development of our two new children who have no known disabilities. How could we afford them opportunities to build relationships in the world when we couldn't do it very well for ourselves? We decided that we needed to suck it up and get to work. Concerned that we might need to go through one hundred rejections to get to one social connection, we decided to get cracking.

We started attending a church and I went to several moms of multiples support groups and got involved in a gym and tried to do anything else I could think of to create connections in my neighborhood. Although people were (and are) generally polite to us, real connections just weren't happening. Dwight had to succumb to being determined "homebound" by Medicare so that he could receive life sustaining medical care. This meant that he was often stuck at or near home. My main problem was that the way people normally meet and develop friendships just wasn't possible for me. I can communicate with people fairly well in a quiet, one on one situation when I am familiar with the context. Essentially, I have to get people into my home in order to communicate, but that isn't the way friendships usually develop. Typically people might start in a large group situation like a church congregation. Then they might join a committee and get better acquainted with a smaller group of people. Eventually, one or two of them might click and go out for coffee together. Finally, people might grow close enough to spend time visiting in each other's homes. I need to go in the opposite direction. If I can get to know a person one on one in my home, then we might be able to enjoy each other's company in a larger group. Meeting people in any kind of large group setting is counter-productive. Others see me at my most challenged and cannot get the answers they need to understand how to accommodate my disability. People seem to need to know my back story and to get information about my disability in order to feel comfortable enough to hang around me. A large church social hall is not the ideal place for me to try to create a sound bite about my deafblindness and my whole strange little family situation. Despite all my efforts, I began to grow disheartened.

Suddenly, however, something unexpected and wonderful started happening. While my invitations to come to my house for coffee were going unanswered, my blogging connections were growing by leaps and bounds. Relationships were blooming both in quantity and quality. Blogging was starting to become less of a hobby and more of a means to develop the much needed community I so strongly desired for me and my children.

With my blog, I can essentially invite people to my "virtual home." I have a chance to tell people my complicated back-story without communication barriers. Readers have a chance to understand who I am and can wait to introduce themselves to me when they feel comfortable enough with me to do so. I have never felt much of the awkwardness of putting all my private business on the Internet that some bloggers feel because I did not have the luxury of hiding my issues in real life. People look at our family and instantly make assumptions and judgments about us that are not fair or accurate. Online, people know *me* and my family: not what we might look like as we walk down the street—a quadriplegic wheelchair user, a blind, white cane user that signs, and a double stroller pulled backwards with children who may or may not look like the strange couple hauling them around. They know *me*, not someone they connect with for three the seconds most people allot me before they cast me off as stupid or pitiful or incompetent. Online, people see me, a mom who loves her kids and all the goofy things they do. An intelligent and coherent communicator with an education and a career. A political activist. A woman with the same dreams and accomplishments and fears and problems others have within their own families.

The risk I take in blogging my life to potentially a whole world of strangers has been offset tenfold by the connections I have made. Since I fit no common demographic, it is difficult to find anyone locally who has much in common with me. When I opened up my life to the whole world, however, I found that there are a lot of people out there like me. Nobody has everything in common with me, but when you cast as wide a net as the Internet allows, you get to make cross-categorical connections while simultaneously sharing, with a variety of different people, such basic human truths as just trying to be a good mom.

When you wake up in the night alone and worried about a problem that no one else understands, the miracle of being able to search for a blog written by someone who has been there means you are never quite alone. If I'm worried about how my sons will react to being conceived through donor insemination, I can find someone who has been there and done that with their own children. If I am unsure of ways to keep track of my children at the playground with low vision, there is another blind mom out there that I can brainstorm with. If I am struggling with the fact that, for all practical purposes, I am a single mom, I can find single moms who can encourage me. Should I potty train my twins at the same time or separately? What has worked for other moms of twins?

These are important assets of blogging, but the overall benefit runs deeper than that the specifics of my situation. My isolation might be extreme, but moms in general are isolated in our society, especially when they, as I have, put their careers on hold when their children are small. Women have traditionally mothered together across generations and within communities. The institution of the nuclear family has made those opportunities to share in parenting less common. The Internet, by contrast, fosters much more of a community approach to parenting. Despite my disabilities and the obvious barriers I have networking in my own physical community, I am extremely surprised by the depth of some of my friendships and alliances in the virtual community.

One of the most rewarding surprises of my blogging experience has been the connections I have made with lesbian moms. I have never considered myself homophobic, but never had any real ties to the gay community either. Within days of starting my second blog after my kids were born, I had a surprise audience of lesbian moms. We found commonalities with each other within the context of fertility and donor issues, the fact that we couldn't legally marry our partners due to arbitrarily ridiculous government regulations, and the fact that we sometimes receive criticism for our decision to become parents. I developed a friendship with one mother in particular that has become so cherished and special to me that my partner and I have asked her family to take over guardianship of our children should something happen to us. Whenever I hear anyone say that online relationships aren't real because they are not with "living, breathing people," I think of her and the fact that she has given me more respect and support than many of the "living, breathing people" in my real life that cannot get past some of their initial perceptions. I have also made many connections and allies within the online adoption community. My partner and I tried to adopt without success prior to pursuing fertility treatments. Although this was infuriating at the time because it was mainly due to prejudice surrounding our disabilities, I now think it was a blessing in disguise. We were too stupid to adopt back then. Through reading about bloggers who have adopted (many of them lesbian moms), I have radically changed my views on adoption, specifically with regards to the rights of birthmothers and their role in the adoption process. Before getting to know people's stories first-hand through their blogs, I never would have considered open adoption or the fact that it is perfectly natural for children to have more than one "real" mother. We do still contemplate the possibility of adoption and/or foster care in the future. Thanks to the blogs I've read, I now feel so much more prepared and open to the possibility of working to develop a fair and trusting relationship with a child's biological family. This feeling didn't come about during all of the research and meetings and classes that we spent hours on when we were in the midst of trying to adopt. This realization only came about by building relationships with a diverse group of bloggers who had real and varying experiences and opinions, and who were open to frank discussions about tough questions.

To know people's individual stories is to break down barriers and bring people together. No other tool can be used as successfully to battle prejudice than to really try to know someone's story from their own point of view. This is often so hard to do in the everyday world. Online, by contrast, there are virtually limitless opportunities to learn about issues from a first person point of view. Not only have other bloggers opened my eyes to some of my own ignorance and prejudices, but I am told all the time that my own writing opens other people's eyes as well.

I pride myself on writing meaty political posts about hard topics like abortion or euthanasia or my (surprisingly controversial) decision to forego circumcising my sons. And although these posts get good responses, I think the posts that have probably broken the most barriers have been the ones I consider the boring "mommyblog" posts. The day-to-day nitty-gritty mommy stuff where I talk about and post pictures of the typical adventures of my two-year-olds have gone a long way toward helping people realize that disabled people *can* be good parents.

When my kids were around nine months old, I made a little book for them full of pictures of them doing their typical daily routines. I decided to post the pictures online and explain the day in the life of infant twins. I figured the post was so mundane that it would bore people to tears. "Here are my kids eating breakfast." "Here are my kids playing on the floor." "Then we go take a bath." Etc., etc. and more boring etc. I received and still receive such a huge response for that post. It was a post that seems to prove to people that my kids are fine and happy and have a good life and do the same things that other kids do. People with disabilities who were told they could never parent wrote to me and thanked me for giving them the courage to fulfill their dreams of becoming parents. Mothers of children with disabilities wrote to me and said that the post made them shed tears of joy that their children might someday be able to have a normal life. I am not a perfect parent and, of course, I make mistakes. But through my blog, I have been able to show a more complete picture that highlights our successes and problem solves our struggles in a way that I just can't pull off when people just catch a glimpse of me on the street or in the grocery store. Blogging has allowed me to show people the most misunderstood truth about my family: that we are just an average, mundane but loving family that has the same joys and struggles as everyone else in this parenting endeavor.

Of course the most fun thing about being a mother who blogs is that you get to show off your children and your love for them and how hard you work for them. Mothers have been compartmentalized and categorized and isolated so much, leading to the so-called "mommy wars" and conflicts about who is a better mom and what method and lifestyle is right or wrong. When we can see past all the media driven labels and really learn how to connect with one another, we learn how committed all mothers are to our essential role in raising the next generation and how hard we work to do it. We learn the value of each mother—lesbian, disabled, single, adoptive, whatever—and only then can we come to know, appreciate, and fight for the value of mothering in and of itself.

The birthday party we went to was the result of a connection I made through my blog. The birthday boy's mother told me that she never would have felt comfortable inviting a deafblind mother of twins to her home before. She wouldn't have even thought it possible for a family like my family to exist in the world. Thankfully, thanks to the Internet, we do exist to a lot of great moms out there. And we like going to birthday parties, too. I'm sure the blog will lead us to many more.

Chapter Five

Marginality in the Mamasphere

Queers Racializing the Family Tree

SHANA L. CALIXTE AND JILLIAN JOHNSON

Here I am, at 29 weeks, feeling our little bub kicking and moving in my tummy. I wonder, what will Black History Month really mean to our mixed race, mixed heritage, various historied, queerly raised child? What will it mean to a child that will probably be seen as Black no matter where they go? What will it mean to a child born into a society, one that believes being "colour blind" is more important than addressing bullshit racism that pervades our everyday lives? What will it mean in a country where his mother's sexuality is outlawed and criminalized? What will it all mean? (*Butch Baby Makin'*, Feb 1, 2006)

I know things like this are likely to happen, but really. Now that I actually look pregnant instead of slightly chubby, I'm starting to realize that strangers in large numbers assume that I'm a sad little teenager who was left by some man. No actually, I WANT this baby, and I don't want a man! And no, the father did not leave me. The father was required for approximately 15 minutes. Do I really seem that incapable of making my own decisions? Do I look that much younger than I am? Or is this just inescapable racism and patriarchy? Probably that. (*Diary of a Pregnant Anarchist*, June 28, 2006)

I think it is difficult to write about feminism and at the same time have the writing be about race. This is perhaps one of the most important concerns for a queer black feminist practice: to make the terrain of feminist sexual politics a discourse on race. (Harris 11)

The blogosphere is large, there is no doubt about that. And it continues to grow, literally, every second. In fact, according to Technorati's 2007 "State of the Blogosphere" report, there are over 70 million weblogs, 120,000 created each day, and 1.4 blogs created each second (*Sifry's Alerts: David Sifry's Musings*, "The State of the Live Web, April 2007," April 5, 2007). The blogosphere continues to be a space where people from all walks of life can find community and share their stories and experiences.

The mamasphere has been described as one such space, where mothers, all over the Internet, have come together around their shared ups and downs around raising little (and big) children. It has been represented as having many voices,[1] as building community around a shared and often maligned experience (mothering) and as opening up spaces for discussions around motherhood that range from the banal to the sublime.

The many great assets of parenting within a digital age are not to be underestimated. The mamasphere has, indeed, bolstered community, generated a new mode of activism and has inhibited the isolation of countless mothers worldwide. The picture, however, is not exclusively rosy. Over the past few years, it seems the great equalizer, the Internet, has not reached its goal of becoming the "inherently democratizing" form of communication that many believed it might be (Huang). Sexism, racism, classism and homophobia are still structural inequalities that continue to keep some voices marginalized online, and in effect, whitewash the realities that are shared over the web (Hoffman and Novak). There have been many discussions about how our cyber identities, the "online face" we chose to share with others, varies dramatically from our actual identities. This means that although many believe that things like gender, race and sexuality are fixed and static to some biological truth online (i.e., you would identify as "black" or "lesbian" or "woman" on the internet if you identify as such IRL—in real life) the reality is that both in our social worlds and online worlds, the way people experience and choose to present their identities varies[2] (for example, a number of people in queer communities who are questioning their gender identity often go online and "try on" their desired gender in the safety of an anonymous world).[3]

Scholars in this school of thought believe that we can choose to be, at anytime, whatever self-identity we wish, which means we can show or hide race, gender, ethnicity and sexuality. However, this utopian ideal of a power free and identity neutral space is challenged when those who experience the day to day realities of oppression away from the keyboard begin to see their experiences replicated in the cyber world

(Nakamura 227). Even though we may leave our corporeal bodies outside of the computer screens, the social and structural oppressions that come along with a white supremacist, heteropatriarchal capitalist society still filter into the world wide web. These oppressions have been experienced by those who realize that even though we may not be talking about identities, we also aren't talking about the impact of those identities (like racism and homophobia for instance); the lack of discussion on these subjects makes it so that the blogosphere begins to look like a whitewashed, heterosexual power free world.

In the mamasphere, a similar concern about a lack of critical attention to diversity and intersectional politics has been made. And even when women of colour are trying to get someone to take notice, the answer is often the colourblind apolitical (and quite racist) "It just shouldn't matter."[4]

What often comes up in discussions about race and sexuality online is that we can't "see" these aspects of identity or that it simply isn't an issue of concern to the (mainly white, mainly straight) readers and writers in the mamasphere. What is problematic about this notion is that it assumes that all of us are white, middle class and heterosexual, as the only ones who can not "see" difference are usually those who don't acknowledge it in their everyday lives. The other question is why do we assume whiteness or straightness or middle class status? The very easy and feminist answer to this question is that we live in a white supremacist, heteropatriarchal capitalist society, where those in power are not required to grapple with the way they experience privilege. When white (or heterosexual or middle/upper class) is the norm, it is easy for the privileged folks to go along with it, and not question the very problematic assumptions that this entails—that they enjoy the benefits of an oppressive system, where others experience marginality.

We should be clear. This isn't the first time discussions about the lack of diversity online, with respect to race, sexuality or class, have arisen. Many top bloggers have asked, "Where are all the black bloggers?"[5]; many lesbians have wondered why their search for pregnant and parenting mamas comes up empty, so it shouldn't be a surprise that the mamasphere has a similar dearth of diverse mamas sharing their thoughts on diaper bags and sleep schedules.

Yet what is of concern is how the mamasphere has handled critiques about this lack of diversity and how of colour and queer mamas survive this once again white washed straight terrain of the Internet. Why is it that white and straight mamas are not identifying their own issues of race and sexuality (normative as they are) in their own discussions of motherhood? Issues that are of concern to us, like the impact of racism on our kid at the playground, or how Mother's Day has been handled by our educational institutions when there are two moms, need room in the larger discussion. Even more importantly, those mamas who have the privilege of living in the normative need to work alongside us to fight these injustices. So many mamas are waiting on that woman of colour to bring up race, or that lesbian mom to talk about sexuality. For those of us who exist in the intersections, it becomes even more of a complicated issue as the quote by Laura Harris at the beginning of the text mentions. How do we look at our of colour mama community and critique their heternormativity, and how do we look at our queer mamas and critique their whiteness?

Many of us have made our own space online,[6] which means there needs to be an acknowledgement that we are here and have always been here. As Daddy in a Strange Land writes about his experiences as a dad of colour online, "That's what we're talking about here, at the root, not advertising dollars or even readership stats, but acknowledged presence in this community we've already called our own, acknowledgement of our diversity and our issues, of our part in all of this."[7] So what is essential in these debates is that we have to stop saying, "where are all the non-white mamas and queer mamas online?" and start realizing that we are here, we are talking and we are tackling issues of sexuality and race head on in our writing and in our chosen communities.

Opening the Conversation: Two Black Queer Mamas Share Their Experiences

In this chapter, we, as two black queer mama bloggers, discuss our own experiences online, examining our relationships to the mamasphere as we attempt to queer and race normative discourses around motherhood. As the mamasphere provides a feminist space to challenge the hegemonic ideologies around motherhood, (in effect, an example of feminism at work) it is not free from infighting, cliques, and popularity contests, where many issues, not only those concerning race and sexuality, can often become marginalized. In this chapter however, our concern, as two blogging mamas to black/mixed race baby boys, is to open up the discussion around race and sexuality, and to insert our voices into the recent literature on mommy blogging that often ignores the realities of those who are queer and of colour. To do so we ask: how have white lesbian mommy blogs ignored important discussions of race as they build their intentional families? How do black het mamas assume a heteronormative framework as they discuss their own communities and family building? Why are the voices of queer mamas of colour marginalized online, and in what ways are they using blogs to challenge the heterocentricity and whiteness of the motherhood blogging world? Our purpose in this chapter is to explore the subversiveness of the mamasphere, while bringing to the forefront the important realities of race, gender and sexuality in the lives of mommy bloggers.

As busy academics and moms, we struggled with the idea of putting this chapter together. Mostly, we wanted it to be engaging and informative, but to provide a critique that we see as missing from other discussions. As a result, we thought it would be pedagogically sound to include our own voices here, in an instant message chat. We see this, as Patricia Hill Collins notes, a "coming to voice" through our own black, queer feminist standpoint, in effect, a challenging of the silence of our marginality online.

Black Mamas to Queerspawn: Who We Are

Shana

For almost three years, I spent most of my days blogging my experiences of conception, pregnancy and parenthood on two blogs: one now defunct called, *Butch Baby Makin'* and another, currently up and running at LesbianFamily.org. As a queer, interracially partnered dyke with, at the time, a mixed raced baby on the way, I wanted my blog to speak to the realities of being queer and of colour and to challenge other mamas, both queer and straight, to think about politicizing their parenting. This included a real commitment to discussing ideas around anti-oppression and to radically rethink what we mean about "family" – not just in terms of sexuality, but also in terms of race and whiteness.

My personal blog ran from October 2004 to fall 2006, when I decided to delete the blog.

Jillian

I decided to start blogging when I got pregnant because I realized that I was going to have a unique story to share. I made the uncommon decision to have a multi-racial baby by a friend donor while in my mid-twenties, and to raise that baby without a partner. I started the blog as a way to catalogue the experience for myself and for the people I knew, but I also wanted to meet other people who were taking non-traditional approaches to becoming mothers and wanted to learn from their experiences.

Our Mamasphere: Centering Race and Sexuality

SC: When did you first start blogging?

JJ: I've had a personal journal blog for about six years, but I started the baby blog the day I found out I was pregnant. One of my friends suggested it and I thought it would be a good way to preserve my pregnancy experience, and keep my family and friends updated, and learn about other people's pregnancies and meet people online.

SC: I started blogging around 2000, well before I had my little one. My blog was on Livejournal, and I went under a pseudonym, black_pearl. I chose this name to mark both my black and gendered identity. It also connected me to a specific black culture (hip hop: it is the name of Yo-Yo's song). I started my trying to conceive (TTC) and baby journal in 2004, after I spent time looking for community on message boards. I wanted to document the journey of making the baby, to also talk through identity stuff, as I was a butch dyke trying to get pregnant. The blog was called Butch Baby Makin'. I made a lot of friends through that blog and we have met up and continue to keep in touch to this day. It provided a really strong community for me. How about you? Did you meet a lot of people through your blog?

JJ: A few. Mostly other mamas or pregnant women who commented on entries they felt they connected with somehow. I was particularly interested in finding other queer families and other single women who were choosing motherhood. The SMCs (Single Mothers By Choice) were particularly lacking, especially in my age group. I found one eventually but she took her blog down a few months later. I also ran around visiting lots of queer blogs and making comments and meeting people that way, but I wasn't able to maintain most of those connections.

SC: Yeah, same for me. At first, it was like a dead zone on my blog. I remember thinking "is anyone really reading?," which I think is a familiar refrain for many people in the blogosphere. And then a few more people started commenting. I then visited those blogs and found a larger and larger circle of queer folks making babies. I also participated in a lot of message boards, so that allowed me to maintain connections. Why do you think you weren't able to maintain the ones you made?

JJ: A combination of factors; people seemed to be pretty transient. For a while they would update every day, and then nothing for months. Or their blogs would just disappear. Some of the people who commented I didn't feel any connection to. They seemed like nice people, but they were white stay-at-home suburbanites and all we could say to each other were exclamations on how cute each other's babies were. Which, after you do it a few times, sort of loses its appeal. Their concerns were just so different from mine.

Being a queer and single mama, you're constantly justifying your existence to people who think you're somehow damaging your child by being what you are. I'm busy enough just trying to get through the day. Also the focus of my life, after my son of course, is politics and activism. Not many people can relate to that either. My best comments were from people who read posts about trying to integrate activism and motherhood and who were able to bring personal experience to my thoughts on that struggle. I like reading comments from people who think my son is cute or that my poop stories are entertaining, but in the end those connections aren't the ones that were sustained.... Also, my computer crashed and I lost all my bookmarks, and I just didn't feel like finding them all over again!

SC: That makes me wonder about something—were you pretty up-front/clear about your identity on your blog? Specifically around race and sexuality?

JJ: Yes, I said I was a queer, black, single mom "by design"—and the title of it was "Diary of a Pregnant Anarchist"—so I stated my politics up front as well. Very few people had anything to say about any of that, though. It was mostly just pregnancy talk, then mama talk.

I think people were uncomfortable discussing the issues of identity that I brought up. It's much easier to have something to say about morning sickness and birthday parties than the ethics of sperm donation or little boys being raised without daddies. It brings up too many deep issues that many people aren't necessarily going to confront. I don't think I was very assertive about my identities in what I wrote either. I focused on my baby, and so did they. What about you?

SC: For me, I was pretty open about being queer/butch, and posted a picture so folks knew I was black. I did spend a significant amount of time talking about race and how it intersected with sexuality on my blog—specifically about being a black butch. While we were actively TTC and looking for a donor, I spent most of the time talking about race and the effects that this choice would have on our baby. I remember also getting my partner to post a bit about her experiences as a future white mom to a kid of colour, and that brought out one or two people. Generally though? Silence around these topics. I got more comments when I brought up my addiction to watching *America's Next Top Model!*

JJ: Yeah, I wrote less often about race/gender/sexuality/politics than I wanted to, but I got a few good responses when I did. My friends and family read my blog and a lot of them are political, so that helped the numbers. Combining my friends with my family in the same space was an interesting experiment though. There were people in my family who didn't know that I identified explicitly as queer or anarchist, or that I was using a donor until I started writing the blog. I had to decide how up-front to be and even whether to let different people in my family know the blog was there. In the end I just wrote whatever I wanted and told them all, and I didn't get any bad reactions. Most of them just didn't mention it actually ... so either they're fine with me or they're in denial. I've actually gotten more challenges from my family about my decision not to circumcise my son than I have about being single or queer or politically radical, which surprised me quite a bit.

SC: So why do you think you wrote less about politics? Do you think politics had or did not have an impact on your baby making/pregnancy discussions?

JJ: I think my politics integrate with my life so much that it's hard to separate them. I chose to become a mother as a single 25 year old because I have always wanted children and I felt stable enough to provide for one. It wasn't an explicitly political decision, but of course it's dependent on a certain political and social outlook.

I don't believe that children need heterosexual two-parent families in order to become functional adults, whatever the Christian conservatives would like us to believe. I don't believe that I need a partner to make my life worth living, or that I should put off doing what I want to do while I sit around and wait for one. I believe that I am perfectly capable of raising a healthy, happy child without insisting on a traditional family structure. I am innovative and resourceful and I can do it. These beliefs are personal, but they're political too. My decision is also strongly a function of my personality. I have a strong independent streak. I wrote less about politics explicitly because I do so much politics, and I wanted to have a space that was just about baby. Of course the politics seeped in. For example I go to political demonstrations with my son all the time. We also go to queer-themed parties thrown by friends and march on picket lines. If I'm writing about what he's done over the last week, at least some of the events are going to be about activism. One thing I never wrote about at all was my choice of a white man as my baby's donor, and thinking about it later, that omission seemed somewhat significant.

SC: That is very true about the politics seeping in. And now, looking back at my blog, I can see that I spent most of my time discussing race in almost every post I put up. The personal is political, as they say! But can you elaborate on that last point? We also chose a white donor, but I spent a lot of time talking about this and working through some serious internalized stuff. Why did you omit the discussion, do you think?

JJ: I'm not entirely sure. One reason was that we were keeping the donor anonymous so I omitted all identifying information about him, but that can't be the whole. Everyone figured it was a white guy as soon as they saw the baby anyway! I think I thought less about race in my decision because any baby I have will be black (one-drop rule, right?[8]), so I didn't have to worry about raising a kid from a different culture or how that would play out. I also wanted to have a kid with a genetically and culturally diverse ancestry to draw on so that he would have different histories and cultures to learn about and feel connected too. I think mixing up the gene pool is a good idea too!

So I've been wondering, why did you take down your blog?

SC: Yeah, good question (and hard one!) There were a number of factors. The first one being that I had a kid and was so so busy and tired and couldn't even find time to pee, I didn't see how I could keep a blog running. I also found myself worried that homophobic family members might find me online, so that was also part of it. But I think the bigger part had to do with that idealized community I was hoping to find and never really did find. When I was around 16 weeks, I entered into a discussion with another queer mom who was white and had a white partner, who had recently had a mixed race baby. We were discussing ideas around identity and whether or not her daughter would identify as white in future. We had some productive discussion, but it quickly developed into a very bitter exchange (mostly with other commenters, but also with her) where people called me quite nasty names because I had been a bit critical of the lack of race politics of the original poster. I think I then realized that my blog was holding back a bit on my real politics, that I was sanitizing it in order to make friends. Like, I don't want to be the angry black dyke in the crowd! But it had already happened, so it was too late. I remember the moments after that exchange, how no one who I had met online wanted to say anything to me, I guess in fear of further upsetting and offending the white mother. It was a harsh reality to see racism so openly displayed and supported by the mainly white queer mama bloggers. I was feeling very vulnerable. I remember I wrote a bit about it on my own blog:

> So I've been taking a break from the Internet, ever since the episode on Friday night (yes, a whole weekend off! imagine!). I have to admit, it has been a long time since I've been involved in Internet fights or arguments, and my reaction to it was very upsetting. Too much stress that I really don't need right now, so

I take a step back and away for now....

But I do want to say that even though this shit is hard, it is cool to talk to folks and to hear the stories from those who spend time thinking of this and many other ways in which society is really fucked up. I appreciate that I have yet to have a child, and that my intense need to theorize this shit gets people riled. I theorize and talk about this and challenge myself and others on this stuff cuz I know, from living it, that it is hard. And I want to make sure that my partner and I are ready ... for everything. Although I disagree vehemently with folks who just want me to chill, I respect your decision to feel so for your own needs. I also appreciate that when folks put themselves out there in ways that make them feel vulnerable, the last thing they expect is someone to disagree with them or call them on stuff. So my anger may be surprising or upsetting or unwanted. And I hear and respect that.

These conversations about race are ways for me to train that anger. If these conversations are enough to make you feel anger, then I believe we are on the right track. Racism, along with many other oppressions, should make us all enraged. And raising a kid of colour (and being queer and raising kids), I believe, will mean you should be ready to be angry and ready to challenge bullshit everyday. (*Butch Baby Makin'*, October 24, 2005)

JJ: When I read this I was really thrown by how much people refused to admit that race mattered at all in their lives and would certainly matter to their black children as they grew up. They seemed to believe that as long as they loved their kids and provided for them well, they would be just fine. I would love to live in a world where you could raise children of color without preparing them for racial oppression and be confident that they would never have to deal with it, but the idea of people doing that in the real world is just terrifying. I was surprised that white people raising black kids didn't make it a point to make themselves more aware of the challenges their kids would face and accept that their kids would have to deal with issues that they don't understand. The defensiveness made it clear that they just hadn't thought through those issues. They were just constantly defending their decision to raise children of color, which is a great decision as long as you can face the reality of what that decision might mean, especially for your kids.

SC: In terms of that idealized community, I should say that I have found since then some pretty great folks willing to question and to interrogate the whiteness of the queer mama blogging space (including, in fact, the original mama with whom I argued). What about you? What have you noticed about the identities of lesbian/queer mamas in the blogosphere? Do you think those of us within the queer mama blogosphere are taking on issues of race? What about those black/of colour mamas? Is there a discussion around heteronormativity?

JJ: I found a few queer blogs of white people raising non-white babies, and it seemed that discussions of race were largely lacking. Or I thought they missed the point. White people talking about their black children would make comments that were just bizarre to me. I remember one post I read on a blog written by a man who was white and gay and who had an adopted daughter who was black. He was discussing a woman he met making a comment that his daughter would be socially advantaged because she would have a "white" accent and how this offended him because he knows there are lots of different kinds of "white" accents, not all of which are socially beneficial. Of course, he's right. White people choose to speak in hundreds of different ways, and if you sound like you're from the South or the mountains or certain other countries, that might reflect negatively. But I felt like he missed the point the woman was making, which was that his daughter WOULD be socially advantaged as a result of her specific "white" accent, taught to her by a highly-educated middle class white couple from a major city. He was so busy defending a plurality of white experiences that he missed the point that his particular experience, and his daughter's, do have real social consequences.

I feel like I have this odd kind of reverse privilege with regard to my baby's ancestry because with a black mama, he's black no matter what. So he can be as ethnically diverse as he wants! White people don't have that privilege. Their kids are white no matter what, and they have to deal with that, or not. I can't actually remember reading any lesbian mamas talking about hetero culture affecting their lives either, which seems odd now that I think of it. I do remember another SMC [Single Mother by Choice] talking about people lauding her decision to "keep her baby" when she had, of course, planned her pregnancy. I think I wrote once also about people thinking I was about ten years younger than I was when I would walk down the street, and how I would get disapproving looks like, oh look at that sad pregnant teenager. I'm sure race affected their perceptions of me as well.

SC: Isn't the SMC community online largely straight? I think you were the first SMC I met who wasn't white, either.

JJ: There are some lesbians as well but the main thing that separated me from them was age. They all seemed to be doing their whole, "I'm turning forty, it's my last chance" TTC runs. And yeah, no one else is a [person of colour]. So speaking of people of colour, does identity matter to you when looking for community online? What is most important to you in terms of a community online? Does mommyblogging apply to what you are doing? Do you attach yourself to that term?

SC: Identity mattered a lot when I started searching for community online. I knew that I wanted to find other pregnant queer folks, but I was on a search for black women in particular. I wasn't surprised that I didn't find any other women ... I did find folks who were willing to "go there" with me though, so that was good. And the community I did find provided essential information for me, specifically around TTC issues, parenting as a queer person, donor sperm etc. My "mommyblogging" moments were brief, so I'm not sure how well I fit into that online identity. I know that I wanted to align myself with other political parenting blogs (like *Republic of T*, have you ever read him?) and focus my blog on more of the politics of parenting, but that never really actualized. I found myself using my blog for the same reasons I find many other mommybloggers do (regardless of race, sexuality, etc.)— to talk about their day to day with their children, to talk about their stresses, their worries. I spent a lot of time theorizing my reality and my future child's reality, specifically about how he/she would exist in a patriarchal and racist society.... I remember vividly writing about that and wondering if this was going to be all I did as a mom online—worry! I did feel, however, limited in my communion around these issues with others. Which made me wonder, beyond the normal blog popularity contests that occurred online, why it was that my blog was relatively popular, at least in the queer mamas set.

JJ: People like to read the unconventional stuff!

SC: Maybe you're right. I guess I wondered, what are people thinking when they read this? Do they think I'm OUT THERE?

JJ: Hee hee, probably. But I have always been thought such, so I embrace it now. For me, identity matters a lot, and I think more so online than in the rest of my life. I have a very diverse set of friends, but none of them are queer black anarchist single moms. Online, I saw an opportunity to find people more like me who I wouldn't meet otherwise. I consider myself a mommyblogger more than any other type of blogger, since my blog is almost entirely about my son. It's almost like an online photo journal for friends and family sometimes, and thus devoid of more meaningful content—but I do use it as a tool for myself to parse through some of the more challenging/interesting bits of being a mama with my various identities, and I find that useful even if no one else reads the thing.

SC: So, in what ways is being a black queer momma disrupt the mommyblogging title? The mamasphere?

JJ: I feel like we're still clawing our way out of the 1950s idea of what mothering and motherhood should be. The smiling white woman in an apron serving cookies or whatever. And even the more backward than that ideas, if you can imagine ideas more backward (barefoot and pregnant in the kitchen!). And being queer and black and single and a mama really throws all that into question. Assuming that the mamasphere is going to reflect of all those existing cultural assumptions, my presence on the Internet has the same effect as my existence in general. I find, though, that I don't get challenged so much—and I'd like to think that's a reflection of changes in culture, but maybe its really just a reflection of the people I choose to surround myself with.

SC: Yeah, for this project, I was searching for images of "mommybloggers" and the first image that comes up is of a black mommyblogging site. Heterosexual and coupled, but woah, was I ever surprised. I want to be challenged in this way. I want people to ask me hard questions, like, "what makes your experience significant in the mamasphere and what are YOU leaving out" and other such things. I don't want folks to be politically lazy around this stuff, because I do want to feel ownership of the title [of mommyblogger], even when the assumption is that I'm not.

So do you find blogging valuable to your own sense of self and family? What value does blogging have for you and your queered/racialized notion of motherhood and family?

JJ: I find it valuable primarily as a form of self-expression and communication with friends and family; and I think its good for people who are considering various nontraditional ways of creating family that it doesn't have to be just theory, that there are people out there raising healthy happy children in a variety of family structures. I always knew that my approach to parenting would be unconventional, and that scared me sometimes. I wondered if I shouldn't just revert to a socially acceptable format to be safe. I think it's good to be open about what I'm doing so that people can see that it's possible and doesn't have to be so scary. Your kid will not turn out all messed up because he doesn't have a standard two-parent middle class white family.

SC: Does it work? Because I agree, it provides a picture of the alternatives, but do we get to be the freak show (or the canceled show)? I know from my experience, I had quite a few people feel the need to question my parenting choices, even before I made them! I know that a lot of queers run across this stuff online. Do we get as much cred for mommyblogging as the straight white mamas do? I am not sure if some of the major parenting websites like *Literary Mama* or *The Mom Blogs* would even think of recruiting one of us. Which makes me sad ... and mad.

JJ: Yeah, I'm not sure. I love it when I find other unconventional parenting blogs, and it makes me feel affirmed, so I think it does at least within our community. I haven't had anyone question my choices. It may be because my blog is less popular.

SC: It makes me wonder, you know? Especially since the mamasphere is so situated within whiteness and straightness, I wonder if that famous *NY Times* piece, which said that Mommy bloggers are all navel gazers,[9] it made me wonder if you can make the same statement about folks critically discussing race, gender and sexuality, that it's just self-indulgent. I mean, many in the mamasphere do navel gaze, but it is probably easier to make that sweeping generalization of a group of people who seem to be so uniform or homogeneous. I'm wondering if more mommybloggers were critically examining these issues and how they affect their families, if that wouldn't have been as easy to say. Like, who is gonna call someone a navel gazer when they are talking about how their kid was called the N-word at school? But you know, even if it wasn't that extreme, mommybloggers still get no cred for doing the basic—you know, putting their personal into politics. I just wished many of them would push a bit more in that area.

JJ: I think the blogosphere inspires quite a bit of narcissism in general honestly, people are really just talking about themselves, but that's kind of the point. People's lives are inherently political and social and it's interesting to draw those nuances out.

SC: So what have been the challenges of blogging within the mamasphere and as a mama for you? What have been the uplifting moments?

JJ: Hmm, I think the most challenging things are 1) finding time to do it and 2) not being nervous about my relatives reading it. The best parts have been comments by random strangers who connected with what I was writing somehow. Even if they were very unlike me. There are several people that I keep in touch with online now that I met though their visits to my blog or my visits to theirs. I also managed to meet one other queer single mama who was close to my age, which was great. And you?

SC: For me, the challenges have been finding time, not getting ahead of myself in terms of theorizing before experiencing and keeping myself sane during conflicts. The great things have been finding people like you! And finding community that I feel comfortable pushing my politics on. It is slow going, but it is nice to share the experience with others who get what it means to be a mama, even if they aren't necessarily ready to go all the way to where I am in terms of race and queerness.

Any last questions for us?

JJ: Well, where do we go from here? Should we be pushing mama blogging to be a more culturally and politically challenging experience?

SC: Indeed. I don't know how that would look, beyond us already existing, you know? I don't know if it means that we need to critically engage with the mainstream mommybloggers and do "sit ins" so to speak (blog ins?) I think for me it means just pushing the agenda, one day at a time. Because the rest of the time, I've got this little boy to think of, and to engage with and to ask questions of and with. You know? Cuz sooner than later, it will be his reality that will come face to face with this marginalization, and I've got to be ready for it. Hmm ... not a good note to finish on.... How about you? Anything more uplifting?

JJ: LOL. No, I think you're right, and I think my blog will become more of a political tool when he starts to confront the issues of his birth and parenting as he grows up. But my main priority in blogging, as in life, is making sure he grows up happy and strong and ready to deal with whatever gets thrown at him, and that's enough work for any one person.

[1]See Ann Kroeker who states, "In my wanderings, I'm amazed by all the questions, opinions and ideas. I'm struck by *all those voices*. Skilled wordsmiths are telling their stories or calling out for truth." (*Ann Kroeker,* "Cruising the Mamasphere," January 18, 2007.)

[2]See Nakamura where she discusses how online, people can 'pass' and become 'identity tourists', where race, gender, sexuality and class (among other social locations) become spaces of liminality, available to anyone by virtue of choice. Nakamura does, of course, see the dangers in assuming that power does not still reside within these spaces, stating: "One of the dangers of identity tourism is that it ... [reduces] non-white identity positions as part of a costume or masquerade to be used by curious vacationers in cyberspace ... race is 'whited out' in the name of cybersocial hygiene" (233).

[3] See Gautier and Chaudoir who talk about the use of the Internet for FTM (female to male) trans folks who use "cyber communities" for tips on passing and other ways to socially mark their bodies as masculine.

[4]See the discussion on *Mocha Momma*'s blog about the lack of attention to moms of colour by marketers where commenter Leah states, "I, for one, am beyond tired of obsession over appearance as if it matters for *anything*..." (*Mocha Mamma,* "Marginalization and Marketing," July 30, 2007.)

[5]See *The News Blog*, "Us Coloreds don't be bloggin'," February 22, 2006; *Khanya*, "Where are the black bloggers?" March 26, 2007; *Republic of T*, "Blogging While Brown," March 30, 2007; and an interview from *Feministing* with Nubian from *blac(k)ademic* on "Blogging While Black," which has generated significant controversy, and has since been taken down (http://www.feministing.com/archives/007085.html).

[6]See, among others, *Lesbianfamily.org, Mombian, MochaMomma; KimchiMamas;* and *One Tenacious Baby Mama* (which has since gone private, but snippets can be found using Google's cached pages).

[7]Daddy in Strange Land, on *RiceDaddies,* "What's Race Got to Do With It?" August 6, 2007.

[8]The one-drop rule is the historical racialized ideology and legal codification during slavery that one drop of black blood would mark a person's racial identity as black, regardless of their outward appearances or self-identification (Roth 2005).

[9]See David Hochman's piece entitled, "Mommy (and Me)," *New York Times*, January 30, 2005, where he stated that mommyblogs are an, "online shrine to parental self-absorption."

Works Cited

Ann Kroeker. Retrieved May 10, 2007. <http://annkroeker.wordpress.com>.

Butch Baby Makin'. Retrieved from Way Back Machine, May 10, 2007. <http://kwynne.blogspot.com>.

Daddy in a Strange Land. Retrieved May 11, 2007. <http://web.mac.com/quioguesperber/iWeb/daddyinastrangeland/blog/blog.html>.

Diary of a Pregnant Anarchist. Retrieved May 10, 2007. <http:// diaryofapregnantanarchist.blogspot.com>.

Feministing. Retrieved May 11, 2007. http://www.feministing.com/

Gauthier, DeAnn K. and Nancy K. Chaudoir. "Tranny Boyz: Cyber Community Support in Negotiating Sex and Gender Mobility Among Female to Male Transsexuals." *Deviant Behavior* 25 (4) (2004): 375-398.

Harris Laura Alexandra. "Queer Black Feminism: The Pleasure Principle." *Feminist Review* 54 (1996): 3-30.

Hill Collins, Patricia. *Fighting Words: Black Women and the Search for Justice*. Minneapolis : University of Minnesota Press, 1998.

Hochman, David. "Mommy and Me." *New York Times,* 30 January 2005, Style. Retrieved from <http://www.nytimes.com/2005/01/30/fashion/30moms.html>.

Hoffman, D. L. and T. P. Novak. "Bridging the Racial Divide on the

Internet," *SCIENCE* 280 (1998): 390-391.

Huang, Edgar. "Flying Freely but in the Cage: An Empirical Study of Using Internet for the Democratic Development in China." *Information Technology for Development* 8 (1999): 145-162.

Khanya. Retrieved May 20, 2007. <http://khanya.wordpress.com>.

Kimchi Mamas. Retrieved May 11, 2007. <http://kimchimamas.typepad.com>.

LesbianFamily.org. Retrieved May 11, 2007. <http://lesbianfamily.org>.

Mocha Momma. Retrieved May 11, 2007. <http://www.mochamomma.com>.

Mombian. Retrieved May 11, 2007. <http://www.mombian.com/>.

Nakamura, Lisa. "Race In/For Cyberspace: Identity Tourism and Racial Passing on the Internet." *Reading Digital Culture*. Ed. David Trend. Malden, Mass: Blackwell Publishers, 2001. 226-235.

One Tenacious Baby Mama. Retrieved May 11, 2007. <http://dark-daughta.blogspot.com>.

Republic of T. Retrieved May 20, 2007. <http://www.republicoft.com/>.

Roth, Wendy D. "The End of the One-Drop Rule? Labeling of Multiracial Children in Black Intermarriages." *Sociological Forum* 20 (1) (2005): 35-67.

Sifry's Alerts: David Sifry's Musings. Retrieved May 16, 2007. <http://www.sifry.com/alerts/archives/000493.htm>.

The News Blog, Retrieved May 20, 2007. <http:// stevegilliard.blogspot.com>.

Chapter Six

Meter Politikon

On the "Politics" of Mommyblogging

CATHERINE CONNORS

The niche of mom blogging, especially, is fucking weird. Because it's female driven, there's a lot of bullshit underlying politics. Everyone tries to act like it's all "sister, sister" but there are camps, there are cool girls, and damn you if you read but don't comment! When I started this blog two years ago, you could just read freely, write when you had the time and comment when you wanted. Now, as the popularity of blogging has increased, so has the clique-y-ness of bloggers. (*Martinis for Milk*, "Blogging Is Not Cool Anymore," June 15, 2006)

I was doing some googling around yesterday, and I found some bloggers who seem to have ingested a large serving of Hater-ade.... I'm not even going to bother to link those people.... Now I know how dumb I looked in high school when I was sitting in the stands throwing mustard packets at the cheerleaders. YOU SOUND DUMB. I just thought you should know. (*I, Asshole*, "Snakes On A Motherfucking BlogHer: Part Two," August 2, 2006)

The classical political philosophers held that "politics" referred to the condition and circumstances of social discourse within a human community. For Aristotle, humans are political animals for the simple reasons that we must live in community to survive, and that we require discourse to live in such community. Politics, in other words, is how, where, when and why humans substantively communicate with each other; it is how we establish and negotiate shared meaning of the concepts and ideas that hold our communities together—justice, rights, citizenship.

In late modernity the term "politics" has, however, come to carry a somewhat different meaning when used in descriptions of social life. When we talk about politics—when, that is, we are not talking about formal political systems and structures, like elections—we are usually talking about the exercise of ambition in pursuit of some power over others. To say that someone is political, or that a particular circumstance is political, is usually to say that that someone is ambitious, or that a given circumstance is defined by, or can be characterized by, the social exercise of such ambition. To the casual observer or commentator, it is not only formal politics that is political: the boardroom is political, as is the schoolyard and the playground and the cocktail party. Everything, as they say, is political, and by this we usually mean that every social interaction is characterized and/or delimited by some exercise of ambition among and between individuals and groups.

This is certainly the case in online communities—not least the community of mothers who write online, or "blog." In the so-called mamasphere, the "politics" of mommyblogging is a frequent—and controversial—topic of discussion. Mommybloggers (and it is worth noting that the term itself is sometimes called "political," insofar as some believe it to exclude mothers who do not identify as "mommies")[1] accuse each other of "playing politics" or "being political" with some frequency. By this they usually mean that certain bloggers are organizing their blogging behaviour (the topics that they are posting about, who they are linking to, who they are adding to their blogrolls, which sites they are visiting and commenting at) according to some strategy driven by ambition. The tacit ideal that such bloggers abandon is seen as a more authentic posture, one better suited to a community understand to be largely based on shared experience (in particular, the shared experience of motherhood, which is often assumed to establish a priority of shared values around cooperation and norms of maternal virtue and self-sacrifice) mutual esteem, and friendship. When mommybloggers lodge such complaints—the complaint that others are being "political"—they often do so by saying that the mamasphere is or is becoming like high school.

"Just like high school" has become convenient shorthand for charges of politics in the blogosphere, not least because it seems to capture the informal nature of the seeming hierarchies and sub-groups formed within the mommyblogging community. These seeming hierarchies and "cliques" are disparaged as running counter to the principles of amity and equality that are understood, however implicitly, to define the mommyblogging community. Many mommybloggers understand themselves to be, as members of the general mommyblogging community, participants in a community that is more or less defined by the common experience of motherhood, rather than a common experience of writing and publishing.[2] Accordingly, there is often some wariness expressed when other mommybloggers pursue—and celebrate—larger reading audiences and/or advertising dollars and/or writing assignments at established parenting websites. Any online behaviour that suggests a desire on the part of the blogger for greater popularity risks, from at least some quarters, condemnation. It risks being seen as an effort to join the elite ranks of "popular" bloggers and to turn one's back on "smaller" bloggers; it risks being seen as a demonstration of ambition of the sort that characterizes high-school corridors and schoolyards. That is to say, it risks characterization as political.

It is the pursuit of popularity within the mamasphere that draws most—if not all accusations—of politics, because it is popularity, defined by levels of traffic and degrees of virtual visibility, that determines perceived degrees of inclusion: who gets to participate most fully, and what is the character of that participation? There are few, if any, "real" barriers to participation beyond those imposed by the technology.[3] Limits to participation, such as there are, tend rather to be related to one's exposure—and, some would say, one's status—within the community.[4] Blogs with very limited readerships have very little reach in the mamasphere, which is to say, they have very little influence or impact upon the content and character of the discussions that take place therein, outside of what limited contribution those bloggers make by way of comments at other blogs. Blogs with extensive readerships, on the other hand, are generally more influential in contributing to and even shaping the discourse of the mamasphere: because they are widely linked to and widely read, the topics that they introduce and issues that they take up on their own blogs tend to be the topics and issues taken up by other blogs throughout the community. So it is that the "bigger" blogs—and the bloggers that author them—are often seen as gatekeepers to, and mediators of, discussion. This has been particularly evident in two areas of discussion recently: the first concerning the norms and ethics of pursuing revenue from one's blog, and the second concerning the question of race and identity in the mamasphere.

The Politics of Commerce

I'm not saying that popular blogs are bad. I'm not even saying that we should do away with advertising on blogs, per se. What I am saying, rather, is that the blogging world (and the "mommyblogging" world in particular, I think) could do with some reality checks in this regard. We need to shine a very strong light on the fact that these popularity contests take the focus away from the actual "product" of a blog and more towards pleasing a "buyer," or "buyers." The whole idea of blogging to please or blogging for links is disturbing at the very least. (*Tripping The Life Unbalanced*, "This Space For Rant," September 18, 2006)

The bigger point for me, and one that I think is more or less settled for many established bloggers, is this: we're writers. Why shouldn't we receive recognition and—where possible—compensation for what we produce?... Earning money from blogging doesn't undermine the integrity of the blogger any more than having a book published by Random House or an article printed in Vanity Fair undermines the integrity of any other writer. And as for our ability to be good blog citizens—well, the so-called "professional" or semi-professional bloggers demonstrate time and time again, through their community-building efforts, that they're leaders in this community. (*MommyBlogsToronto*, "Show Me The Money," May 13, 2007)

The debate over the so-called "commercialization" of mommyblogs centers around one key issue: whether the pursuit of revenue from one's blog undermines one's authenticity as a mommyblogger, and so as a member of the community. Once a blog has been "commercialized," according to the argument against revenue-seeking, the blogger in question is no longer motivated to blog simply for the rewards of self-expression and being a member of the community: they become motivated to increase traffic in order to increase revenue. Accordingly, the argument goes, commercialized mommyblogs can no longer be assumed to be sincere expressions and articulations of the experience of motherhood, inasmuch as they seem to violate certain implicit codes of virtue and self-sacrifice that are understood to be embedded within the culture of mothering.

For proponents of this argument, revenue-seeking brings out the worst political impulses of mommybloggers: in their pursuit of the higher traffic that will earn them more advertising dollars, such bloggers are more inclined to comport themselves (in the posts that they write about, the blogs that they link to, the blogs that they comment upon) in such a manner as to boost their popularity. Such bloggers, it is believed, will be more likely to try to participate in the discussions generated and fostered by more popular bloggers, in order to benefit from the flow of traffic generated by such discussions. In this way, the argument goes, community discourse becomes driven by revenue concerns, rather than by the genuine concerns of parents. And those bloggers who opt out of this flow of discussion risk being marginalized or excluded from full community participation, inasmuch as they choose to not play the "popularity game."[5] Essentially, for those opposed to revenue-seeking in the mamasphere, commercialization transforms the mamasphere into high school with marketing incentives: the "queen bees" attract "wannabes" not only because of the pure appeal of popularity and status, but also because they represent opportunities to earn money, and so the norms, mores and terms of discourse of these particular high school corridors are shaped according to exercises and demonstrations of mercenary ambition. It's high school on capitalist steroids.

The problem is that the claim that commerce in the mamasphere turns that community into some sort of devilish hybrid of high school and marketplace ignores or discounts two very important problems with any wholesale condemnation of mommybloggers seeking revenue from their blogs. The first is that objections to revenue-seeking by mommybloggers represents a sort of oppression, in that such objections demand that mothers "sacrifice" the creative and discursive work that they do on their blogs in the name of some vague notions of non-profit-driven (and so, presumably, more virtuous) craft and authenticity. The demand seems to be that mommybloggers should *not* put a value upon their written work, in much the same way that mothers generally are expected to *not* put a value upon the work that they do in the home. The rejection of revenue-seeking is, in other words, a luxury that only bloggers of a certain class—the class that has the means to expend energy and resources on the craft of blogging without any expectation of recompense—can enjoy. Most mothers stand to really benefit—as both bloggers *and* mothers—from earning revenue from their blogs, inasmuch as such revenue might go toward the childcare or household support or technology that facilitates pursuit of their craft. And for some mommybloggers, making money from blogging—which is to say, from *writing*, which in most other spheres is paid work—allows them to stay home with their children *and* launch careers as part-time or full-time writers.[6]

The second problem with arguments against revenue-seeking is, simply, that it overlooks or ignores the possibility—some would say the fact—that the so-called commercialization of blogs does not corrupt the practices of blogging as these apply to individual bloggers and to the community at large. Most bloggers, arguably, will not change their blogging style or the content of their writing for the paltry earnings that advertising usually provides, both because it is not worth the extra effort and because it erodes one's enjoyment of blogging. More problematically, however, arguments which hold that commercialization compels bloggers to seek larger audiences overlook the fact that most bloggers, regardless of revenue opportunities, write for an audience and aim to maintain (and, where possible, increase) that audience, simply because a larger audience represents a larger *readership*. Mommybloggers are, for the most part, mothers who love writing and who hold some ambition for their writing to be enjoyed and respected; to that end, they usually write with their audience in mind and aspire to expand that audience. More traffic equals, simply, more readers, and because all writers want readers, it is disingenuous to suggest that bloggers who have no concern for making money from their blogs are, on the whole, any less likely to pursue the popularity that brings greater traffic—and so more readers—than are bloggers who desire or depend upon advertising dollars or other forms of revenue.

Although the pursuit of some measure of popularity is a very real element of blogging, it is simply not as mercilessly ambitious—which is to say, as political—as its detractors make it out to be. Most bloggers, regardless of the revenue opportunities open to them, endeavour to increase their traffic within the context of their own niches and preferred sub-groups within the community, but they tend *not* to do so to any extent that diminishes their enjoyment of blogging. For the most part, bloggers gravitate toward other like-minded bloggers, are active in interacting with the bloggers that they like—by commenting and exchanging links and suggesting topics for discussion—and enjoy the consistent traffic levels that such interaction provides. Even very popular bloggers, many of whom earn real income from their blogs, tend to limit activities that are solely intended to increase traffic (dabbling in "search optimization," for example—a practice that can be very useful for maximizing traffic but labour-intensive and mind-numbingly boring) in favour of activity that is both rewarding in its own right—enjoyable or satisfying—*and* good for traffic (participating in "hot" topics of discussion, for example, or reciprocating comments). Most bloggers resist having their blogs become workmanlike; once one stops enjoying the writing and the involvement in the community, there is little incentive to continue, given the limited potential for significant income from individual blogs.[7] To the extent that mommybloggers pursue popularity in the form of larger readerships, they do so for the inherent rewards—the satisfaction that comes from being read, for example, and from honing one's skill as a writer—and do so, ordinarily, by means of reaching out to the community and making themselves heard (again, by commenting and linking and participating in "blog blasts'). Pecuniary reward is, more often than not, a secondary concern, and so does little to alter the blogging practices that are already directed, in some part, toward building audience.

It can be argued, then, that there is very little "politicking" occurring in the mamasphere that is directly related to pecuniary ambition. And to the extent that some bloggers *perceive* others to be driven by fiscal imperatives, complaints that are rooted in this perception can be explained in simple terms of hurt feelings and sensitivities concerning seeming exclusion from certain social circles, wherein the perceived exclusion is explained away as a byproduct of the "exclusive" group's concern for strategic advancement.[8] Mommybloggers—and, one assumes, bloggers in general—are sensitive to the location of their place in the virtual crowd, and are attentive to the advantages and disadvantages of that location; they are therefore alert to any real or perceived efforts by others to shift location.

Earning revenue from one's blog—and "socializing" with bloggers who make extensive use of advertising and/or who are associated with revenue-generating websites—is often perceived as such an effort. It is understood by some to be a signifier of an ambition to move, because it seems to represent an effort to attain the status of the "A-list" bloggers who (it is widely and not always correctly assumed) earn real income from their blogs. Revenue-seeking is not only criticized for being an end in itself; it is often criticized—identified as political—because it is understood to be a signifier of an ambition toward the end of popularity. That is, it marks a blogger as one who aspires to be the type of blogger that is sufficiently popular that others *assume* she is making money. The presence of advertising on a blog, or random product reviews (which indicate that public relations professionals have sought out that blogger to promote their products) is, in other words, viewed as a real or aspirant status symbol, one that reveals a blogger's desire to garner attention beyond her immediate community circle.

That perceived attempts at upward mobility are viewed as problematic is, of course, due almost entirely to perceptions within the community that demonstrations of ambition violate certain unspoken mores within the community; that, specifically, such practices that are rooted in or seem to demonstrate ambition are responsible for turning the mamasphere into a community that is more like high school (socially competitive to a fault), and less like the egalitarian community-of-peers that many assume it to be. The great benefit of the mamasphere, for many, is that it does, or seems to, avoid the "politics'—the competitive status-seeking, the sizing-up, the constant comparing of one's mothering abilities or one's children with those of others—of mom-groups and playgroups and schoolyards and the other "real-life" spaces in which parents socialize, and which are understood to reflect yet more perfectly the dynamics of high school.[9] In the mamasphere, it is assumed and expected that everyone speaks honestly, revealing their weaknesses and vulnerabilities and generally interacting on the basis of an assumption that other mommybloggers sympathize with and relate to one's weaknesses and vulnerabilities as equals in the experience of motherhood.[10] Any perceived dynamics of ranking or demonstrations of status-seeking in this environment are perceived by some to be threats to the sanctity of the community's greatest asset: its open and (seemingly) egalitarian inclusivity (especially with respect to participation in driving and determining content of community discourse). If some bloggers are understood to be better than others, won't those bloggers exert undue influence, set standards and compel others to conform, rather than allow for the co-operative and non-judgmental individualism that does, or did, or should define the mamasphere?[11] Won't the mamasphere, under these circumstances, turn into high school, full of queen bees and wannabes and defined entirely by social competition and exclusion?

What this concern ignores, of course, is the fact that any community will of necessity organize itself in such a way that patterns of inclusion and exclusion are fluid. There is, simply, no such thing as a perfectly inclusive community: all communities negotiate issues concerning limits to inclusion and participation, and even the most putatively egalitarian communities negotiate issues concerning status and hierarchy. This is politics as the canonical political philosophers—Plato, Aristotle, Rousseau, Mill, Hegel—understood it: the discursive negotiation of social relationships within formal and informal communities. No single individual in any given community can be a part of all conversations, nor participate in all relationships, and as such, any one individual is likely to feel, at some time, excluded from some interaction in which he or she would prefer to be included. The important question concerning inclusion and exclusion and the politics of popularity in the mamasphere—in any community—is not whether all members are at all times made to feel perfectly socially comfortable in the community, but whether there are larger social patterns of inclusion and exclusion that consistently impose exclusion on certain members of that community.

The Politics of Race and Identity

Why aren't the Top Bloggers people of color? Where is the Black/Hispanic/Asian/Indian Dooce? Is there a mommyblogger

(I think I will just ~~pick on~~ stick with that one genre for the moment to make a point) of color who is considered an "expert"? The reason I ask this has to do with a question someone posed to me in a private email: "Are you a mommyblogger?" Well, that was rather pointed. I mean, it reads "Mocha *MOMMA*" on my address bar and my banner. To be fair I *have* children. They aren't the focus of *everything* I write about so does that make me less of a mom? (*Mocha Momma*, "Inclusion and Exclusion," August 2, 2007)

One of the thoughts that's been rolling around in my head is the idea that race is invisible or non-noticeable on the blogosphere. On one hand, I get it. I want you to see me as "Tere"—mother, wife, writer, all-around interesting human being. I want you to read me and email me and be my friend regardless of whether I'm white or olive or bi-cultural or speak English with a distinctive "Miami accent." On the other hand, I can't shake the feeling that only white people don't see color because well, they don't have to. (*BlogRhet* "Race And Ethnicity: It Matters," August 6, 2007)

Debates in the mamasphere about race and identity emerged from the above debate about inclusivity and commerce, when a blogger asked, during a panel discussion on mommyblogging at a leading conference for women who blog, why it was that advertisers and marketing representatives seemed to reach out to bloggers of colour *less* than they did to bloggers who are, or seemed to be, white.[12] And why, this blogger later asked in a blog post, did her mommyblogger peers not come to her aid in getting this topic onto the virtual table for discussion and debate?[13] The topic very quickly gained discursive ground in the mamasphere, but its focus became more concentrated on the latter concern—why did the "gatekeeper" (popular) bloggers not talk about this? And why did there seem to be no women of colour among the gatekeepers?[14] ("Where is the Black/Hispanic/Asian/Indian Dooce?").[15]

Bloggers involved in this discussion agreed upon two things: one, that the mamasphere seems to be an overwhelmingly white, middle-class community, and two, that this seems to be the case, if only in part, because there is an overwhelming silence on the subject of race.[16] In the course of the debate, it became clear that a significant number of popular "gatekeeper" bloggers were, in fact, women of color, but that they, for the most part, did not make issues of race central concerns on their blogs.[17] The questions that emerged, then, were these: did these gatekeeper bloggers bear responsibility for raising and fostering discussions about race and identity, or was it the responsibility of all bloggers, popular or otherwise, to maintain a sensitivity to issues of race and identity, and to demonstrate such sensitivity by raising the subject whenever the opportunity arose? And if bloggers did not raise such discussion, was it because such discussion might not be "popular" (that is, amenable to maximizing traffic)? Here, then, was the potentially dark underbelly of the impulse of bloggers to maintain and expand their audience: was it possible that some subjects were avoided because they were believed to be "audience-unfriendly," and so some bloggers (bloggers invested in those subjects) marginalized within the community as a result?

Issues concerning race and identity in the blogosphere are difficult to navigate, not least because anonymity and pseudonymity are the norm, rather than the exception, in virtual communities: anonymous/pseudonymous bloggers by definition do not reveal much about their identities. Even bloggers who blog under their real names might never, or only rarely, post pictures or write about subjects that reveal their race (or religious beliefs, or ability, or sexuality, etc).[18] The mamasphere, and the blogosphere more generally, is, as a virtual space, a space in which identities are fluid and malleable. What members of the community "see" when they approach each other is lines of code or text—not facial features or color. Still, the blogosphere is not entirely blind: there are many bloggers who blog about their race and/or cultural identity and who raise questions concerning identity on a regular basis, and so the original questions were good ones: why does the mamasphere seem so overwhelmingly "white," and why is "whiteness" sometimes assumed (rightly or wrongly)—by bloggers within the community as much as by interested outsiders like PR flacks—to be a prerequisite for popularity? And is it because there is an assumption of homogeneity in the mamasphere that bloggers avoid, for the most part, discussion about the politics of diversity?

The immediate answers again came back to the issue of popularity and its effect upon inclusion: most of the visibly popular mommybloggers are or seem to be white, and, as the collective "face" of the mamasphere, these bloggers project an image of middle-class Caucasian uniformity.[19] And to the extent that these bloggers rarely, if ever, raise questions concerning race and identity on their blogs, those questions rarely receive widespread discursive treatment in the mainstream mamasphere. But again, *why* do popular bloggers—even those who do not fit the perceived mainstream profile of "white, straight, middle-class mom"—neglect, for the most part, to regularly address issues of race and identity in their writing? And does this neglect represent some sort of insidious politics—an effort to avoid controversial or potentially alienating subjects so as to preserve or better advance one's popularity?

The fast—and probably unsatisfying answer—begins with the fact that although the mamasphere seems to be a cohesive community with norms and mores and collective values and concerns, it is, at its core, simply a collection of individuals whose first priorities are to express their own concerns and values and to reflect upon ideas that are of interest to them, rather than to see those concerns and ideas cohere meaningfully within the context of a larger community. In other words, mommybloggers, for the most part, tend to write about whatever it is that is holding their attention—as individuals, as mothers—at any given moment, not about whatever issues might need addressing within the community.[20] If a mommyblogger—of colour or otherwise—is interested in questions concerning race, she might write about those issues regularly. If she's not interested in those questions, she won't.

Alternatively, she might write about those issues within the confines of smaller communities within the mamasphere, or in communities outside of the mamasphere, where she might share those interests with others who are more explicitly interested in the same issues. To this end, many mommybloggers—and parent bloggers generally—set up secondary or tertiary blogs on which to write about these issues, or join group blogs that address these issues. Blogs such as *KimchiMamas* and *RiceDaddies* provide a forum in which parent-bloggers can write about issues of racial and cultural identity in a community of peers and receive commentary from parents with similar concerns, while allowing those bloggers to preserve their main-blog space for writing that is accessible to a broader audience.

Does this "ghetto-ize" certain communities of discourse within the mamasphere and within the blogosphere more generally? It almost certainly does, but again, the difficulty is that the "ghetto-ized" bloggers are also members of the mainstream, and make the choice themselves to compartmentalize certain of their interests and concerns. Obviously, there is broader pressure within the larger community—especially for a blogger who wants to attain and maintain a widespread and broad-based readership—for mommybloggers to *not* structure their blogs around topics that do not have a broad appeal (whether those topics be related to race and identity, or to disability or religious belief or an interest in knitting), but I contend that this is an issue that emanates from a broader societal tendency to privilege discourse that is non-specialized—and, certainly, from a broader social tendency to privilege white heteronormativity and/or the appearance thereof—and not from a failing that is particular to the mamasphere. I will address this in more detail below.

The mamasphere itself is perceived by many—including many of the mothers who write within it—as a kind of ghetto, one that is defined almost entirely by the written experience of motherhood. Mommybloggers are defined as "mommybloggers" because they are understood to write almost exclusively about and from the perspective of experience of motherhood. Other issues and concerns are certainly raised, but these are usually situated firmly within that specific experience and perspective. The most active bloggers blog, for the most part, as diarists—as opposed to essayists—and, as mommybloggers, they are more likely than not to devote most of their attention to issues concerning motherhood (rather than to, say, issues of importance to political scientists or academics or devotees of celebrity gossip). Perhaps bloggers of color ignore questions of race and identity because those questions do not bear upon their experience of motherhood in a way that is easily documented within a mommyblog. It may be that such issues do not cohere with the theme or "vibe" that a blogger has established for her blog. And it may be, of course, that those bloggers do not wish to alienate their broader audience and/or compromise their popularity in the broader "sphere," or that mommybloggers with divergent identities have internalized the need to conform, in order to preserve both emotional and physical safety, in contexts both real and virtual. Whatever the case, the fact remains that questions of race and identity are not widely discussed in the mainstream mamasphere—just as issues of motherhood are not widely discussed in the blogosphere outside of the mommyblogging community—and so that sphere continues to appear, despite evidence to the contrary, homogenous.[21]

Whether this silence on questions of race and identity represents a social problem for the mamasphere has, as I have outlined above, been hotly debated. Some see the mamasphere as colour-blind; others see it as racist. For some, it is a reflection of a broader societal unwillingness to address these issues, and has the effect of excluding parents of colour from full involvement in the community (inasmuch as silence on issues of identity seems to be the norm in the community). For others, it is a reflection of the inclusivity of the mamasphere, and the blogosphere generally. No-one talks much about race, according to this argument, because race is simply not an issue in an arena where the participants have very little idea of each others' physical profiles: as one commenter noted in response to a post about race and blogging, "What about those of us who simply don't care about race? It's not about white liberal guilt or anything else. We simply *don't care*. Speaking only for me, I care about the ideas presented. I care whether those ideas are interesting, exciting or teach me something." (comment at *BlogRhet*, "Race and Ethnicity: It Matters," August 6, 2007)

At the end of the day, it is difficult to escape the fact that "colour-blindness" all too often translates into a presumption of whiteness: if no-one knows that *CityMama* or *MotherhoodUncensored* are women of colour, does that mean that their readers acknowledge, however subconsciously, the rainbow of possibilities around the racial/cultural identities of these women, or does it mean, simply, that their readers assume them to be white?[22] And is such a default assumption of whiteness—if there is in fact such an assumption—due to some social failing of the mamasphere, or is it a by-product of broader social forces (or, to return to the topic of blog commercialization, a by-product of virtual market forces: the more generic the blog content, the more saleable or appealing it is to a broader—presumably predominantly white—audience?)

Whether or not there is a widespread assumption of whiteness in the mamasphere, the relative silence in that sphere, on questions concerning race and identity, nonetheless seems to translate into a discursive marginalization of those bloggers who might otherwise write more freely on those subjects. It is easy to dismiss the seeming silence of the mamasphere on matters of race and identity as simply a choice made by the bloggers for whom those topics are relevant—in much the same manner as mommybloggers might dismiss their own (albeit infrequent) complaints about being marginalized within the larger blogosphere as complaints borne of their own choice ("I might get more traffic/respect if I wrote on gossip or politics or tech, but writing about being a mom is what I *love*")—but the fact remains that that silence is a sort of self-fulfilling prophecy. So long as such discourse remains absent from this community, the less likely it is that anyone will feel comfortable asserting a need for its presence. And that, inevitably, makes the playground-slash-cocktail-party-slash-symposium that is the mamasphere a little less welcoming, and—perhaps—a lot less inclusive.

Conclusion

The mamasphere is *not* like high school. We might end up in all variety of social clusters here, but those clusters are in no way like the tribes of adolescence. In my experience, no one excludes anyone else because they aren't wearing their collar properly or lacking the requisite scrunchy. (*Her Bad Mother*, "High School Confidential," July 31, 2007)

The question of politics in the mamasphere comes back, always, to issues concerning how mommybloggers understand their community, and whether certain perceptions of the community accord with the actual dynamics of this group. That some bloggers are more popular than others is an undeniable fact of the mamasphere, as are the practices that are driven by the desire for popularity—practices that are often identified as "political" within that community. But is popularity, and its pursuit, a problem? The great appeal of the mamasphere to many is that it seems at first glance to be an *a*political space. That is to say, it seems to be a community in which conventional politics (in the modern understanding of ambition or pursuit of power and influence) has little hold: anyone (with the means) can participate, all are welcomed and no-one rules.[23] But the mamasphere is also an exceedingly social space, one in which friendships and collaborations are regularly made and broken, in which participants group and un-group themselves in and out of like-minded clusters, and in which there are rewards—social and otherwise—for participants who distinguish themselves. In such social spaces competition for inclusion, attention and distinction is inevitable. This, then, is the great difficulty faced by anyone wishing to settle upon a clear characterization of the mamasphere as a political community: it is both anarchic, inasmuch as there are no formal, or even informal, systems of "rule" (even if understood broadly as a kind of far-reaching social influence), and polyarchic, inasmuch as there are a variety of forms of influence and status within the community, most of which limit full substantive equality among members and unfettered universal inclusivity. Mommybloggers both identify as equals; and strive to distinguish themselves as *individuals* among equals. The tension between these impulses yields, at times, certain individual and collective discomforts.[24] But mommybloggers are uniquely situated to navigate and negotiate these discomforts, for the simple reason that they recognize, explicitly, the opportunities that these discomforts yield. Mommybloggers often say that they thrive upon self-reflection, debate and discussion—participation in discursive community is, after all, one of the most-cited reasons for why they blog[25]—and claim to welcome opportunities to flex their discursive and reflective muscles (they do, of course, also welcome the minor surges in traffic that participation in such discussion brings.) Speaking one's truth to power on matters of exclusion and social discomfort within the mamasphere is, perhaps ironically, a sure-fire means of drawing a significant virtual crowd around oneself. Feeling marginalized? Write a post, and watch the discussion take off!

The mamasphere cannot be understood to be as mercilessly political as the average high school community with respect to the negotiation of popularity among its members, because those members, for the most part, remain in consistent sympathy with each other and openly regard one another as fundamental equals as writers and as mothers—regardless of differences in quote-unquote popularity. There are (as any cursory evaluation of the social dynamics of the mamasphere shows) rarely, if ever, any active efforts to exclude "others" from the sub-networks and niche-groups of the mamasphere, and, for the most part, mommybloggers who reap rewards in terms of popularity or pecuniary advantage are eager to share them.[26] Inclusion in the mamasphere is a much more effective—and more rewarding—means of securing one's popularity than exclusion: the more a blogger actively embraces and engages other members of the community, the more others will congregate around that blogger, and so the faster (and bigger) that blogger's audience will grow. Does it matter that there is this reward attached to social generosity in the blogosphere? Arguably, no: this is how all communities survive and thrive, through the mutual recognition of the advantages of social cooperation.

To the extent that members of the community need to be alert to the dynamics of inclusion and exclusion, it is to be alert to certain such dynamics becoming entrenched or systemic. Any such dynamics that systemically silence certain members of the community, or marginalize sub-groups within the community, need to be interrogated early and often. This is not to say that such dynamics will be easily rectifiable—or rectifiable at all—but the community needs to be alert their presence when they persist, so that their effects can be mitigated by ongoing discourse.

If anything, then, the politics of the mamasphere are less like high school and more like that of a (very, very big) cocktail party: the social clustering and manouevering that occurs here is not the clustering and manouevering of adolescent tribes. The social clusters in the mamasphere are fluid, dynamic—the type of the clusters that form in really big, really good parties where there is a fascinating mix of people who are meeting for the first time and who fully intend to make full and open benefit of both the social and networking possibilities that such a gathering provides. The mamasphere, in other words, is not high school by any stretch: it is a massive salon-slash-symposium-slash-agora-slash-playgroup. And if it is, in fact, political, it is politics of the very best kind.

> The thing about this grown-up party that we call the mamasphere: it's a party full of people that we like—a lot—or will like or could like or maybe would like if they stopped swearing so much. We have the most important things in common. We love

our children. We love to write. We are smart and funny. And so a strange intimacy develops. We share more with each other than many do in their real life friendships. We make meaning together. For better or for worse, we're close.

And so we're able to hurt each other. Not in the sticks-and-stones way, or the high-school-politics way, but in the way that friends and would-be friends and intimate strangers do. Accidentally. By forgetting or overlooking or neglecting. It stings a little when someone you like stops coming 'round. It's uncomfortable to turn up at a party and not be noticed. It sucks to tell a story, start a conversation, and get no response.

That stuff feels bad. But it's not politics. It's the natural discomfort that comes from being in community, from interaction and discourse and friendship. Community is great, but it's not going to make us feel great all of the time. That's life. (*Her Bad Mother*, "Meter Politikon, Part II," June 17, 2006).

[1] I will use the term "mommyblogger" throughout this paper, both because it is the term by which I identify myself as a blogger, and because it is the term most frequently used within and outside of the mamasphere. For an overview of the debate, see my post: "A Mommy By Any Other Name Would Still Smell Like Spit-Up" at *Her Bad Mother*, March 27, 2006, and Kristen Chase's "The 'MY' Factor" at *Motherhood Uncensored* (March 19, 2006)

[2] *Mom-101* has argued that the mommyblogging community is actually divided in this regard:

"There isn't mommyblogging, there is *mommybloggings*... There are two groups as far as I can see. There are writers who came to blogs as another medium in which to hone their craft. The community of kindred spirits found through blogging is a wonderful and rewarding but altogether unexpected side benefit. These are the women—me included—for whom the term (mommyblogger) is inherently limiting. It tells men, older parents, the childless, *this writing is not for you*. And there is no writer who wants to alienate a potential reader before he or she has even read word one.... The second group of mommybloggers are women who came to blogs as a way to find a community of like-minded people and develop more meaningful relationships than those found in a chat room or an online message board. The writing itself was perhaps secondary to the friendships—or maybe it became more important as time went on. For these women, mommyblogging is entirely the opposite of limiting. It's downright freeing. It's a portal to wonderful things, opening far more doors than it closes." See Liz Gumbinner, "Mommybloggings," at *Mom-101* (July 31, 2006)

[3]Because readers of blogs very often cannot tell—especially with pseudonymous blogs—whether the blogger is black or white or able or differently-abled or heterosexual or homosexual or atheist or Christian, it is difficult to argue that participation in the blogging community is less accessible to members of non-mainstream "real life" communities (I will address this issue in much greater detail below). There are, however, other barriers: that access to blogging is, in practice, limited to those with access to the necessary technology (a computer and an Internet connection, at minimum), time (time to maintain a website, write posts and to interact with others in the community), and some degree of literacy and technical skill, and that this necessarily limits participation to persons of certain social and economic means is well-acknowledged within the community. See, for example, my post "My Bad Mother, Keeping Me On My Toes" at *Her Bad Mother* (March 15, 2007), especially discussion in comments to that post; "The Back Of The (Upper) Class" at *Bub And Pie* (March, 17, 2007); Joy Palmer's "Big Fat Caveat" at *GingaJoy* (March 13, 2007); and, "Mad's Big Bloggy Thinkfest, Part 3" at *Under The Mad Hat* (March 14, 2007)

[4]The mamasphere is generally understood to be comprised mostly of women with access to and the ability to use the relevant technology—computers and the Internet—which is to say, women with a certain minimum level of education and of some economic means. See note 5, above.

[5]Proponents of this argument also argue that "full community participation" itself risks decline: they point to certain popular mommybloggers who earn income from their blogs, and accuse these bloggers of not participating extensively within the community, i.e. not fully reciprocating comments and links. A difficulty here, however, is that the more popular a blog, the more difficult it is for that blogger to keep a niche audience happy: it is very nearly impossible for a blogger who regularly receives upwards of 50 or 100 comments per post to respond to every commenter, let alone link to every commenter. Such bloggers therefore participate in the community in different ways; for example, by organizing collective activities such as "blog blasts, (in which a group of bloggers all post on a specific, assigned topic on a specified date), promoting social causes or by linking to and/or otherwise promoting new bloggers through awards, etc.

[6]This raises the question: why shouldn't quality writing in the mamasphere be accorded the same kind of monetary value that is accorded writing in,

say, *The New Yorker*? See Mom-101's comments on mommyblogging as writerly practice in "MommyBloggings," cited in note 4 above. See also my post, "You Know What? We All DO Get Along" at BlogRhet on the same subject (June 26, 2007).

[7]Very few bloggers outside of the tech and gossip corners of the blogosphere make significant income from advertising on their blogs alone. Where real income can be earned, however, is through paid writing assignments or regular "blog" columns at high-profile websites (in the parenting blogosphere, examples of such sites include *Babble.com*, *ClubMom*, and Disney's *Family* pages.) Bloggers with significant traffic and/or impressive Technorati rankings are frequently solicited for such opportunities.

[8]For an overview of this debate, see my posts on the subject: "Politics 101: A MommyBlogging Seminar," at *The Mother 'Hood* (September 15, 2006), and "Meter Politikon, Part I," (June 16, 2006) and "Meter Politikon, Part II," (June 17, 2006) at *Her Bad Mother*.

[9]The idea that the real-life spaces of socialization for mothers—playgroups, playgrounds and "mom's groups"—is wholly akin in its politics to high school is one that has been well-explored in such novels as Tom Perrota's *Little Children* and Jennifer Weiner's *Goodnight, Nobody*, and one that is referenced frequently in the mamasphere. See Liz Gumbinner's"The Competimommy" at *Mom-101* (June 12, 2006) and *Sunshine Scribe*'s "Wishing It Were A Flashback Friday" (June 16, 2006).

[10]Witness debates about the so-called "mommy wars" (that hypothetical phenomenon in which mothers criticize and judge each other relentlessly for their parenting decisions): the dominant response, within the mamasphere, to such debates is that any "judgment" of each other as mothers is "bad," or at least contrary to the ethos of community that is understood to permeate the mamasphere. For an interesting take on this debate, see *IzzyMom*'s "Mommy War? Or Momism?" (April 27, 2006).

[11]Some mommybloggers suggest that the "early days" of mommyblogging were "a time of idealism and mutual support and sharing," and that that time has passed. See Ann Douglas, "Magazines and Mommyblogs: The Parenting Media Revolution" at *The Mother Of All Blogs* (September 13, 2006) and Jen Lawrence's "Back To (Blog) Basics" at (September 10, 2006).

[12]This discussion took place at BlogHer's Annual Conference "07, July 27-29, 2007, "The State Of The Mamasphere." (Disclosure: I was a featured speaker on that panel.)

[13]See *Mocha Momma*, "Marginalization And Marketing," (July 30, 2007).

[14]See *Daddy In A Strange Land*, "What's Race Got To Do With It?" (Au-

gust 6, 2007), *BlogRhet*, "Race And Collaborative Blogging" (August 15, 2007), *BlogRhet*, "Race And Ethnicity: It Matters" (August 6, 2007).

[15]*Dooce.com*, the blog of Utah-based writer Heather Armstrong, is, by any informal standard of measurement, the best-known of the "mommyblogs." It attained notoriety in 2002 when Armstrong—then an L.A.-based web designer who blogged about her work and life in L.A.—was fired for writing about her employer.

[16]See sources cited in notes 18 through 20, above.

[17]See *Daddy In A Strange Land*, "What's Race Got To Do With It?" (cited in note 20 above).

[18]Glennia of *The Silent I* wrote in a guest post at *BlogRhet* that "I don't hide the fact that I'm half-Korean on my blog, but I don't have many pictures of myself, and it's not the subject of every blog post. I see that as part of my identity as writer, mother, wife, citizen, traveler, lawyer, and all the other aspects of myself." "Race and Collaborative Blogging" at *BlogRhet* (cited in note 20, above).

[19]As *Daddy In A Strange Land* notes in his post on race and blogging (cited in note 20, above), some very popular bloggers, like Kristen Chase of *Motherhood Uncensored* and Stefania Pomponi-Butler of *CityMama*, are *not* white, but are widely assumed to be white.

[20]See the comment in note 23, above.

[21]No formal statistical analysis has been done on this question that I know of, but a random sampling would probably show that most mommybloggers are white. There is, however, as noted above, a significant proportion of the most popular parent bloggers—moms and dads—that are persons of colour.

[22]Stefania Pomponi Butler, the writer behind *CityMama* and a contributor to *KimchiMamas*, has suggested that *CityMama* receives more solicitations from PR firms and marketers than does *KimchiMamas* precisely because they believe her to be—in the absence of any explicit blog evidence to the contrary—white.

[23]See note 5, above.

[24]This is, of course, the great tension at the core of democracy, as understood by the classical political philosophers: inasmuch as democracy promises, and relies upon, both individual freedom and equality, it exists in a state of tension, because those impulses more often than not contradict each other (the desire for freedom often manifests as a desire to distinguish one's self; the desire for equality manifests as a desire that others not distinguish themselves to such a degree that they set themselves above us.) See Aristotle's *Politics*.

[25]See the collection of posts—on the topic of "why moms love blog-

ging'—at "The Great Mommyblogger Love In," a blog blast conducted at Her Bad Mother in May 2006.

[26]There is an undisputed positive feedback loop in the mamasphere when it comes to the perks of popularity: sharing these perks—referrals to ad networks, reciprocal linking, cross-promotion of others' blogs and blog-related projects—almost always yields more such perks for all parties, because these perks—being for the most part "virtual"—are nearly infinite and self-perpetuating.

Works Cited

Armstrong, Heather. *Dooce*. Accessed from February 2006. <www.dooce.com>.

BlogHer. Accessed from April 2006. <www.blogher.com>.

BlogRhet. Accessed from June 2007. <www.blogrhet.blogspot.com>.

Bub And Pie. Accessed from April 2006. <www.bubandpie.blogspot.com>.

Chase, Kristen. *Motherhood Uncensored*. Accessed from February 2006. <www.motherhooduncensored.net>.

Connors, Catherine. *Her Bad Mother*. Accessed from January 2006. <www.badladies.blogspot.com>.

Connors, Catherine. *The Mother 'Hood*. Accessed from September 2006. <ww.urbanmoms.typepad.com/the_mother_hood>.

Daddy In A Strange Land. Accessed August 2007. <www.web.mac.com/quioguesperber/iWeb/daddyinastrangeland/blog>.

Douglas, Ann. *The Mother Of All Blogs*. Accessed from September 2006. <www.anndouglas.blogspot.com>.

Gumbinner, Liz. *Mom-101*. Accessed from February 2006.<www.mom-101.blogspot.com>.

I, Asshole. Accessed August 2006. <ww.iasshole.com>.

Izzy Mom. Accessed from March 2006. <www.izzymom.com>.

Kimchi Mamas. Accessed from June 2006. <www.kimchimamas.com>.

Lawrence, Jen. *MUBAR*. Accessed from April 2006. <www.tomama.blogs.com>.

Mocha Momma. Accessed from May 2006. <www.mochamomma.com>.

Mommyblogs Toronto. <www.mommyblogstoronto.com> (archived, now Better Than A Playdate, Accessed from May 2006. <www.betterthanaplaydate.com>).

Palmer, Joy. *Gingajoy*. Accessed from July 2006. <www.gingajoy.blogspot.com>.

Pomponi-Butler, Stefania. *CityMama*. Accessed from June 2006. <www. citymama.typepad.com>.

Rice Daddies. Accessed from May 2006. <www.ricedaddies.com>.

Silverthorne, Nadine. *Martinis for Milk*. Accessed from April 2006. <www.scarbiedoll.blogspot.com>.

Sunshine Scribe. <www.sunshinescribe.blogspot.com> (archived; now Blog Chocolate, <http://www.blogchocolate.typepad.com/>).

Tripping The Life Unbalanced. <www.trippingthelifeunbalanced.word-press.com>.

Under The Mad Hat. <www.madhattermommy.blogspot.com>.

Chapter Seven

Web 2.0, Meet the Mommyblogger

ANN DOUGLAS

Mothers who have spent a lot of time online creating blogs and participating in social networking communities have a vested interest in seeing the mamasphere (the mother-focused portion of the blogging world) and the world of social networking sites for mothers through rose-tinted glasses. Likewise, marketers who hope to attract and retain huge numbers of mothers to the online communities that they have created have a vested interest in highlighting the positive aspects of mom-to-mom connections online. Is it any wonder, then, that a powerful mythology about the online world of mothers has been created?—an oxytocin-powered virtual universe in which all mothers are kind, good, and mutually supportive—and morally superior to those other non-mother bloggers who simply don't know how to get along?

It's a compelling mythology. Unfortunately, it also happens to be untrue—and the recipe for 1950s-style major disappointment. Just as those stereotypes about perfect wives and perfect mothers felt like straitjackets to the women who felt forced to try to fit inside them, trying to make the mamasphere out to be something it's not—all-perfect, all the time—is misleading, dishonest, unhelpful, and selling mothers short. Besides, emphasizing only the positive aspects of relationships between mommybloggers reeks of marketing spin.

Speaking openly about the full range of behaviors that can and do occur between mommybloggers—the good, the bad, and the ugly—is the only way to start the kind of dialogue that allows for change. After all, until mothers have a chance to talk about the role that horizontal violence[1] plays in causing mothers to lash out at one another online and off, vitriolic flame wars on blogs and grade-school-like exclusionary behavior at social networking sites will remain totally mystifying, particularly to the mother on the receiving end of such attacks—the poorly-connected mommyblogger.

Ad pitches aimed at mothers have been becoming more intense and more intrusive ever since marketers discovered the influence and reach of the well-connected mommyblogger and her new sidekick, Mom 2.0. Now, every marketer wants to be that mom's best online friend. As Maria Bailey, CEO of BSM Media and author of *Trillion Dollar Moms: Marketing to a New Generation of Mothers*, told Theresa Howard of *USA Today*, "(Marketers) are scurrying to be part of the mom dialogues." And Web 2.0 entrepreneurs, in turn, are eager to be part of any conversation that even hints at mothers, marketers, and money. The net result? When moms attempt to connect online, there's increasingly a third party sitting in (or eavesdropping on) those conversations, eager to find ways to cash in on the increasing presence of mothers online.

It took a technological evolution for mothers to become the darlings of Web 2.0. The Internet had to evolve to the point where any user—as opposed to a technologically-savvy few—were capable of generating sophisticated online content with a few keystrokes or clicks of the mouse.[2]

Not surprisingly, Web 2.0 has ushered in an explosion of user-generated content.[3] Now that Jane or Joe User are able to generate content with an ease that they couldn't have even imagined a few years ago, the Internet has become any user's oyster: easily accessible to even the least experienced and most time-pressed Internet surfer. Thanks to push-and-play scripts that are invisible to the end consumer, any user with high-speed broadband (the new Internet great divide in terms of status) can carry off ever-more-complex acts of online wizardly. As a result, uploading photos and videos to popular media-sharing sites such as YouTube and Flickr; sharing opinions on books, movies, and other goods and services and sites maintained by retailers; and creating online profiles in wildly popular social networking sites such as Twitter, Facebook, and LinkedIn have become almost commonplace activities in the Web 2.0 era.

If mothers feel at home in the world of Web 2.0, it's certainly for good reason. Long before anyone had coined the term *social networking*, moms were finding ways to connect with one another via email lists, usenet groups, bulletin boards, and chat rooms. And group moderators were painstakingly compiling and uploading text-only FAQs[4] into the Internet attic, hoping that the collective words of wisdom from their online mothers' groups would be stumbled upon by the next group of mothers desperate to hit the online advice motherlode.

As web development software became more user-friendly, mothers began sharing photos of their families via email groups and online message boards; creating elaborate profiles at their favorite web sites; and establishing mini-communities within social networking sites as they arrived on the scene.

As the era of user-generated content emerged (with its overriding emphasis on social networking), a large number of social networking sites for mothers or parents began to emerge. Some sites were created by parents. Others were created by technology companies, marketing companies, or individual consumer product companies who had a vested interest in building relationships with mothers. And still other sites were created by consortiums of investors and quickly sold off to other interested parties interested in capturing their own piece of the motherhood pie. As Theresa Howard noted in a recent article in *USA Today,* "Every day is Mother's Day for advertisers using digital marketing to attract today's moms and their command of $1.7 trillion in annual spending."

Mommy Boom

For love or money (or both), there have been a large number of social networking sites for moms launched over the past two years. Most social networking sites for mothers provide users with a variety of different methods of interacting with one another via the site, in an effort to maximize user visits, page views, and advertiser revenue. Common site features include the ability to comment on other journals/blogs, send private messages to other users, participate in online groups hosted on community message boards, and vote on (or comment on) one another's photos. Beyond that, each site has its own unique features.

At *CafeMom* (heralded as the largest and fastest growing social networking site for moms, with 2.1 million unique visitors in October 2007, according to comScore MediaMetrix) moms are able to connect through groups, journals, private messages and by viewing one another's photos. Users can also communicate via thought bubbles that surf a map of the world, picking up random comments from moms on the site, ideally enticing users to click through and join the conversation. There is a much more entrenched corporate presence at *CafeMom* than at most other social networking sites. The "About *CafeMom*" page at the site states that *CafeMom* offers "a series of cutting edge sponsorship programs that allow leading brands to join the consumer conversation, add value to members' lives, and get members talking about sponsor brands in an authentic and viral way." Advertising partner JC Penney recently handed out $100 gift cards to one hundred moms on the site and asked them to write about (and upload photos of) the gifts that they bought with the cards. Similarly WalMart had CafeMoms create a holiday gift guide by recommending their favorite product picks (all WalMart products, of course).

Endorsements in which real moms talk about their experiences with products and then recommend those products to their online friends are the ultimate way of generating online buzz. And given the ease with which recommendations can be passed along in the click-and-connect world of Web 2.0, it's no wonder marketers see social networking sites for moms as the ultimate online paradise for themselves and their products.

Three's a Crowd

Ultimately, how much of the world of Web 2.0 is about marketing and how much is about moms having conversations with other moms? And to what extent does the growing presence of marketers affect online conversations between moms, both on the social networking sites themselves and in the once sacrosanct space of moms' blogs?

Mom-to-mom conversation that is free of product mentions and endorsements still makes up the majority of the dialogue in the online world of mothers.[5] If you're an exhausted new mother and you've been up all night with a crying baby, your brain is on one channel and one channel only: make my life better now.

Of course, a mother in need presents an irresistible target to a marketer with a product that promises to meet that need. All they've got to do is make the pitch. And, in recent years, marketers have cranked the emotional pitch up to a scream in advertising campaigns targeted at mothers. Consumer product giant Procter and Gamble has taken the lead in this area, developing ads that use highly emotive and sensory language and that tap into very real worries and concerns of mothers. One of the most offensive examples of ads in this genre was the infamous Tide with Febreze ad which implied that mothers stink (*"There's a difference between smelling like a mom, and smelling like a woman."*)[6]

Of course, marketers aren't above using information gleaned from moms to market products back to moms. Moms were invited to participate in a contest sponsored by Suave shampoo and Sprint long distance at a special contest website called *In the Motherhood*. More than three thousand moms submitted contest entries sharing slice-of-life moments from their own lives as mothers, in the hope that these scenarios would be developed into "webisodes" of an online show. The contest attracted 3,000 submissions and 50,000 unique visitors.

The beauty of the contest from the sponsors' perspective was that they were able to attract mom visitors and harvest mom data. "People who create online content (as opposed to those who merely view and rate content) can be particularly valuable to marketers," Kevin Townsend, managing partner for Science + Fiction, San Francisco, the company which designed the site, explained to the advertising industry publication *AdWeek* ("MotherHood Site Suggests the Strength of Numbers," *Adweek,* June 18, 2007). If "family-oriented extroverts" who create content online can draw other moms to the site, they draw in their own personal networks. From the 3,000 women who contributed, the site thus tapped into 50,000 additional contacts. What's more, getting women to contribute content about their lives produces a data goldmine that can be used for future marketing campaigns.

Stats and Status

Now that marketers have joined in the dialogue, stats and status have become an important part of the conversation about mothers online. Marketers' attempts to profit from mothers' conversations online have led to a need to quantify the worth of any particular mother using terms that are more traditionally used to measure success in the world of business—measures such as blog ranking and popularity (as ranked by sites such as Technorati), number of online friends/contacts, incoming vs. outgoing blog-links,[7] the number of unique visitors and page views, and (where applicable) ad click through rates and blog revenues.

Statistics are also used to measure success in the highly competitive world of social networking: how well the site as a whole is performing against its various competitors and how well individual groups and site members are measuring up against one another within the site population.

The concept of popularity is built into the very architecture of most social networking sites, with members being asked to rate everything from individual photos and posts to, in the world of parenting social networks, cute kid quotes so that these ratings can generate rankings for content, members, and groups. Members who hope to rank highly within each social networking site need to create a lot of content (post frequently, share a lot of photographs, participate in groups and site contents, etc.) They are rewarded (through points) for site contributions and votes on those contributions; the more content created, the more contributions pay off for members, in terms of added popularity.

Popularity has a built-in multiplier effect at many of these sites: mothers can easily forward posts to an extended network of contacts using the "share this" feature. (In many sites, users can instantly forward posts within the network or via email to mom-contacts who have yet to join the network.) Of course, this all means added revenue for the site. To date, not one of the social networks for moms has proposed any sort of ad revenue sharing arrangement with even their most prolific site users,[8] even though this arrangement would pick up on the precedent established by blog ad revenue sharing arrangements. This means that social networking sites are able to attract hundreds of thousands of members who are willing to accept popularity—or even the promise of popularity—in lieu of cash payment for the content they provide to these sites. That's a deal that social networking site operators are happy to leverage and profit on, with great success.

The emphasis on ranking and popularity can encourage mothers to begin to use the same measures as marketers as they assess the value of their online communication, rather than looking at non-quantifiable measures such as the enjoyment they derive from their online activities and how other mothers are positively affected by their online connections and contributions. This can, in turn, create an atmosphere of competition rather than cooperation between mothers.

Some mothers who blog and/or participate in social networking sites take blog rank and social networking ranks very seriously, musing about their popularity relative to others. Consider this comment, which was posted to a discussion thread at *BlogRhet*:

> I have a few regular commenters that I can count on [to comment] almost every time I post. I have come to view these women as my friends, even if it is only online, and I always try to reciprocate [by commenting on their posts]. I try really hard not to see blogging as a popularity thing. It should and is a place to express myself and meet some neat people at the same time. (*BlogRhet*, "Belonging" September 14, 2007)

There are some clearly defined, albeit tacit, rules of engagement when it comes to interacting with other mothers online. At social networking sites, these rules are set and enforced by the site's administrators. In the world of mommybloggers, these rules are much debated by bloggers themselves. It's possible to gain a lot of insight into mom culture (the raw, unedited, unmoderated version) by considering the kinds of comments that come up in discussions of mommyblogging etiquette. Consider this comment from a discussion on blog etiquette posted to the blog ... *and I wasted all that birth control*:

Most of the writers of blogs that I read already seem to have a 'core' group of commenters and friends, and I totally feel like I'm butting in on private conversations, so I often don't comment. Other places, I'll only comment if I feel I have something unique to add to the discussion.... I'm still working on trying to overcome the 'not a cool kid' syndrome here. (...*and I wasted all that birth control*, "Blog Etiquette (and I'm feeling much better, thank you)," August 11, 2005.)

It's worth noting that many conversations on mommyblogs tend to be more genuine and authentic than conversations in third-party controlled social networking spaces. Most social networking sites are moderated by a community manager or by users themselves (through a "report offensive content mechanism"), and most sites have explicit rules about the content of posts[9] and, in some cases, the use of profanity. By contrast, a blogger sets her own rules, although she may feel pressured to adhere to implicit or explicit policies set by her fellow bloggers and, of course, she will have to adhere to any policies set by her blog host or Internet Service Provider. That said, blog posts tend to be more raw and authentic. This can be both a good thing (in terms of mothers sharing) and a bad thing (if a herd mentality sets in and the group decides to circle around a particular mom). Of course, this isn't new or unique to the Internet. "Any expression of anger or the introduction of a tabooed subject may result in the group's scape-goating of one or two of its members," wrote Phyllis Chesler in *Woman's Inhumanity to Woman*. "Most women have a repertoire of techniques with which to weaken, disorient, humiliate or banish other female group members." The Internet isn't the exclusive domain of viciousness between mothers. Just ask any mother who has had a bad experience serving on the parent-teacher committee at her child's school—or the fundraising committee for her child's hockey or gymnastics team—and she will tell you: motherhood doesn't make you immune to the nastiness you experienced during your growing up years. If anything, it causes some of it to boomerang back for another round.

People start speaking in contradictions when the subject of women and bullying—and mothers and bullying—arises. On the one hand, they like to pretend that mother-on-mother bullying doesn't exist. After all, isn't bullying terribly unmotherlike? On another level, mother-on-mother bullying has become such a fact of life in the online world that most online communities for mothers have had to establish formal policies to deal with it.[10]

Group Think

Group think[11]—and a tendency to attack dissenters—tends to be a problem in both blogs and social networking communities, as this commenter to the previously cited discussion thread at ...*and I wasted all that birth control* notes:

> I especially dislike it when someone just respectfully posts a dissenting opinion, and then 100 commenters come out of the woodwork to call her names. It really stifles that free and open communication thing we're supposed to be standing for, [in my humble opinion]. And to be quite honest, it's the reason why I've gone from fairly active commenting on some blogs, to not even reading or posting in the comments anymore. A lot of the comments just degenerate into junior high us vs. them-ness for no reason. I get the impression that the words have lost meaning for people when they can so carelessly and venomously throw around "bitch" and the c-word with other women they don't even know; I guess I'm too sensitive, words have meaning and power for me, and watching the lions gather to tear into a hapless Internet poster just doesn't do it for me. (...*and I wasted all that birth control*, "Blog Etiquette (and I'm feeling much better, thank you)," August 11, 2005)

The group think phenomenon isn't limited to mommyblogs, however. As this commenter to the *Free Think Blog* notes, it's a common problem throughout the online world:

> In social networks, group think runs rampant ... when a person or group of people who don't agree infiltrate the group think party, they are labeled as haters, offenders, etc., and the group does their best to kick them out or ignore them.... After scrolling through hundreds of butt-kissing comments, if you see one that is negative or that doesn't agree with the status quo, it is immediately followed by a ton of comments that either insult the infidel, or comfort the party that was "wronged" by the negative commenter. (*FreeThinkBlog*, "The Dark Side of Social Networking," July 10, 2007)

While group think is hardly unique to the mamasphere, then, disagreements have a tendency to become particularly high-stakes and personal in the online world of mothers. This can be explained by two factors. First, the importance of popularity as a measure of success in mommyblog-ging and maternal social networking (in lieu of more material rewards) and second, the phenomenon of horizontal violence, when members of groups with low status display hostile behaviors toward their fellow group members

Given that getting rich in the world of mommybloggers has traditionally been defined as being able to quit your job and being able to afford health insurance (that was A-list mommyblogger *Dooce*'s measure of success, anyway), moms are unlikely to "get rich" online anytime soon—unless, of course, they are operating or flipping the social networking sites that are profiting off the super-hot Mom 2.0 demographic. (As noted above, social networking sites have yet to show any willingness of sharing revenue with even the most prolific of their content producers.)[12]

Because huge paycheques and revenue streams aren't the perks being offered to moms online, mothers have had instead to rely on social rec-ognition to keep them going: blog ranking, popular post awards, and being invited into the inner circle of alpha bloggers. Is it any wonder that horizontal violence—a behavior associated with oppressed groups who are eager to get ahead—is commonplace in the mamasphere?

There's no denying that mommybloggers command less respect in the mainstream blogging community than the majority of other bloggers. In fact, if you have to place them on the blogging food chain, they'd end up being placed just above spammers and multilevel-marketers in the eyes of most business and techie bloggers.[13] Case in point? The 2007 BlogHer Convention (for women, both moms and non) barely attracted any national mainstream media attention at all, while even the most fringe techie blog convention warrants some coverage by the major newspapers.

Marketers have been able to use this craving for attention in the on-line world to their advantage in dealing with moms online. They have discovered that handing out token freebies or letting a mother know that she'll be first in the know about a product coming down the pipeline—or securing her an exclusive invite to a product launch in her community or, better yet, to some chi-chi event an airplane ride's away—is a powerful incentive to generating online buzz. That can lead to resentment between mommybloggers who are perceived to being "on the take" (even if the "take" amounts to free soup or cleaning products) and mommybloggers who find it annoying to find product pitches weaved into the tapestry of ordinary conversations between mothers, all because someone else feels like they "owe" a big multi-national company a free plug in exchange for sweet-talk and swag. This is yet another way that intrusions into the world of mommybloggers by marketers have caused dissension between mothers.[14] Rather than directing their feelings of resentment about these intrusions towards the intruders (the marketers), they have misdirected these feelings of resentment towards other mothers.

While this behavior may seem puzzling at first, it becomes more understandable when it is viewed as an example of horizontal violence: dismissive, negative, demeaning, or hostile behaviors that occur between members of oppressed groups. Instead of lashing out at their oppressors, members of oppressed groups are more likely to lash out at their peers. Horizontal violence can be conscious or unconscious; overt or covert. It may include gossip, sarcasm, snark, name calling, belittling, dismissive comments, fault-finding and nit-picking that go above and beyond the boundaries of constructive criticism; undermining a person's credibility; making comments that devalue people's areas of expertise; ignoring anyone who is different from "the norm"; ignoring or minimizing a person's concerns; withholding support for (or actively rallying support against) someone's project or opinion; limiting the right to free speech and the right to have an opinion; seeking to control someone; using "humorous" put downs that feel anything but funny to the group member being targeted; excluding someone (particularly when such exclusion could be socially, academically, or career limiting); and/or threatening or intimidating someone.[15]

Regardless of the specific techniques that are used, the effects of horizontal violence can be devastating. Victims report feelings of humiliation and a lack of respect; a sense of powerlessness; and a sense that they have become invisible within the group.

The concept of horizontal violence is useful in explaining the hostile and even hateful behavior that can be witnessed between mothers online. It can consist of an explicit attack on someone's credibility on a blog or at a social networking site or it can be a matter of shunning someone: shutting them out of discussions, blocking their comments, or de-friending them or making use of the technological tools that make it so easy to "manage" friendships, for better and for worse, in the world of Mom 2.0.

Horizontal violence is a problem on the larger social networking sites for moms—but you have to be quick to spot out-and-out attacks. Most sites have rules that ban posts flaming fellow members as well as anonymous posts; and they forbid the use of fake accounts ("sock puppetry"), and members are quick to police the rules. The result is a much more friendly atmosphere, although with a slightly Stepford-ish edge. Big Sister is keeping the peace, but that peace is less than genuine.

The problem is bigger than Mom 2.0 or even the Internet itself, of course—a point that Lyn Mikel Brown, Ed.D and Meda Chesney-Lind,

Ph.D. make in their cultural critique *Bad Girls, Bad Girls, Watcha Gonna Do.* "The problem is a culture that commodifies and denigrates women and then gets a kick out of watching the divide and conquer consequences." (2)

If calling yourself a mommyblogger is done with the same embarrassed shrug with which some women call themselves a feminist—or is rejected altogether for the same reasons—discovering horizontal violence in the Land of MommyBlogs shouldn't be any surprise either.

Conclusions

In venturing into this brave new world, mothers need to keep a number of conclusions in mind. First of all, the online world of mothers is being transformed by marketers with their own specific agendas. These marketers—who are eager to tap into the $1.7 trillion market that mothers represent—have the budgets to ensure that they are able to tap into the conversation of mothers, wherever those conversations happen to be taking place online. Web 2.0 sites are eager to find ways to generate revenue from their operations and marketers are the source of that revenue, so their needs will often eclipse the needs of mothers in online communities. Often what works well from a revenue generation perspective by meeting the needs and wishes of advertisers is at direct odds with the needs of mothers. Web 2.0 sites claim to pay attention to privacy concerns because users control how much or how little information they choose to share with the site. In reality, however, at social networking sites both content contributions and contacts are valued, so that users who choose to make family privacy a priority quickly become invisible within the Mom 2.0 machine. The message is clear: if mothers want to reap the benefits that the marketers are dangling before them, they need to be willing to bring what the marketers are asking them to bring to the table: whatever detailed demographic information the marketers are hoping to harvest from this crop of moms.

Moms have always been generous about sharing their wisdom and ideas with other mothers, but now a third party is privy to those conversations. In the world of Web 2.0, there's a third party sitting (or eavesdropping) at the table—a marketer who is taking notes and looking for ways to use mothers' ideas to sell products back to mothers. More often than not, moms are not being compensated for these intellectual property contributions in any meaningful way. Rather than paying cash—the traditional currency of business—marketers and the mega-corporations that they front for offer fleeting fame and freebies. On a per-hour basis, these "pay rates" can amount to lower rates of compensation than the rates paid to workers in third-world sweat shops—working conditions these mega-corporations go to great lengths to distance themselves from.

Horizontal violence between mothers online is the result of the lack of respect shown to mothers by other online users. This type of hostile activity between mothers is at its rawest in the blogging community ("the wild west") as compared to in the highly moderated (and much less authentic) world of social networking sites aimed at mothers. When horizontal violence does occur on social networking sites, the social networking tools that are built into the site architecture can be used with merciless effectiveness (at least until a site moderator steps in). Rumors and misinformation can be forwarded to an entire network of contacts (both on-site and off-site) with a mouse-click. Deleting someone from a list of friends can be accomplished with equal ease (and, in many cases, that former "friend" won't even realize that they have been de-friended).

Perhaps the most important conclusion that web-savvy mothers must keep in mind is that horizontal violence will become less of a problem when the status of mothers and women is improved both online and in the real world. Until this happens, it is important for mothers to acknowledge its existence and to work toward collective solutions. In "Horizontal violence in the workplace," Carolyn Hastie recommends a series of strategies that appear to be just as practical and relevant to the world of mothers: recognizing and acknowledging that horizontal violence occurs between mothers and using the term "horizontal violence" to name the problem; raising awareness of this issue and addressing the cultural issues that allow horizontal violence to continue to be a problem between mothers and women; speaking out against instances of horizontal violence whenever they occur; addressing individual attitudes and behaviors; and practicing self-nurturing and self-care so that each woman is able to "do the things that help [her] to be healthy and happy in all aspects of [her] human-ness." Once she applies that age-old common sense to dealing with a computer-age online problem, Mom 2.0 will have more to give to her Web 2.0 girlfriends. And it's a 100% product-free solution, to boot.

[1]The term horizontal violence is used when members of groups with low status display hostile behaviors toward their fellow group members as opposed to lashing out at their oppressors.
[2]It was O'Reilly Media Inc. VP Dale Dougherty who first coined the term Web 2.0 back in 2001—to describe the new era of user-generated

content. O'Reilly Media Inc. founder and CEO, Tim O'Reilly, describes the conference call in which this conversation occurred in an online essay entitled "What is Web 2.0?"

[3] *User-generated content* is a decidedly geeky term that is used to describe content that is generated by the user while she navigates the Internet. These content contributions can require anything from a mouse-click or two (tagging an item at del.icio.us, rating the helpfulness of a review at Amazon.com, or making someone your friend at Facebook, or clicking on the "metoo" button at www.truuconfessions.com, or sending a tweet from Twitter) to adding a comment (on blogs, on videos at YouTube, on photos at Flickr, on book reviews at Amazon.com) to creating content that is either posted at a website or blog you host and control or to a third party site (posting videos to YouTube, photos to Flickr, adding content to online journals and blogs and otherwise using the user tools at social networking sites for mothers; creating detailed lists of product recommendations on user lists at shopping sites).

[4] FAQs are lists of Frequently Asked Questions.

[5] For a discussion of the kinds of conversations that occur between mothers and how blogging about motherhood affects the experience of mothering, see the notes from my Association for Research in Mothering presentation "Mothering in the Age of the Blog" and my *Canadian Family* magazine article "Moms Who Blog."

[6] For more about this campaign and the related "Have a Happy Period" campaign for Always feminine pads, see Berner.

[7] Andrea McDowell's analysis of the blogging experiences of mothers of children with physical differences reveals that their blogs are less likely to be linked to and read than the blogs of other mothers. She argues that mothers of children with special needs are frequently marginalized and excluded and that the rhetoric that the mamasphere is all-inclusive is simply rhetoric. "If the voices of Canadian mothers with children who have special needs are not represented in the mamasphere, then the discourse is lacking a vital element that reduces its ability to represent Canadian mothers as a group."

[8] It takes an enormous amount of time to be a "successful" social networker. If a social networker really want to get noticed, that person needs to have a presence in multiple communities. According to a study conducted by Dallas based Parks Associates, which researches social media space and other consumer behavior, 45 percent of all social network users maintain profiles on more than one site. And some sixteen percent participate on three or more sites. Given the large number of online "friendships" that a user must maintain in order to be socially successful at any given site

(some of the top contributors at Maya's Mom, for example, have over 1,200 friends), the idea of multitasking takes on a whole new dimension. There are emails to send, journal posts to compose, various group memberships to maintain, friends' content to vote on—and all this across multiple sites.

[9]There's a greater expectation that a member will share information (and create content) on social networking sites than there is in the world of mom blogs. What a blogger does or doesn't share on her blog is up to her. She is the web-mistress of her own web domain. Fitting into someone else's social networking web template is an entirely different matter. If she isn't willing to complete any of the profile creation prompts (e.g., "Thing I don't want to forget" "Little known fact" "Biggest wish") or contribute photos or other highly personal content about herself or her family, her profile will look empty and she will find it difficult to connect with other site members or attract many online friends. That will drive her ranking on the site down and she will rapidly become more invisible in the world of that site than she ever felt during her most miserable day of junior high.

[10]Most social networking sites targeted at mothers have very specific objectives when they moderate user content. They remove content that contains direct attacks on fellow members (because this type of content can quickly trigger community-wide flame wars). What they don't do is invest the resources in moderating content to ensure factual accuracy of parenting advice (something that has safety implications in areas such as infant sleep practices) or to do even cursory checks to ensure that the copyright and intellectual property rights of others are being respected. (User agreements on most sites place responsibility for posting any copyrighted material on the person who posted the material.)

[11]When a group loses its ability to think critically, weigh the facts, and to consider any opinions that contradict the majority opinion.

[12]When mothers attempt to monetize their online content contributions, they quickly discover that the money on offer tends to be pin money rather than real pay cheques. The key opportunities for generating online income via blogging include selling ad space on their own blogs or podcasts; participating in blog advertising syndicates that sell ads on behalf of a group of bloggers and forward a percentage of revenue to each individual blogger; joining pay-per-post (or pay per click) blog networks; or being hired to blog for a particular website (work which tends to pay considerably less than the rates paid for comparable contributions to print media outlets). Moms who contribute content to Web 2.0 sites by creating profiles, sharing photos, posting to online groups, and us-

ing advertiser-created widgets (such as those available at Maya's Mom) aren't compensated at all, despite the fact that each page of content that women create generates page clicks and ad views which, in turn, generate revenue for the sites being frequented. It's no wonder that marketers are such fans of Mom 2.0. She generates content. She creates connections. And she's giving it away for free.

[13]One of the most notorious examples of the lack of respect accorded to mommy bloggers occurred in a 2005 article by *New York Times* writer David Hochman, who described the "baby blog" as "an online shrine to parental self-absorption." Hochman's comment is frequently cited when mommybloggers want to show how little respect mommy-bloggers receive. Toronto writer Jennifer Lawrence, for example, incorporated Hochman's phrase into the title of her blogging presentation at the Association for Research in Mothering's 2006 Motherlode Conference.

[14]For more on this topic, see Jen Lawrence's chapter in this volume.

[15]This definition of horizontal violence was compiled based on the detailed descriptions provided by Curtis, Bowen and Reid; Epub 2006 Aug 7; and Hastie.

Works Cited

...and I wasted all that birth control. "Blog Etiquette (and I'm feeling much better, thank you)." Aug 11, 2005. Accessed October 28, 2007. <http://zia. blogs.com/wastedbirthcontrol/2005/08/blog_ettiquete_.html>.

Berner, Robert. "Detergent Can Be So Much More." *Business Week*, May 1, 2006.

BlogRhet.com. "Belonging." September 14, 2007. Accessed October 30, 2007. <http://blogrhet.blogspot.com/2007/09/belonging.html>.

Brown, Lyn Mikel, and Meda Chesney-Lind. "Bad Girls, Bad Girls, Watcha Gonna Do." *Hardygirlshealthywomen.org.* n.d. Accessed Oct. 28, 2007. <www.hardygirlshealthywomen.org/docs/BadGirls.pdf>.

CafeMom. "About CafeMom." Accessed January 30, 2008. <www. cafemom.com/about/index.php>.

Chesler, Phyllis. *Woman's Inhumanity to Woman.* New York: Thunder's Mouth Press/Nations Books, 2001.

Curtis, J., I. Bowen, and A. Reid. "You Have No Credibility: Nursing Students' Experiences of Horizontal Violence." *Nurse Education in Practice* 7 (3) (May 2007): 156-63.

Douglas, Ann. "Moms Who Blog." *Canadian Family.* July 2007. Accessed October 28, 2007. <www.canadianfamily.ca/articles/article/moms-who-blog/>.

Douglas, Ann. "Mothering in the Age of the Blog." Paper presented at the ARM Motherlode Conference, October 2006. Online: *The Whole Mom*, November 2006. <http://thewholemom.com/Files/ARM%20Conference/Ann.html>. Accessed January 30, 2008.

Free Think Blog "The Dark Side of Social Networking." July 10, 2007. Accessed October 28, 2007. <http://blog.thinkfree.com/2007/07/10/the-dark-side-of-social-networking-unenlightenment>.

Hastie, Carolyn. "Horizontal Violence in the Workplace." *Birth International*, August 6, 2002. Accessed November 11, 2007. <www.acegraphics.com.au/articles/hastie02.html>.

Hochman, David. "Mommy (and Me)." *New York Times,* January 30, 2005. Accessed January 30, 2008. <www.nytimes.com/2005/01/30/fashion/30moms.html>.

Howard, Theresa. "Internet Becomes Popular Place to Make Pitches to Moms." *USA Today,* 11 May 11, 2006. Accessed January 30, 2008. <www.usatoday.com/tech/news/techinnovations/2006-05-11-wired-moms_x.htm>.

Lawrence, Jennifer. "Tool of Online Revolution or Online Shine to Parental Absorption." Paper presented at the ARM Motherlode Conference, October 2006. Online: *The Whole Mom*, November 2006. <http://thewholemom.com/Files/ARM%20Conference/Jen.html>. Accessed January 30, 2008.

McDowell, Andrea. "On the Internet, Nobody Knows You're a Dog: Blogging About a Child With Physical Differences." Paper presented at the ARM Motherlode Conference, October 2006. Online: *The Whole Mom*, November 2006. <ttp://thewholemom.com/Files/ARM%20Conference/Andrea.html>. Accessed January 30, 2008.

Miller, Laura. "Back Stabbers." *Salon.* Book Review of Phyllis Chesler's *Woman's Inhumanity to Woman.* March 29, 2002. Accessed October 28, 2007. <http://archive.salon.com/books/feature/2002/03/29/girls/index.html>.

"MotherHood Site Suggests the Strength of Numbers." *AdWeek,* June 18, 2007. Accessed January 30, 2008 <www.adweek.com/aw/search/article_display.jsp?vnu_content_id=1003599882>.

O'Reilly, Tim. "What is Web 2.0?" *oreillynet.com.* September 30, 2005. Accessed January 30, 2008. <www.oreillynet.com/pub/a/oreilly/tim/news/2005/09/30/what-is-web-20.html?page=1>.

SociableBlog. "CafeMom Largest and Fastest Growing Social Networking Site for Moms." November 22, 2007. Accessed January 30, 2008. <www.sociableblog.com/2007/11/22/cafemomcom-largest-and-fastest-growing-social-networking-site-for-moms/>.

Chapter Eight

Blog for Rent

How Marketing Is Changing Our Mothering Conversations

JEN LAWRENCE

Once upon a time, "mommy blogs" occupied a quiet little corner of the blogosphere. A general lack of interest in the conversations of mothers, coupled with the relative anonymity of the internet, allowed us to discuss taboo subjects like maternal ambivalence, anger, and depression, without fear of judgment. For women like me who could not identify with the permanently blissful mothers of television and glossy magazines, the raw and honest two-way blogging conversations offered a lifeline.

Then, celebrity babies Shiloh, Violet, and Apple arrived, mummies became Yummy, and advertisers wanted to find new ways to tap into the US$3 trillion mom market. Savvy marketers recognized that the "mamasphere" had a demographically desirable audience and that the very rawness and honesty of the conversations made the medium a highly trusted one. They recognized the influential role that popular mommy bloggers could play in word of mouth marketing efforts and actively courted their favour.

Mommy blogs became big business. While it was positive that mothers could blog professionally for corporate blogging sites, sell ad space, or leverage their blogs into book deals, little attention was paid to how the commercial influence was altering our conversations. Marketers started to look for ways not only to listen to our conversations but to infiltrate them. Tabloid-style "train wreck" blogs attempted to hijack our conversations through attacks on the parenting abilities and integrity of certain high profile mommy bloggers in an attempt to increase their own readership and ad revenue. These elements threaten to spoil the unique ability of the blogging medium to facilitate open and honest conversation among mothers, free from scrutiny and judgment.

I came to blogging in early 2004 out of necessity. When my daughter was three months old, I went through a deep postpartum depression. I felt totally inadequate as a new mother: I could not breastfeed, I was beyond exhausted, and while I loved my daughter (she of the exquisite blue eyes, how could I not?) I was not immediately consumed by the glowy, intoxicating love new mothers are supposed to feel. I could not spend hours smelling her neck, sweet-smelling as it was; I was too darned tired. I had not yet fully immersed myself in texts like Andrea Buchanan's *Mother Shock* (a book which, literally, saved my sanity) or Anne Lamott's *Operating Instructions* and I feared that my maternal ambivalence put me on the same path as a Susan Smith or Andrea Yates, modern day Medeas whose shaky maternal bonds led to murder. I felt very alone.

And then came *Dooce*.

Blogger Heather Armstrong, a blogging pioneer who had been fired spectacularly for blogging unflattering things about her employer, had recently given birth and had been hit with debilitating depression (www.dooce.com). Suddenly, I was not alone—Heather and I were on the same real-time, white-knuckle ride together. And there were other Heathers out there, bold, funny, flesh and bone women who served as a perfect counterbalance to the smiling celebrity moms served up on a plate in the Mother's Day issues of *In Style* magazine. The relative anonymity of the blogosphere made women feel free to share the dark secrets of mothering that used to be shared in whispers over the coffee pot while the kids played in the backyard, but which rarely get mentioned in this day of Gymboree, formal Mommy and Me groups, and scheduled playdates.

Eventually I started blogging myself in part as a therapeutic exercise and in part as a way to share my story with other mothers who might feel alone. I blogged about breastfeeding pressure, the hard unsung work of mothering, postpartum depression and the desire to chuck it all, change my name and simply run away. It took me a long time to enable the "comments" function that allows readers to respond, but since the emails I received had all been positive, I made that leap. The comments were heartfelt and positive and the acknowledgement gave me a sense of identity in that difficult first year of motherhood. For me, blogging had become a wonderful tool of honest communication and support, and I honestly thought that blogging would facilitate a mothering revolution.

As more and more mothers started blogging, something interesting happened: outsiders—non-mothers, non-bloggers—started to pay attention to our conversations. In January 2005, New York Times writer David Hochman wrote "Mommy (and Me)" where he was very critical of mom bloggers (who apparently were guilty of everything from ignoring to exploiting their children) and in the shot heard around the mamasphere, indicated that mommy blogs were "an online shrine to parental self-absorption" (Hochman 2005). Certainly it must have come as a shock to many that mothers have thoughts of their own; that we are not simply extensions of our children. As I wrote on my blog in response to his article: "For me, the question is not whether blogging about parenting is self-absorbed but why blogging about parenting is considered more self absorbed than writing about, say, one's trip to the North Pole by dogsled?" (*MUBAR: Mothered Up Beyond All Recognition*, "The Politics of Blogging" January 29, 2005). A number of bloggers felt angry that our world had been invaded, and that social critics reading us not as a source of comfort, but in order to glean evidence to prove a certain point: "look at the bad mommy typing instead of reading *Guess How Much I Love You* for the 423rd time that afternoon, *see* how ambivalent she is?" I for one, started to feel the need to self-censor.

And social critics were not the only ones reading and taking notes. On May 25, 2005, I wrote a post titled "Tom Cruise is an idiot" (*MUBAR: Mothered Up Beyond All Recognition*, "Tom Cruise is an Idiot," May 26, 2005) at the exact moment that Tom Cruise started offering his opinions on psychiatry and leaping on Oprah's couch. It seemed that a lot of people were typing "Tom Cruise is an idiot" into Google and, low and behold, my post was listed first. Suddenly all sorts of traffic was being driven to my site. My blog was mentioned in the media a couple of times (Gordon 2005). And suddenly—surprisingly—I was on the radar screen of marketers. Would I be interested in sampling a baby blanket worth several hundred dollars? Would I be interested in offering my readers access to "exclusive content" (a.k.a. pictures of television stars using a branded cleaning product at a charity do)? A savvy marketer read about my daughter's favourite TV characters, and then asked if I would like two tickets to their sold-out concert and an invite to an exclusive character meet and greet lunch in the hopes that I might publicize their upcoming tour. I was receiving offers of product daily in the hopes that I might "mention" their merits to my readers.

The interesting thing for me was that even though I passed on the vast majority of offers, the more that marketers viewed my blog as a potential marketing tool, the more I started to view my blog as a potential business. I started to wonder if I should be considering blog ads. I started to track how many people were reading me and started to think about how I could increase my readership. For example, if I were going to be away, I'd pre-write posts so that I did not go for too long without writing. I started to feel pressured to write posts even when I had nothing to say. I noticed that when I referenced a celebrity—P. Diddy or Puffy or whatever he is referring to himself these days in particular—my traffic spiked. A post about JLo's mink eyelashes and Oscar swag generated a groundswell of web traffic. And suddenly blogging seemed much less like a raw journal and much more like, well, work. I started to write more strategically and less from the heart. So I decided to make a few changes. I unplugged my sitemeter. I stopped linking to other blogs. And in September 2006, I wrote about why I did it because, well, that's what bloggers do:

> Content used to read as raw and fresh, no one was trying to sell you something or increase their site traffic. There was collaboration among bloggers, not competition, because, well, there was nothing to compete over. But now, money and fame has entered into the equation and because we bloggers, enemy of the ad-driven mass media, are not supposed to be thinking of this like a business, we hide our underlying intentions. Instead of competing directly for market share, for advertising dollars, for readers, and then sitting down to have a friendly beer at the end of the day, we seem to be doing the frenemy thing and write mean comments and parody blogs and leave throwaway comments designed simply to promote our own urls. It's a trend that threatens the very goodness of the blogosphere: Goodbye Children's Television Workshop; hello Maury Povich. (*MUBAR: Mothered Up Beyond All Recognition*, "Back to (Blog) Basics," September 26, 2006)

The reaction of the local mamasphere surprised me. I thought there would be a conversation about how others felt the same way. How the commercial aspect was distracting them from the writing. I thought that readers might chime in about how blog ads were ruining the aesthetics of their favourite pages. And indeed, I did receive a lot of support. But more interesting were the voices of dissent. Bloggers passionately defended a mother's choice to feature blog ads. To not encourage blog ads, some argued, was to keep the blogosphere in the hands of the elite. To not encourage blog ads was to support the notion that the work of mothers does not deserve remuneration. Most surprisingly, people were denying that marketers had negatively influenced the "mamasphere" in any way.

So I decided to dig a little into marketers' efforts to infiltrate the mamasphere and made a few discoveries.

Blogging Is Big Business

More and more companies are using blogs as a way to reach their target markets. September 2006's *Business 2.0* cover article explains the appeal: "Blogs offer a personal touch in the mediascape; small sites have become our guides to a content-saturated world. As such, their recommendations are highly valued by readers—which naturally has made advertisers take notice" (Sloan and Kaila 2006). Bloggers are being remunerated for putting ads up on their sites. Others blog for ad revenue-driven community blog sites like Café Mom (formerly Club Mom, www.cafemom.com) or ParentDish/Blogging Baby (www.parentdish.com). Success stories abound: Dooce's Heather Armstrong now supports her husband and daughter by blogging full time. Bloggers have received mid-six figure book deals. Weblogs, Inc. (owner of ParentDish/Blogging Baby.com) was sold to AOL for an estimated $25 million netting its founder a tidy profit. There was $40 million in advertising dollars up for grabs in 2006, and an expected $23.6 billion (yes billion) by 2010, in addition to book contracts, speaking fees etc. (Sloan and Kaila 2006).

For the average person, however, blogging does not lead to fame and fortune: 69 percent of bloggers using blog ads make less than $20 per month (Qumana Official Blog "Blog Advertising Earnings: Qumana Survey," October 5, 2005). Marketers often dangle the potential upside in front of bloggers, many of whom are mothers who would love nothing more than to find a job they could do from home in the off hours. So we agree to share our stories about our children for a modest sum—much less than if we sold the piece in other commercial markets. Frankly, we're just happy someone is listening to us.

Marketers Are Actively Targeting the Mamasphere

Oh, and they are. As Maria Bailey, CEO of Blue Suit Moms, a firm that helps marketers tap into the three trillion dollar mom market, posted on her website:

> Marketers are increasingly trying to understand how to engage Mom Bloggers. These influential moms not only have large loyal audiences but give credibility to the brands and products they mention in their blogs. The challenge is to balance commercialism with information sharing. BSM Media has over 400 active relationships with mom bloggers around the globe.... Through online media tours with Mom Bloggers, BSM Media has been

able to generate millions of page views and blog mentions for their clients. *(BSM Media: Specializing in Marketing to Moms,* "Mom Bloggers and Online Media Tours")

They are targeting us because we influence a three trillion dollar market and because we are willing to promote their products very, very cheaply. A number of the community blog sites encourage readers to join up to be eligible for contests or to receive email updates. This information is then sometimes being sold to marketers who mine it to find out how to better dip into your pocketbook. Buyer beware.

Interestingly, only middle class white mothers are being targeted. As blogger Stefania Pomponi Butler commented at BlogHer 2007, her blog City Mama (citymana.typepad.com) is approached by marketers daily whereas her group blog focused on Korean mothers, Kimchi Mamas (kimchimamas.typepad.com), has yet to be approached. In her follow-up blog entry about her experience with marketers, she describes how a marketer revealed that they do not market to bloggers of colour as they "just don't know what to do with them" (*City Mama: Always Cooking Something Up,* "Putting PR people on notice," July 28, 2007). The underlying assumption is that a blogger's talent with words and photos is not as important as the perceived demographic of her readership. White, middle class women are a key consumer group and it is assumed that it is the white, middle class blogger who can influence them.

Corporations Are Actively Fostering Blogging

Billed as "the premier online destination for moms, by moms," Cafe Mom is headed up by CEO Michael Sanchez and Andrew Shue (formerly of *Melrose Place*)—neither of whom, to my knowledge, is a mom. In an interview in the *New York Times,* Sanchez discussed their key advertisers such as Johnson & Johnson and Home Depot, "Moms are their key customers, and they're extremely interested in figuring out an authentic way to fit into social networks and sites with user-generated content" (Tedeschi 2006). Over the past several months, Cafe Mom has actively recruited a number of mom bloggers to help them with this task.

BlogHer, one of the leading networks for women bloggers, whose 2006 conference was partly underwritten by Johnson & Johnson, describes the benefits of its Blogher Ads program to potential advertisers on their site, www.blogher.com: "53 percent of BlogHer Parenting Network readers have their own blogs with which to publish and amplify their recommendations and referrals" (Camahort 2006). Oglivy, Johnson &

Johnson's ad agency, sent a team to the BlogHer conference. As Rohit Bhargava of Oglivy blogged:

> Mom bloggers are an emerging audience that we firmly believe in. We have conducted significant research to understand this audience, and have developed personal relationships with many mom bloggers. Several of my teammates are at BlogHer [conference] right now, sharing their insights and observations about the event. Mom bloggers, as you can imagine, will be big there—and a hot topic for many marketers is going to be finding authentic ways to connect with them. This is a group that will continue to grow in volume, influence and prominence. It won't be long before you see more bloggers joining the "A-list" right beside Dooce." (*Influential Marketing Blog*, "Understanding the Mom Blogger Revolution," July 28, 2006)

Following on this heels of Ogilvy's work, Johnson & Johnson announced the plan to launch a mom blog directory in the fall of 2006: "JOHNSON'S® recognizes that today's moms are connecting in entirely new ways.... The blogosphere, open for conversation day or night, is the modern mom's park bench.... With this mom blogger directory, we are bringing moms together to share and support, converse and communicate—enabling unprecedented conversations to take place" (Johnson & Johnson). While the blogger directory still has yet to go live as of Fall 2007, Johnson & Johnson is acquiring some mom blogs outright (like the popular Maya's Mom[1]) and folding them under its online portal Babycenter.com. And although bloggers say that it will make no difference to their writing, one wonders.

Bloggers Are Responding to Marketing Efforts.

The data shows that mothers with an audience are helping the marketer spread the message. Blue Suit Mom's (www.bluesuitmom.com) Maria Bailey runs The Guerilla Mom Network[2] which for a fee connects marketers with a network of websites owned and operated by mothers. In her report, "Trillion Dollar Moms: Marketing to a New Generation of Mothers," Bailey revealed the success she has had with Mom Mavens, a pilot group of 125 web site/blog founders, 75 authors, 225 mom group leaders and 11 media producers/writers, who collectively influence 20,000 other moms (Bailey). After receiving a product and product information, 47 percent of Mavens recommended the brand in question to 20-30 other mothers, 26 percent mentioned the brand to 50 other mothers. 32 percent posted something on a website, 12 percent blogged about the brand, and 11 percent chatted in a chat room about the brand (Bailey).

Bailey outlined exactly what would entice these Mom Mavens to spread the word and the interesting thing is that direct remuneration is not the key driver. Bloggers are more interested in membership to a group that elevates her rank among peers, a brand she can attach to her resume, simple ways for her to share messages that are impressive to her peers, something that gives here an exclusive nugget of information, and something that empowers her child within his/her circles. In the beginning I was flattered when I'd be invited to join an exclusive ad network, or was given hot off the press information to share with my readers, or when someone took the time to find out what band my kids liked—little did I know it was all part of a broader marketing strategy.

I believe that it is not an entirely bad thing that marketers have infiltrated the mamasphere. Corporate involvement is allowing more and more women to join the conversation as they are setting up portals to publicize our efforts. Supporters of marketers' initiatives argue that corporate involvement is subsidizing the cost of blogging, offering free blog software, subsidizing conferences and allowing women who might not otherwise be able to afford the luxury of blogging to add their voices to the mix. Many bloggers believe commerce and honest conversation can coexist. One such advocate is Dawn Constantini, a blogger and consultant with Lucid Marketing (www.lucidmarketing.com), a firm that helps clients like P&G, Disney, and AOL connect with moms:

> It's ironic that most women bloggers create blogs for personal reasons rather than building a business endeavor, because they are a highly coveted group by marketers. In this age, women, (moms in particular) could create a strong platform that would attract more women to their conversations. Given the proper tools, they could offer marketers the chance to join the conversations as well. My hat will go off to the woman who can take these genuine discussions and successfully build a business from it! (*Lucid Marketing to Moms*, "Women Bloggers," August 11, 2006)

A year after doing my initial research, I contemplated Constantini's challenge to bloggers to monetize their blogs without compromise. Certainly, I think that people are talking about the issue a lot more: certainly it was a hot topic at the Mom Bloggers panel at 2007's BlogHer conference. Many mom bloggers have fully embraced the marketers and are blogging for sites such as Parent Dish and including ads on their websites. Some are taking on paid work as blogging consultants, helping marketers reach their target groups. Others turned away from marketing. They unplugged, ignored their statistics, and took down their blogrolls. Some password protected their blogs just as one might put a lock on a diary, giving access only to faithful readers and friends. Some quit blogging altogether.

A lot of bloggers out there, including me, continue to straddle both camps. Many of us are interested in finding ways of monetizing our blogs without compromising our ethics or losing our credibility. Certainly, I have been open to monetizing my blog. I have done book reviews for a book publicity firm whereby I am paid an honorarium ($20 in gift certificates is the norm) and given a copy of the book. I also accepted free theatre tickets and blogged a mini review of the show. I also use my blog to showcase my other writing, and to help me land paid writing gigs. I am open with my readers and disclose whenever I receive free product. And I give my honest opinion—good, bad or ugly. And yet even my minor brush with marketers changed the way I write.

As an example, even though I will only review books that interest me, I might read a book I might not otherwise have come across. Certainly I read the books more quickly than I might otherwise as my normal tendency is to have several books on the go at the same time, reading certain pieces more intensely depending on my mood. And if I have committed to writing a review on a certain date, I write my review on that date. I have written as part of blog blasts wherein bloggers are invited to post about a set topic to create buzz for a particular product. My personal blog entries are much more subject to mood. I also tend to proofread my entries and play a little less fast and loose with conventional spellings. I also write a little more cautiously, knowing that my readers are not the same small group of like-minded souls who found my blog by googling "postpartum depression" or "gross motor delay in toddlers" or "choroid plexus cysts in utero." I write knowing that a marketer, a talk show producer, or a social critic might be taking notes. So while I am not doing anything wrong or misleading, I am not writing as authentically as I might without the influence of marketers.

I also think that the influence of marketers has changed the way we read blogs. When I started blogging, I'd be thrilled if I received the occasional comment or email. The comments were always thoughtful and I always responded personally and often reciprocated by reading and leaving a comment on their blogs. Over time, I started to notice people leaving short and less-than-sincere comments on my blog simply to advertise their own blog's url. Some smart cookie had figured out that the way to build search engine visibility and blog traffic—traffic that could be monetized—was to link to as many other blogs as possible. The comments field, once a place of conversation, had become a subtle method of advertising.

All of these things started to depersonalize the blogosphere. For me, a blog used to be like someone's home. Reading someone's blog was like being invited into someone's home for a cup of tea and a chat. I found that people were very respectful of each other's spaces. You would no more advertise something in their comments field or promote your own agenda, than you would stick a bumper sticker on their sofa. But monetizing one's blog was not unlike sticking a For Sale sign up on your front lawn. Suddenly there was a lot more traffic going through your house, but not everyone was a welcomed guest. Some people were there simply to make snide comments about the ugly decor. To me, it is not a coincidence that as marketing influences grew, so too did snark blogs like the now defunct Trainwrecks.com, which used mom bloggers' words and pictures against them in extreme acts of mother judgment—the very mother judgment that drew so many of us to blog in the first place.

I'm sure that there are people who can combine the commerce of blogging with the art, who can be savvy and marketing focused on the one hand and then incredibly raw and honest on the other. But I think it's tough. I am not saying that as moms, as women, we ought to separate ourselves from that filthy lucre and donate our services as has been expected of us historically on so many other fronts. But instead, we need to think about how this approach is watering down a very important medium. We have the chance to reach other mothers. We have a chance to break down the isolation that is mothering in North America. We have a chance to talk honestly about the lack of licensed daycare, the lack of services for at risk mothers, the lack of fairness in the workplace and on the domestic front.

I do believe that there is a way to have honest conversations about mothering in a world that is increasingly becoming saturated with marketing messages, but we won't find that balance if we deny that the potential for conflict exists. I think that as guardians of the blogosphere we have an obligation to preserve its goodness through awareness and self-reflection and discussion. We need to address how marketers are trying to play us and make a conscious decision to accept or reject their advances. And if we do blog or foster online community for money or other perks, we need to do so openly and unapologetically And if what drew us to the blogosphere in the first place was the presence of so many diverse voices—voices ignored by the mainstream media—we need to find ways to ensure that these voices are not silenced by the presence of marketers who seek to increase the profile of only those bloggers who reach their desired consumer demographic. Part of that process involves the often uncomfortable realization that it might not be our scintillating prose that has drawn their interest so much as the perceived colour of our skin, sexual orientation and tax bracket.

I think that blogging can be an incredibly powerful tool when it comes to building community, even if there are blog ads running down the side-bar. It can be a way to further the mothering conversation when we are just too tired at night to sit in one another's living rooms and jam. But I don't want blogging to become just another guerilla marketing technique. I don't want to be invited to a friend's home, only to discover that I was *really* invited to a Tupperware party.

In the end, the decision to embrace or reject the marketers may not be ours to make. As the blogosphere becomes diluted by the marketing messages, so to does its power. As marketer's efforts become more apparent, the medium becomes a less trusted source of information. And as bloggers become less like the mom next door, their opinions carry less weight. The marketers are no longer as anxious to woo us. Johnson & Johnson has yet to launch a web portal for mom bloggers. On the heels of poor sales on books by bloggers, publishers are no longer tossing six figure deals our way. For me, a leading indicator was the BlogHer 2007 conference, which I attended. While the previous year's conference had a strong focus on mom bloggers, at this conference, the mom marketers simply were not there. Only one company offered swag specifically for moms (onesies advertising their online scrapbooking site). Johnson & Johnson had no visible presence and the one session on The State of the Mamasphere was sponsored by 5 Moms, a not for profit organization whose ad spend budget would have been significantly less than J&J's. Marketers seem to want to pay in coupons instead of in cash and remuneration has, if anything, decreased. Instead of paying bloggers, now it is common for marketers to offer moms a chance to win a prize. One such recent example was to a book publicity stunt inviting bloggers to post about "the one item in your closet you are most ashamed of" in exchange for a chance to win a $250 handbag. It seems that marketers are interested in the mom bloggers only if they are willing to work cheap.

I do not think that all is lost in the mamasphere. At BlogHer I was thrilled to see activist mom bloggers Cooper Monroe and Emily McKhann launch BlogHers Act,[3] whereby bloggers will use our collective voices to push for social change. If we can harness all of the interest in the mamasphere and direct it towards improving the world for ourselves and our children, blogging will become a truly radical act.

[1] See here: <http://splash.babycenter.com/maintenance/sp-mym/> for the redirect of Maya's Mom to BabyCenter.

[2] See here: <http://www.bsmmedia.com/services/onlinemarketing.php>.

[3] See here for the "Bloghers Act," <http://www.blogher.com/introducing-new-blogher-community-initiative-bloghers-act>.

Works Cited

Bailey, Maria. "Trillion Dollar Moms: Marketing to a New Generation of Mothers." BSM Media presentation to International Dairy Foods Association, Smart Marketing 2006 Conference, Westin Casuarina Hotel and Spa, Las Vegas, NV, March 15-16, 2006. Retrieved May 20, 2007. <http://www.idfa.org/meetings/presentations/smartmkt2006_bailey.ppt>.

BlogHer. "Introducing a new BlogHer Community Initiative: BlogHers Act." Retrieved May 30, 2007. <http://www.blogher.com/introducing-new-blogher-community-initiative-bloghers-act>.

BlueSuitMom.com. Retrieved May 20, 2007. <http://www.bluesuitmom.com>.

BSM Media: Specializing in Marketing to Moms. Retrieved July 4, 2008. <http://www.bsmmedia.com/services/bloggers.php>.

Cafe Mom. Retrieved May 20, 2007. <http://www.cafemom.com/>.

Camahort, Elisa. "BlogHer blog readers: Loyal, vocal, highly educated... and shopping online." Blogherads. September 11, 2006. Retrieved on May 20, 2007. <http://www.blogherads.com/blogher-blog-readers-loyal-vocal-highly-educated-and-shopping-online>.

City Mama: Always Cooking Something Up. Retrieved May 30, 2007. <http://citymama.typepad.com/citymama/>.

Gordon, Andrea. "Moms find safety Net." Toronto Star, Dec 17, 2005: L.01. Online: <http://www.tomama.com/star.htm>.

Hochman, David. "Mommy (and Me)." New York Times, 30 January 2005. Retrieved from <http://www.nytimes.com/2005/01/30/fashion/30moms.html>.

Influential Marketing Blog. Retrieved May 20, 2007. <http://rohitbhargava.typepad.com/>.

Johnson & Johnson. "Johnson's Baby Unveils Plans to Launch a Mom Blog

Directory a Whole New Way for Moms to Connect and Communicate in the Blogosphere." *PR Newswire*, July 28, 2006. Retrieved May 20, 2007. <http://www.prnewswire.com/cgi-bin/stories.pl?ACCT=104&STORY=/www/story/07-28-2006/0004405683&EDATE>. *Kimchi Mamas: Burn Your Tongue.* <http://kimchimamas.typepad.com/>.Retrieved May 30, 2007.

Lucid Marketing to Moms. Retrieved May 20, 2007. <http://marketing-tomoms.blogspot.com/>.

MUBAR: Mothered Up Beyond All Recognition. Retrieved May 30, 2007. <http://tomama.blogs.com/mubar/>.

ParentDish. Retrieved May 20, 2007. <http://www.parentdish.com>.

Qumana Official Blog. Retrieved May 30, 2007. <http://blog.qumana.com/blog/_archives/2005/10/5/1282559.html>.

Sloan, Paul and Paul Kaila, "Blogging for dollars." *Business 2.0 Magazine.* Oct. 2, 2006. Online: <http://money.cnn.com/magazines/business2/business2_archive/2006/09/01/8384325/index.htm>.

Tedeschi, Bob. "M" Is for the Many Ways Marketers Court Her." *The New York Times*, May 8, 2006. Retrieved May 30, 2007. <http://www.nytimes.com/2006/05/08/technology/08ecom.html?ei=5088&en=4093d637477dd527&ex=1304740800&adxnnl=1&partner=rssnyt&emc=rss&adxnnlx=1162866719-fVzRVM4dVlTur2AB2RZAnw>.

Chapter Nine

LesbianFamily.org

Expanding the Understanding of Motherhood and Visibility of Lesbians, or, "Um. If You Don't Mind My Asking ... How Does a Lesbian Get Pregnant?"

LIZA BARRY-KESSLER

Within hours of finding out that I was pregnant, I scoured Technorati and Google for blogs written by pregnant lesbians. Surely I was not alone on the Internet! I had friends in real life who were pregnant, and some who even had children. No matter how obscure your interest, you can find your people online, right? Not as easily as I had imagined.

Searching for "pregnant" and "lesbian" is not for the faint of heart. My confidence that a community can be found on any topic may only be true online for interests of a prurient nature, but that confidence has been shaken as far as less lucrative interests are concerned. And those allegedly pregnant alleged lesbians were not what I was hoping to find. Certainly there were no lesbian bloggers on the major mommy or parenting websites.[1] Even the diverse and inclusive site for women bloggers, *BlogHer*, didn't produce many results back in 2005.

The first few blogs I was able to identify as being written by lesbian bloggers who were pregnant or trying to conceive (*Addition Problems*, and *Hydrangeas Are Pretty*) I found through comments and blogrolls on infertility blogs written by heterosexual women. *Addition Problems* is written jointly by both partners in a lesbian couple. At the time I found them, they were trying to get pregnant against medical advice, a few months after surviving an agonizingly complex partial molar pregnancy and miscarriage. *Hydrangeas Are Pretty* is written, as are the majority of lesbian parenting, pregnancy, and trying to conceive blogs, by one member of a couple. When I first began to read her blog, she had been trying to get pregnant for more than a year, and was beginning the open adoption process. Through their blogrolls, I found a few more, including *An Accident of Hope*. This blog is also written by one member of a couple; at that time, her partner was pregnant. I also found and regularly read innumerable blogs by heterosexual mothers and women hoping to become mothers—single, married, and partnered; stay at home moms, waitresses, graduate students, and professionals; Orthodox Jews, Mormons, Christians, and non-religious bloggers. Gradually my bookmark list became crowded and confusing, full of pregnant and trying to conceive women from all walks of life—including a few on paths similar to mine.

Occasionally and frustratedly, I thought, "There has to be an easier way to find these blogs!" I'm no expert on search engine optimization, but I know these algorithms are failing the lesbian family blogosphere. I suspect that abuse of "lesbian" as a keyword in the metatags of far too many pornographic web sites is to blame. I couldn't imagine any way to solve the problem.

I also found *Babes in Blogland*, a work of love that made it easy for me to find other bloggers with due dates near my own. Shana, the blogger behind *Babes in Blogland*, made it her mission to list every blog about being pregnant on the Internet, sorted by due date. Much like how I became driven to find blogs by other pregnant lesbians, when Shana discovered that she was pregnant with her youngest child, she also found herself urgently wanting to connect with women who were due near the same time. Very quickly, she expanded to include parenting blogs (obviously), blogs by people trying to conceive, and those trying to adopt (unfortunately, Shana had to take down this blog, as she no longer had the time to update it).

"There should be something like this for lesbian mommyblogs!" I thought.

Months passed. During the first few of them, like many pregnant women, I mostly spent my free time sleeping. When I could muster the energy to sit at the computer, I commented on other lesbian blogs, and on the blogs of women with due dates near mine, and on the occasional other blogs whose writing caught my attention while I was frantically attempting to determine whether it was in either of the first two categories.

During all of this, Shana and I struck up a friendship, eventually leading to a long discussion about the value and ethics of sorting mommybloggers by sexual orientation. We even discussed whether making it easier to find lesbian family blogs might be dangerous or lead to an increase in harassment of those bloggers. On a lighter note, we also giggled imagining a hypothetical conservative Christian and homophobic mommyblogger recoiling in horror as she discovered, through *Babes in Blogland*, that she shared a due date with a lesbian.

Ultimately, we both reached the conclusion that the value to the community of lesbian families was greater than the risk or the discomfort we felt with this kind of blog "segregation." That's when I registered the domain LesbianFamily.org, and when Shana added—among other expansion categories—a list of LGBT families to *Babes in Blogland*. Shana designed both the site and the logo for me, because she believed in the vision (and because she saw what my pitiable technical skills were able to produce.)

My top priority was to create a long and useful blogroll. It was also very important to me for this site to be as inclusive as possible, without losing focus as a resource for the lesbian community. My primary goal was to include the blogs of as many self-defined lesbian parents, pregnant lesbians, partners of pregnant lesbians, lesbians who were trying to become pregnant ("trying to conceive" or "TTC" in the language of the blogosphere), partners of lesbians trying to conceive, lesbians who have or are attempting to adopt, and lesbians who are parenting in the foster care system. But I wanted the site to include listings for any blog that asked, and I knew that there would be supportive heterosexual friends and allies who would want to be visible as such, and that there would be resources that lesbian families would want to share, so I also created categories for those blogs. While I didn't create categories for bisexual or polyamorous parenting blogs, had I encountered any in my original search, I would have considered it.

I knew, both from my own experience and from reading the few blogs I'd found by lesbian families, that in spite of many common interests and concerns of lesbian parents, some of these experiences raised unique and emotionally charged issues. In particular, those lesbians whose partners were pregnant or who had been pregnant, face the difficulty of often having their very motherhood challenged—casually by strangers ("which of you is the real mother?"), viciously by family members ("that woman's child is not my grandson!"), and even by their own self-doubt, particularly in those early and exhausting months of parenting a newborn. I also imagined that issues of race, nationality, and gender identity might be as important for some potential readers as finding lesbians who were currently pregnant had been for me, and wanted to make blogs by parents of color, interracial families, parents outside of the U.S., and parents who had undergone gender transition, easily visible within the site.

Having first created numerous categories, I then scoured the Internet[2] looking for blogs to put in them, some unsuccessfully. Generally, I only included blogs that included a clear self-reference to the author being lesbian, queer, or the blog being about two women trying to have a child together.[3] Some results were not surprising—the largest category was *Trying to Conceive*. I never found a *parenting* blog by someone who was out as a transperson, either male to female or female to male.[4] Many blogs are listed in more than one category, such as *Babies* and *Non-Bio*, or *Interracial Families* and *Adoption*. I was surprised to find that nearly all of the parenting blogs by lesbians of color were in interracial relationships. I don't think I ever found more than one blog by a lesbian of color in a family where both parents were African-American or both were Asian-American, for example. That is why the only category with a clear reference to race is *Interracial Families*, which also includes blogs by white lesbian parents who have children of another race.

In *LesbianFamily.org*'s core categories there are well over 300 blogs! While some are listed in multiple categories, there are certainly at least 250 blogs in total. It could never be a representative depiction of the lesbian parenting world, particularly given the class issues involved with Internet access, technical knowledge, and the leisure time to write. It skews white, well-educated, and urban, particularly within the United States and Canada—and although I haven't attempted a statistical analysis, my impression is that it is more white than the blogosphere as a whole. According to the Pew Internet & American Life Project:

> Another distinguishing characteristic is that bloggers are less likely to be white than the general Internet population. Sixty percent of bloggers are white, 11 percent are African American, 19 percent are English-speaking Hispanic and 10 percent identify as some other race. By contrast, 74 percent of Internet users are white, 9 percent are African American, 11 percent are English-speaking Hispanic and 6 percent identify as some other race. (Lenhart and Fox)

The Pew study did not analyze bloggers by sexual orientation, much less sexual orientation broken down by race, so there is no way to know whether the lesbian mothers who blog are in fact less diverse than people who blog as a whole, or whether *LesbianFamily.org* has failed to find them. In spite of being somewhat less diverse than the blogosphere at large, most *LesbianFamily.org* readers will be able to find someone with a story to which they can relate.

Through the "Related Categories" lists, I attempted to include other voices and resources that I felt would be helpful and supportive of lesbian families. While the "KidSpeak" category, for children of lesbian families, is small today, I expect it to grow from year to year as the many babies and little kids listed grow into tweens and teens who blog themselves.

I also wanted to include a category where we could acknowledge the many wonderful allies and "Friends of the Family" in the blogosphere. This began as a place for those blogs in my personal blogroll that were not lesbian family blogs, then expanded to include anyone who asked to be listed or who posted something that I felt screamed to be explicitly recognized as a "Friend of the Family." This is probably the broadest category within the site, including, for example, political blogs, heterosexual mommyblogs and daddyblogs, and blogs where one parent is trans, so that the family appears to be a traditional heterosexual family, but obviously has a more complex relationship to gender and sexual orientation than appearance might suggest. Some blogs were listed by *LesbianFamily* authors on their own initiative, while others were listed by requests from others.

The other way that I tried to make sure diverse voices were included in the blog at launch was through the "Resources" category. It includes links to sites like *Sayoni*, a lesbian blog portal & forum for queer Asian women from all over the world, and the *2 Spirit Press Room*, a GLBT Native media & cultural literacy project. Although neither of these sites explicitly addresses lesbians as parents, they represent important constituencies within the lesbian community which are under-represented in the blogosphere. While there may not be many Asian lesbian mothers blogging, an Asian woman considering parenthood, or considering coming out, will at least gain some assurance that she is not entirely alone. In my opinion, that is the most valuable service that the Internet can provide.

Within the first few months of the launch, it became obvious that *LesbianFamily.org* would never be able to be the valuable resource I imagined it if I continued to try to do everything myself. I am not a professional web designer, and the combination of a demanding day job and a demanding baby crowded out the demands of the blog.

In December 2006, I expanded *LesbianFamily.org* into a team effort. I recruited a few of my favorite bloggers, who I thought might do it, and asked them to join me. My original invitations were extended to the authors of *An Accident of Hope*; *Butch Baby Makin'* (who had closed her personal blog out of the same post-partum reprioritization), *Lesbian Dad* (lesbiandad.net/) and *Artificially Sweetened* (artsweet.wordpress.com). The authors of *Accident* and *Lesbian Dad* were both non-bio mothers, although the mom from *An Accident of Hope* planned to begin trying to conceive.

Mostly by luck, but partially on purpose, this shift resulted in a crew with diverse families and experiences: Bio and "Non-Bio" parents, interracial and white families, adopting and gestating families; but it was not sufficiently representative of the bloggers using the site. I totally got called out on it, which was tough but so valuable as the criticism was spot on. The site readers wanted the site to reflect their families, wherever they are in their family experience. So I added more team members, including *Round is Funny* and *Cheese and Whine*, giving us two very different experiences of adoption, international closed and domestic open, both transracial, and a family that was still trying to conceive.

For awhile, we had a very lively crew updating the site, generating discussions on everything from hypocrisy in politics, how GLBT families create and redefine extended families, the power and privilege available to certain elite GLBT families, race and attempting to teach and model anti-oppression behavior for our children, the concerns lesbian mothers have about raising boy children, news coverage of lesbian mothers, and ways that biological mothers can help counter social habits that diminish the full recognition of their partners as equally real mothers, among many others.[5]

Later that year, *Clare Says* joined the team with a commitment to finding and adding Spanish language blogs by lesbian parents, and *Some Random Chic* came on board as a pregnant academic expert in child development.

During 2007, the site thrived. It was a finalist for the 2007 Bloggies, in the "Best GLBT Weblog" category (it lost to *Perez Hilton*). It receives more than five thousand unique visitors per month, with visitors returning an average of just under three times per month, and joined the *BlogHer* Ad Network. Visitors posted comments such as:

> I totally love your site, I am so glad there is something out there where all the blogs of Lesbian Families are listed together. (*Lesbianfamily.org: Find blogs from all kinds of lesbian families*, "Another Reason I started this," September 7, 2006)

> This has been very inspiring for us. Thanks for posting so many blogs. It is great to see that we aren't alone in our journey even though we should know better it often feels like we are. (*Lesbianfamily.org: Find blogs from all kinds of lesbian families*, "Trying")

> This is such a great resource. Thank you for establishing this list and thanks to all the contributors out there! What a great way to find community. (*Lesbianfamily.org: Find blogs from all kinds of lesbian families*, "Trying")

Lesbianfamily.org has been such a valuable resource for my partner and I on our TTC journey. We are now 7 months pregnant, and I think I'm ready to make my blog public, especially in appreciation for all the blogs that have helped me along so far. (*Lesbianfamily.org: Find blogs from all kinds of lesbian families*, "Expecting")

As of this writing, the site is languishing again. People continue to visit in large numbers, many from predictable Internet searches like "lesbian family" but new posts are only added occasionally. The blogroll is updated, but also erratically. Perhaps the site's value is as a blogroll, and there isn't a need to add commentary. Although the choice to join a blog advertising network has not yet generated the kind of income that could pay for a single cycle of medicated IUI with sperm from an unknown donor, it has earned enough in one quarter to cover the cost of hosting for the year. Perhaps adding a small economic incentive for the authors would make a difference. I don't know the answer, but I do know that the Internet and the blogosphere, particularly the mamasphere, continue to need sites like *LesbianFamily.org* and the hundreds of blogs on our blogroll.

The world of "mommyblogs" needs *LesbianFamily.org*: all of the isolation new mothers face, the overwhelming roller-coaster of early and first-time parenthood, and the sense of connectivity and support that mothers have found through blogging are exacerbated for many lesbian mothers.

While some of us are fortunate enough to live in communities with other lesbian families, have civil rights protections, and are confident that our children will not face discrimination or hatefulness in day care and elementary school, many more of us are not. Finding other bloggers whose families are similar, who face the struggles we face, can help us feel less alone and develop strategies for coping with homophobic discrimination. They can also help us figure out how to talk about issues we face far more frequently than heterosexual parents—paternity through sperm donation, for example, and how anonymous donors, ID release donors, and known donors play roles in our families that are often very distinct from "fathers."

The world of "mommyblogs" also needs *LesbianFamily.org* and the myriad blogs listed in our blogrolls because of our role as the public voices of lesbian parents. I believe that being out in public helps change the perception of lesbians, and helps so-called "ordinary people" understand why same sex marriage and same sex adoptions are so important to us.

While nothing can replace direct relationships as a way to move people from neutral-to-vaguely-homophobic to being active and understanding allies, blogs can make a difference. When all of us are struggling with sleep deprivation, returning to work, or getting partners to share parenting and household responsibilities, it is easier to see the commonalities we share as mothers and human beings—and harder to make lesbian families so "Other."

I hope that my co-contributors and I can find ways to re-energize the *LesbianFamily.org* site, but even if it continues to limp along, I will keep it up as a resource. The lesbian community deserves ways to make connections between families, and the Internet is one of the easiest ways to do that, however imperfectly.

But wait! I never answered the title question in this essay: How does a lesbian get pregnant? For that answer, you'll have to check the blogroll. You may be surprised by how many different answers there are. I'd start with the "Expecting" section, and also browse the "Trying to Conceive" section. If you're a blogger who would like to be listed as a "Friend of the Family" or in any of the other categories, leave a comment on the blog.

[1]Parents.com had Harlyn Aizley's "Are you my mothers?" for approximately six months during 2007, but did not renew her blogging contract. *ClubMom* (now *CafeMom*) had Denise's "FastTimes at Homeschool High," which was then moved and abandoned after *ClubMom* removed its mom bloggers. See here: <http://gimleteye.clubmom.com/the_gimlet_eye/2007/11/if-i-hadnt-alre.html> and here <http://blogs.clubmom.com/daily_dose/2007/11/fare-thee-well.htm/> for more commentary on the switch.

[2]The bulk of the research took place between August-November, 2006. There is a clear opportunity to update the blogroll, especially in underrepresented areas.

[3]This methodology is far from perfect. However, only one originally listed blog, *Unwellness*, <http://www.unwellness.com/unwellness>, indicated that the author did not consider hers to be a lesbian family, and requested that the blog be moved from the category "Trying to Conceive" to "Friend of the Family."

[4]Many readers in the infertility blogosphere are regular readers of the mommyblog *Unwellness*, a blog whose author is partnered with an out transman (female-to-male). While he also blogs, he has not blogged about parenting.

[5]To see these and other discussions, see lesbianfamily.org.

Works Cited

2SPR—Two Spirit Press Room. Retrieved November 8, 2007. <http://home.earthlink.net/~lafor002>.

Addition Problems. Retrieved November 8, 2007. <http://additionproblems.wordpress.com>.

An Accident of Hope. Retrieved November 8, 2007. <http://anaccidentofhope.com/>.

Artificially Sweetened: Because I like the Bitter Aftertaste. Retrieved November 8, 2007. <http://artsweet.wordpress.com/>.

Blogher. Retrieved November 8, 2007. <http://www.blogher.com/>.

CaféMom. Retrieved November 8, 2007. <http://www.cafemom.com/>.

Cheese and Whine: Deconstructing the Minutiae. Retrieved November 8, 2007. <http://littlestpea.com>.

Clare Says: Musings from Inside, Outside and Underneath. Retrieved November 8, 2007. <http://claresays.wordpress.com/>.

Hydrangeas Are Pretty. Retrieved November 8, 2007. <http://hydrangeasarepretty.wordpress.com/>.

Lenhart, Amanda and Susannah Fox. 2006. "Bloggers: A portrait of the internet's new storytellers." PEW/Internet and American Life Project. Retrieved November 8, 2007. <http://www.pewinternet.org/pdfs/PIP percent20Bloggers percent20Report percent20July percent2019 percent202006.pdf>.

Lesbian Dad: Notes from the Crossroads of Mother and Father. Retrieved November 8, 2007. <http://www.lesbiandad.net>.

Lesbianfamily.org: Find blogs from all kinds of lesbian families. Retrieved November 8, 2007. <http://lesbianfamily.org/>.

Mom's Daily Dose. Retrieved November 8, 2007. <http://blogs.clubmom.com/daily_dose>.

Parents.com: The Online Home of American Baby, Parents and Family Circle. Retrieved November 8, 2007. http://www.parents.com/

Perez Hilton: Celebrity Juice, Not from Concentrate. Retrieved November 8, 2007. <http://www.perezhilton.com/>.

Probably Boring Ramblings: Radical. Queer. Infertile. Research. Psychologist. Retrieved November 8, 2007. <http://somerandomchic.livejournal.com/>.

Round is Funny: Adventures in queer transracial adoptive parenting and other mundane things. Retrieved November 8, 2007. <http://roundisfunny1.wordpress.com>.

Sanyoni: A Platform Based in Singapore to Empower Lesbian, Bisexual,

Transgender and Queer Asian Women. Retrieved November 8, 2007. <http://sayoni.com>.

The Gimlet Eye. Retrieved November 8, 2007. <http://gimleteye.club-mom.com>.

Unwellness. Retrieved November 8, 2007. <http://www.unwellness.com/unwellness>.

Chapter Ten

Beyond Cute

A Mom, a Blog, and a Question of Content

MELISSA CAMARA WILKINS

I'm sitting at my desk, sipping hot tea and checking my email, when my seven-year-old peeks over my shoulder to see what I'm working on. My younger kids are napping, so I'm trying to grab a few minutes of screen time; besides the mail program, I've got a couple of news pages and my blog dashboard open in my Internet browser.

"Will you put a picture of me on your blog today?" my daughter asks, twirling on tiptoe behind me, first to my left, then to my right.

I smile and blow on my tea. "No, not today."

She shrugs. "Okay." My answer isn't unexpected. I rarely post pictures of my kids. On their birthdays, maybe, or on the occasional holiday, but today isn't either of those. I offer instead to email her grandparents some photos of her and her siblings, which she decides is an exciting alternative. She helps choose a couple of recent shots before wandering down the hallway in search of a book to read while I'm typing. Instead of turning my attention back to the screen, though, I lean back heavily in my chair. Now that we've determined that I'm not posting pictures, what am I going to write about today?

My blog is a small one, by which I mean that it's infrequently trafficked. To date I have a few dozen subscribers, a few hundred page-views a week—more if I manage to post every day, which I often don't. My sidebar includes links to literary magazines, political organizations, and communities for parents. And the posts? Well, they're mostly about me, and about mothering. It's *that* kind of a blog. This week's posts discussed my inability to carry on a proper email conversation, my mistaking dirty laundry for clean, and my (ahem, *failed*) attempts to model appropriate problem-solving behaviours for my kids. But my posts haven't always been quite this mother-centric. When my blog was still fresh-faced and new, a friend suggested that I send the URL to a variety of far-flung friends and relations, since the blog was all about my kids—and distant relatives love my kids. *What? No!* I thought. Clearly my friend didn't appreciate the difference between a blog about kids and a blog about mothering! I was confident in my self-righteous annoyance ... for about five minutes, until I looked back through my archives and realized that my children did, in fact, make more than the occasional appearance in my content. There was a post about Abigail, then five, insisting that she would "die of death" if I made her stay in her car seat; a post about Owen, then two, explaining that he was "not a fan of stripey shirts"; posts about baby Audrey learning to grab toys and crawl and break Mommy's reading glasses. Sometimes I would offer commentary on the childhood antics of the day, but often enough I didn't even do that. *What was I writing,* I wondered, *and for whom?* Was my personal mothering blog a private memento, or did it have value in the public sphere?

In examining the blog I write alongside the blogs I read, I began to suspect that mothering blogs—in addition to providing a momentary escape from the stress of having toddlers underfoot—serve their readers in several ways. Bloggers willing to write with transparency about motherhood provide a place of community for readers; within that community, blogs are often consciousness-raising; and, when taken as a group, these blogs change our understanding of normative motherhood. The personal motherhood blog is political.

If I was writing for an audience of just my family and friends, a blog about my kids would be fine. It would be better than fine, really—it would keep everyone abreast of all the latest milestones and achievements in the kids' lives with a minimum of effort on my part. But really, if someone wants to know how tall my kids are, they can call and check. (And they do; just ask my mother.) Plenty of "mommyblogs" do keep track of just this type of statistic, with photos and first words and weight checks all duly recorded—but that was never my intention for my blog.

I blog primarily for my own benefit, of course. Every day—or however often I please—I have a chance to sift through the activities and emotions of the day to create my own story and meaning. I understand that normal people write such things in private journals. I never claimed to be normal. Perhaps other people harbour less suspicion that the world wants to read about their daily travails, or perhaps they're more private. Perhaps they don't need validation in the form of reader comments. Or perhaps they keep anonymous blogs. I really couldn't say. Personally, I find the writing of my own stories to be cathartic, and made more so by connecting with readers. And if my readers' comments—as well as my own experience as a blog reader—are any indication, blogging can be therapeutic in both the uploading and the downloading.

I started blogging to join the conversation mothers were already having online—women were voicing their opinions and sharing their experiences on various blogs, as well as in essays and poetry on such sites as *The Mothers Movement Online, Literary Mama, Hip Mama,* and *Mamazine,* and I wanted to be a part of that community of reading, writing, and thinking mothers. Of course, the very fact of community begs the question of inclusion: of whom is this online community comprised? Perhaps not surprisingly, the accessible voices overwhelmingly belong to white, middle-class, heterosexual women, a demographic of which I am a member. An exploration of the reasons for and the results of the homogeneity of this virtual mothers' group would constitute an essay in and of itself, and it deserves treatment by an author with more authority to speak to the topic than I have. For our purposes here, I would submit that joining a community that already identifies with you or your positions is easier than trying to educate its members about alternative points of view; that joining a homogenous group may not appeal to members of other demographics, especially when there is a perception that the duty to bridge any experience gap falls primarily upon new members; and that communities and coalitions formed online are therefore likely to lack representatives of certain groups of mothers.

My own entry to the online mothers' community was fairly straightforward. I started a blog on a free hosting platform; I submitted essays to various websites; I left comments on blogs I already read, and slowly developed a small audience and social network. It is impossible to know who exactly that audience comprises, as many of its members choose to remain anonymous, but those who do identify themselves tend to fall within the same general demographic as myself.

But even in light of the similar backgrounds of the women authoring "mainstream" mothers' blogs and literature, there is value in this online representation of motherhood. Blogs in particular are able to present a more complete and nuanced account of motherhood—or at the very least, of white, middle-class, heterosexual motherhood—than is available elsewhere. The ongoing nature of the blog allows for change and growth and complexity not easily achieved in other media.

Complex and varied accounts of birth have long been popular and available—Ina May Gaskin's classic *Spiritual Midwifery,* for example, was first published in 1975 and remains in print decades later. The narrative of what happens after the cord is cut has not been as readily accessible in recent generations, but parenting blogs are beginning to fill this void. In addition to chronicling pregnancy and birth (whether medicalized or au naturel), blogs preserve the gamut of parenting experiences. Anytime I feel isolated as a suburban mother, or inadequate as a parent—I'm not Martha Stewart or Rachel Ray or even the nice lady on Sesame Street who patiently teaches kids to count to twenty, after all—I know I can turn to other bloggers for much-needed comfort and camaraderie. Reading reminds me that I'm not alone, that others are walking the same path—a point that my own readers frequently comment on as well.

Within the community of blogging mothers, the posts aren't always anecdotal and reflective. Sometimes, in fact, the content is explicitly political. I might direct my readers to current articles at the Mothers Movement Online, for example, or suggest a cause worthy of their philanthropy. My own daily blog reading might bring me up to speed on the FDA's current rulings on cloned animal foods, or provide me with a link to *MOMocrats*, where I can keep abreast of current electoral politics. Even aside from forwarding specific political agendas and calls to action, though, the public recording of a personal life can be consciousness-raising by providing a window into unfamiliar situations. If you want to know what it's like to be a married twenty-something at home with four small children, stop by my blog any time. Other blogs I frequent help me to understand how my experience overlaps with that of mothers parenting under different circumstances: my daily blog reading might bring me to an account of parenting a child with Down Syndrome (for example, Jennifer Graf Groneberg's *Pinwheels*), parenting in the foster care system (*My Life in a Foster Care Space Warp*), or parenting via transracial adoption (Dawn Friedman's *This Woman's Work*). Though perhaps not as prolific, more-diverse communities do exist in the realm of parenting blogs; *Anti-Racist Parent*, for example, provides parenting resources along with a platform for diverse viewpoints and a welcoming community of parents of varying backgrounds.

Bloggers are, as a general rule, real people, unlike the hypothetical, idealized parents found in modern how-to manuals, or the one-dimensional mother stereotypes provided by mass media and marketers. My readers can see, for example, that while I embrace an attachment parenting philosophy, I certainly make no attempt to live by any parenting rule book. While vanity may be among my faults, I'm certainly not a yummy mummy. I didn't really opt-out. I'm not a mommy warrior, and I don't think I've ever met one; most women I know combine family and paid work or other intellectual endeavours in creative ways, and don't have energy to spend worrying over the semantics of stay-at-home versus go-to-work mothering (Belkin). Are we hyperscheduled parents, or earth mamas, or soccer moms, or security moms? Yes, sometimes, but those sound-bite descriptions lack the nuance that an individual record of mothering provides. When my experience is placed alongside that of dozens or hundreds or thousands of other blogging mothers, each of whom has her own way of loving, disciplining, and interacting with her children, it becomes clear that motherhood is not as neatly packaged as parenting experts would lead us to believe. Our collected voices—both more representative and more realistic than those seen in most parenting manuals, in commercial advertisements, on daytime television or the nightly news—thus serve to subvert cultural norms of motherhood.

The personal mothering blog, then, is not so much a private record as it is a public statement. The promise and the potential of the medium—the possibility for community, the confronting of popular stereotypes of mothers and motherhood, the connection and reassurance provided to readers—define my purpose. I'm not narcissistically writing about myself; I am recording my personal narrative and contributing to a collective, descriptive understanding of contemporary motherhood.

So I've made some changes from my early blogging days. The focus has shifted from the children's experience of being mothered, to my experience of mothering them. I've admitted to jealousy:

> I've been envying all my mom friends who suddenly seem to have gads of free time now that their children are off to full-day school. I know it's a silly bit of envy—I actually like the arrangement I've got going on. But the free time sounds so enticing. (*Making Things Up*, "fall envy," September 8, 2006)

I've confessed to being a neurotic blogger:

> I have been trying to comment on blogs more lately, but you know what? It's harder than it looks ... [as it involves] writing a witty comment that someone will not be embarrassed to have in their inbox and also that will not cause anyone to think I'm an idiot. I do not mostly succeed. (*Making Things Up*, "ridiculous difficulties," June 25, 2007)

I've bemoaned my need to overthink, well, everything, including trimming my hair:

But actually GETTING [a haircut] seems like such a drain on the emotional resources, what with the calling to schedule and the figuring out when I can go, not to mention the actually showing up and having it cut and then deciding whether to buy the product that will make my everyday hair somewhat resemble the hair I walk out of the salon with. (*Making Things Up*, "it's the hair," June 21, 2007)

I've discussed why I choose to give birth at home, ranted about guilt-inducing parenting articles, complained about the fact that the university where I spent my undergraduate days doesn't accept homeschooled students, recounted the tale of running into neighbours when out and about with my tantrumming two-year-old, in which I "smiled and chatted politely like a normal not-crazy mother neighbour," when I felt like anything but (*Making Things Up*, "tricks," July 17, 2006).

By now I've learned that for almost any post I want to write, some subset of readers will be able to relate. When I write that "I suspect how 'easy' one finds the experience [of parenting a second baby] depends in large part on the personalities of the kids and parents in question, but let me just say: I did not find it to be a walk in the park on a breezy spring day," I can reasonably expect that someone reading will identify and heave a sigh of relief (*Making Things Up*, "the second," June 20, 2007).

As I write, I can process my own remembered difficulty at parenting that second newborn, while also acknowledging that newborns grow, that parenting gets to be more familiar and less difficult as one gains experience, and that my lack of bliss did not indicate a personal failing. My life experience insists that parenting defies the definitive solutions of glossy magazine articles; mothering can't be prescribed by a ten-point bullet list. I can connect with other mothers who feel similarly—or provide a more detailed picture than might otherwise have been available to someone just starting down the path I am walking. There is value in that. And none of it depends on my children being cute for me to record.

Does this mean I'll refrain from quoting my deliciously endearing children from now on?

Well ... probably not. Occasional posts devoted to the children's silliness and sweetness will still appear. I might want to remember some of these details—and it is my blog, after all. But they're unlikely to dominate, and indeed, they ought not to; if my kids want their own stories told, perhaps they'd better start their own blogs.

Works Cited

Anti-Racist Parent. Retrieved February 20, 2007. <http://www.antira-cistparent.com>.

Belkin, Lisa. "The Opt-Out Revolution." *New York Times Magazine* 26 Oct. 2003.

Blogflux: Parenting Blogs. Retrieved February 20, 2007. <http://topsites. blogflux.com/parents>.

Friedman, Dawn. *This Woman's Work*. Retrieved February 20, 2007. <http://thiswomanswork.com>.

Gaskin, Ina May. *Spiritual Midwifery*. Summertown, TN: Book Publishing Company, 1975.

Granju, Katie Allison. *Attachment Parenting: Instinctive Care For Your Baby and Young Child*. New York: Pocket Books, 1999.

Groneberg, Jennifer Graf. *Pinwheels*. Retrieved February 20, 2007. <http://jennifergrafgroneberg.wordpress.com>.

Hip Mama. Retrieved February 20, 2007. <http://www.hipmama. com/>.

Literary Mama. Retrieved February 20, 2007. <http://www.literarymama. com>.

Making Things Up. Retrieved February 20, 2007. <http://makingthing-sup.com>.

Mamazine: Where Mamas can get real and get happy. Retrieved February 20, 2007. <http://www.mamazine.com/>.

Mothers Movement Online. Retrieved February 20, 2007. <http://www. mothersmovement.org/>.

MOMocrats: Raising the Next Level of Blue. Retrieved February 20, 2007. <http://momocrats.typepad.com/momocrats>.

My Life in a Foster Care Space Warp. Retrieved February 20, 2007. <http://fostercarespacewarp.blogspot.com/>.

Peskowitz, Miriam. *The Truth Behind the "Mommy Wars": Who Decides What Makes a Good Mother?* Emeryville, CA: Seal Press, 2005.

Sears, William. *The Baby Book: Everything You Need to Know About Your Baby from Birth to Age Two* (Revised and Updated Edition). USA: Little, Brown and Company, 2003.

Chapter Eleven

Blogging the Romanian Mother

"Motherhood" and "Mothering" Intertwined

OANA PETRICA

Blogging may be considered one of the most empowering tools through which people can exercise and strengthen their freedom of expression. While freedom of speech has been viewed as an inalienable right in liberal "Westernized" countries, it has never been an implicit and taken for granted reality in the communist countries of Eastern Europe where censorship and state control of discourses ruled. (Tismaneanu 109). At the same time, scholars have long argued that socialist states constructed women as workers and mothers in order to fit ideological interests (Einhorn 64). Arguably since the communist regimes in Russia and Eastern Europe collapsed in December 1989, women have been in the position to construct and represent their own identities without any barriers of repressive censorship and state-mediated representations. This paper will analyze the ways through which a Romanian woman constructs her maternal identity by making use of the blog as a medium of expression. Specifically, the chapter will consider how an individual, subjective discourse on maternity is created in the context of 45 years of censorship and state-imposed female constructions, and how the institution of "motherhood" is shaped, lived or contested after it is no longer embedded in a national, political, and ideological agenda. In the new context of the blog, can mothers provoke a rupture with socialist prescribed gendered roles, or will they perpetuate the same conventional hypostasis? Is a previous ideology undermined? And, if it is undermined, how, and under which conditions, is this accomplished?

When she started writing her mothering blog, Ada Demirgian titled it *The First One Thousand and One Nights*. In its immediate meaning the blog's title might refer to the first 1001 days of Demirgian's child's life. The intertextual reference, however, was to the famous anonymous collection of ancient Arabic stories, dated around 800-900 C.E. The collection has at its centre a new bride, Scheherazade, who, in order to avoid execution by her husband, the king Shahryar, starts telling him tales. Scheherazade's artifice consists of never ending her story so that the king cannot kill her at the end of any night but must rather keep her alive in order to hear the conclusion. Each subsequent night, as soon as she finishes the previous tale, she starts another and leaves it unfinished. Scheherazade's tales exceed the 1001 nights of the story's title. On the 1001st night the king expressed his wish to hear again the first narrated story. The reader is left to presume that the story is left unfinished and that the rhetorical spiral of never-ending stories or infinite tales therefore continues. In contemporary thought the *Arabian Nights* stand as a metaphor for an infinite process or for an endlessly self-reproductive phenomenon. When Demirgian titled her mothering blog *The First One Thousand and One Nights*, she suggested a representation of motherhood as a never-ending practice.

In the former Romanian communist regime (1944–1989) the maternalization of women and emphasis on their reproductive functions were ideological priorities. Women's identities in the communist political agenda of Romania were basically constructed as workers and mothers. It was essential for the ideology of the communist party in Romania to mobilize women's potential as "women-producers" and "women-reproducers/women-mothers" (Kligman 112). As the socialist economies did not function on the capitalist logic of profit and consumption, but that of accumulation and preservation, the labour force was continuously needed to produce resources that the socialist state had an interest in preserving and maintaining. The state further needed to ensure that these resources were not consumed by the population. In the Cold War context, and after internationally denouncing Soviet's invasion of Czechoslovakia, the Romanian communist leader, Nicolae Ceausescu started to build up his own vision of communism that later would be considered as "nationalist communism" (Verdery 25). Many propaganda strategies were used in order to forge a legitimizing nationalist communist system. Ceausescu focused on how best to represent the "Romanian identity" and the "Romanian nation" (Verdery 27). One of the features of the constructed "Romanian identity" was the representation of women as good wives and mothers, as well as model workers. However, what seems to be a common agreement in the feminist scholarship in this field is the fact that the socialist states, while resorting to female hypostasis as exemplary workers and mothers, did not emancipate women, nor stimulate their personal autonomy, or render their voices visible (Einhorn 66; Magyari-Vincze 201; Miroiu 196).

The full participation in the labour process was part of a political ideology that defined women's subject position as equally subordinated to the masculine in aid of the projects of a national "paternalist" state (Verdery 63). Therefore, the so-called "emancipation" of women was stimulated as long as female subjects were needed in the economy production (Einhorn 66; Magyari-Vincze 86). In the end, this presumed "emancipation" just equalized a triple burden on women as mothers, wives, and workers. Women were homogenized within the monolith category of producer-reproducer and instrumentalized by the state ideology. Due to this homogenization and to forceful censorship politics, personalized and individualized female voices were rarely expressed.

In 2005, when Ada Demirgian gave birth to her first child, Irina, she started a mothering blog. Demirgian is a 31-year-old Romanian writer, radio producer, and journalist. Her intention with the blog was to describe her daily, subjective, maternal experiences. After 45 years of communist imposed ideology and censorship, Ada Demirgian's blog attempts to disrupt previous official and formal rhetorics of motherhood by presenting an individual, personal representation of mothering rather than a state sanctioned view. Her writing about the experience of maternity is not mediated by the state anymore, but is rather drawn through her own subjectivity. The surprise is that Demirgian's portrayal of herself seems to largely succumb to maternal roles and the "good mother" icon already prescribed by the former communist apparatus. She disrupts a genealogy of state-imposed discourses, but in her subjective, individualized writing narrative she seems to mainly adhere to previously prescribed domestic roles, perpetuating, in this way, "motherhood" as institution (Rich 13). Nevertheless, there are some breaks and ruptures in her motherhood narrative (e.g. when she tears apart pictures and leaves her husband); only then does she break with the "motherhood" ideology, and begin a more empowering maternal practice. Ada Demirgian has the power and agency to write about her maternal experiences, but the ideology of a previous State-imposed "motherhood" is so powerful that she mainly perpetuates gendered maternal characteristics forged by the communist system. However, there are several paradoxical ruptures of her discourse, and in these contradictions and inconsistencies one can find the blogging author switching to a more empowering maternal practice.

Mothering and Motherhood

In 1976 Adrienne Rich published her book *Of Woman Born: Motherhood as Experience and Institution*, and previous feminist frames of analysis, which argued that motherhood was a universally oppressive practice, were shaken. Rich made the argument that not all maternal experiences were pernicious for women's spiritual growth and intellectual development. According to Rich, only the "male-defined and controlled" maternal experiences, and those externally prescribed by the "institution of motherhood" (13) were considered abusive and intrusive. The author maintained that maternity had, at its core, an empowering potentiality when it could be "female-defined and centred" (14). Therefore, the variable of her theoretical framing was the existence of a female construction of the maternal experience. In this respect, she coined two different concepts: "motherhood," for the maternal experiences as they were "defined and restricted under patriarchy" (Rich 14) and "mothering" for the same practices, but as female- determined and circumscribed.

Recent scholarship on the subject of maternity reconfigures and resignifies Adrienne Rich's terminology as "patriarchal motherhood," on one hand, and "empowered mothering" on the other (O'Reilly 4, 12). Andrea O'Reilly considers that "patriarchal motherhood" is still a dominant and prevalent ideology that instils a set of expectations by which "all mothers are regulated and judged" (5). Moreover, current social expectations such as the sacrificial mother, the selfless and the totally family-devoted, the altruistic, patient and all-cheerful mother are constructions of this type of ideology. To this subordinating ideology, O'Reilly opposes a narrative of "empowered mothering" seen as a way through which mothers are given back agency, authority, autonomy, and authenticity (13). According to O'Reilly's theory, mothers should denounce the externally imposed institution of "motherhood," with its alienating standards and characteristics of sacrifice and boundless devotion, and instead look at the way maternity can be a site of power. Socializing and educating children in a gender-sensitive manner with a commitment to social justice ideals; and enforcing maternal authority and the value of motherwork, are methods through which maternity empowers women, and "motherhood" as institution converts into "mothering" practice.

Empowered mothering discourse and practice and motherhood ideology and performance are rarely considered as possible accidental allies. What about the possibility, however, that they can go along together, or that the ideology of "motherhood" can be intersected and crossed by that of "mothering?" Without universalizing the phenomenon, we can take Ada Demirgian as an example. Demirgian, through her blogging on maternal experiences, starts defining something that, for 50 years, was defined and constructed by others, in mothers' names, and presumably for mothers' own good. Demirgian takes this narrative power while

simultaneously promoting maternal characteristics such as self-sacrifice and unlimited devotion. Still, her narratives of "motherhood" are
not uniform and consistent in their content. There are moments when
these celebrations of maternity are broken, allowing clear potential for
"mothering" seeds to grow.

Blogging the Self-Sacrificing Woman

The 31-year-old Romanian writer and journalist, Ada Demirgian, graduated from the Faculty of Arts of the University of Bucharest and immediately started working as a journalist at Radio Romania International
in Bucharest where she continues to work at present.

At the beginning of 2004 Demirgian gave birth to her first child,
Irina. Two months later, she started her blog *The First One Thousand
and One Nights* and dedicated it to her experiences as a new mother.
Her perspective is extremely original, as the Romanian literary market
lacks such subjective discourses on mothering. Although there are many
popular books about how to be a mother or how to raise your children
properly, these books are excessively didactic and normative. They are
also known for removing the authority of mothering from actual mothers to "expert knowledge" (Miller 64). Ada Demirgian presents one of
the first attempts to narrate a practice of Romanian mothering. After
decades of censorship and imposed ideology, Ada Demirgian gives voice
publicly to her own vision of mothering. Her *First One Thousand and
One Nights* are an example of how some Romanian mothers make sense
of and narrate their experiences.

Surprisingly enough, while Demirgian takes the power to build up
her own narration of maternal experience (a discourse that previously
belonged to the official ideology of the state), her agency is hijacked by
the maternal characteristics that she portrays in her blog. However, there
are several instances when her story subverts conventional gender roles,
troubling the reader, and letting us know that the blog might be more
than the perpetuation of the "motherhood" institution.

Generally Demirgian's renderings of maternal events are imbued with
high levels of romanticization and sentimentalization[1]: the act of giving
birth is portrayed as a "definitive metamorphosis" after previously dream-
ing about reading bedtime stories to "conical [pregnant] bodies." In this
sequence, her first efforts at being a mother are quickly reprimanded in
the moment the child "smiles at you, with one eye half closed, and the
other one closed" or when he/ she "looks at you innocently below the
giant breast" ("So This Is the Thing Everyone Has Spoken About..."

April 2, 2005). Permeated with these romanticized visions are not just her child's descriptions, but also that of her husband and father of the child or that of the Demirgian's mother-in-law, grandma Gabica who, for a while, would play the role of nanny to Irina. Her husband, better known in her stories as either "Valu" or "Irina's father" seems anxious "to know why the baby sneezes, hiccups, quivers, or has cold hands!" ("Seven Days with Irina," April 9, 2005). Moreover, during these first nights that are "so beautiful in our home" the baby looks him "directly in the eye, with a limitless admiration" ("I Still Feel that Place Where the Needle Entered," April 23, 2005). Similarly, Gabica appears to be portrayed as the ideal family grandmother who knows whenever the baby is "warm or cold," brings dolls every time she passes by, and impatiently waits for the baby to grow older so they may go out together. Gabica would cross the entire city to bring Ada "three packages of dried milk powder, for which she stood in line, shoulder to shoulder, with other grandmas and mothers." The Grandma gives the impression that she is so much into the grandmothering role that her next step could easily be to move from helping with swinging and carrying the baby to "sewing the baby to her coat" ("The Girl with Many Grandparents," April 30, 2005). In fact, all of the maternal practices described seem to be done in celebration of abnegation and self-sacrifice:

> Three months ago I passed through a definitive metamorphosis.... My body secretes strange hormones that give me unusual powers: that of confronting everyone, of saying things that in other circumstances I would not have said, the power not to sleep during the night for more than two hours, the capacity to endure hunger and thirst when I have more important things to do—and I always have more important things to do. No, I'm not sick, but I've entered a club into which I've always wanted to be included: the club of women with large circles around their eyes, the club of the eternally worried, the club of those who speak in highly-pitched voices, the club of those who are suddenly fearful of everything, but who are able to fight anyone that would dare put in danger the deity to which we all surrender: Our Majesty, the Baby. ("So this is the thing everyone has spoken about..." April 2, 2005)

The passage above depicts the mother's character as a heroic one, and, moreover, as an eternally available one. Mothering is assumed as a continuous state of emergency, with all the senses tuned for the sound "of being needed" (Rich 37). Using a rhetorical device that seems to be taken from children's tales, Ada Demirgian's mothering is a radical metamorphosis: in circumstances of crisis, the fairy tale protagonist can become more powerful and resistant. Experiencing motherhood is hence a state of siege where women are expected to pass through a ritual of physical suffering and physiological deprivations of food and liquids. A psychological weakening parallels these series of sufferings, translated into anxieties and omnipotent fears without object. This paradigm of maternal sacrifice is couched in the name of her child, raised to the status of sovereign deity. The freshly born child is entitled to subordinate the mother's efforts or to alter her states as she is crowned with the epithet of "Our Majesty, the Baby." Secondly, because of her self-denial, her personal desires either evaporate or metamorphose to become identical to that of her child. When those desires assert themselves, she becomes guilt-ridden:

> I love this silence. It's the sign that I'm off my shift, that I've survived another day in which my baby girl ate for twenty minutes every three or four hours, stained her clothes that are now getting soaked in the red washbasin, cried so much that she broke my heart, smiled at me when I least expected, and melted me in hundreds of ways, in a way that only a baby is capable of doing.... My heart doesn't let me put her in bed ... and in this way, every night, my baby girl steals ten more minutes. In the end, I don't know for which of us this swinging is better.... For her because she doesn't realize that the woman with the swinging and breastfeeding is tender and warm, or for me because I cannot bear putting her in the cradle. ("I Still Feel that Place Where the Needle Entered," April 23, 2005)

Like in the first passage, mothering cautions self-sacrifice. Degree of suffering seems to be the ideal instrument to measure the quality of a good mother, an adequate mother, or a bad mother. Through Demirgian's descriptions we do not see a move from a culture that anticipates and expects suffering and self-sacrifice in motherhood. Indeed, the devoted mother-martyr cannot leave her child in a cradle to sleep without feeling intensely guilty. The temporal continuity of the mother's life and her child's development must not be interrupted: the mother's time can be colonized and subordinated by that of her child. Also, the mother's sleep is allowed to be eroded so that the child feels comfortable. In this way, Ada Demirgian's discourse on motherhood sanctions devaluations of mothers' lives in a culture that has already fixed on maternal self-sac-rifice as a social expectation. Nevertheless, this type of sacrifice has its glowing and celebratory aura, next to the assumption that it cannot be but a noble and sparkling suffering:

> But let's come back to my spring [situation]. Irina is sleeping. The cat is sleeping. My husband is sleeping. I am their guardian. I like protecting them all. From time to time I cover them, then I get up silently and do my things on the sly. Now I fold some of Irina's clothes that are freshly dried. I don't feel like ironing them, I find it useless. ("Don't hit me, Lady!" May 28, 2005)

In the passage above, as in earlier examples, motherhood is portrayed as a task of abnegation. One might argue that it is not just about the protecting, endlessly giving, nurturing role, but also about who is taking a rest and who is doing the laundry. Folding clothes is a maternal task, and is described as an inevitable chore that must be assumed. Doing the laundry is hence framed in the same pattern of maternal sacrificial design. Moreover, it stands as an everyday routine practice. Her attitude legitimates the father's absence and/or his unequal degree of involvement in their child's life. On more than one occasion she justifies her partner's unsuitability to performing domestic chores:

> Three weeks ago I started working again and every morning I leave the house more reluctantly.... Grandma Gabica broke her arm and I have to leave my baby with her father. Who is a man. Who doesn't have patience. Who finds it difficult to be with such a small child, for so many hours.... ("The Bear Industry," May 11, 2005)

Demirgian argues that the only one ennobled to practice parenthood is the mother; that she is the most appropriate person to perform it as she is heroically stimulated by suffering and self-sacrifice. Ada Demirgian's blog ends by constructing and enforcing normative gender roles and defini-tions of motherhood. It is not only about sanctioning domestic chores as a female responsibility, but also about gendering and maternalizing the idea of self-sacrifice for the family. As a consequence, the private sphere is placed along traditional gender divisions. Refusing to create the com-fortable emotional nest at home for your husband and child by folding clothes would be considered unwomanly. Denying your total availability to your family is still not considered as a plausible option. So, while Ada

Demirgian gives visibility to a discourse of mothering as a mother experiences it (and not as it once was, mystified by the official rhetoric of state ideology) she fails to step out of traditional gender divisions. Moreover, she articulates her maternal heroism and duties as a prosaic and unexceptional narrative, enforcing and sanctioning a mother's devotion and sacrifice for the family as a standard social expectation. This phenomenon of maternalizing self-sacrifice obliterates the notion that women should live for themselves. In this way, Demirgian's representations function as a residual mechanism of the previous communist self-sacrificing mother (for the state and state's children) that has not yet been replaced by alternative individualist practices. The problem is not the detail that communist maternal representations are insidiously reproducing at the level of imagery, but the fact that potential readers of Demirgian's blog may reach maternity with the same expectations of self-sacrifice and renunciation, cloaked in the guise of self-representation.

For all the concerns presented by Demirgian's blog there are ruptures and breaks in her narratives of celebrating an idealized maternal devotion. In her glowing and all fulfilling narratives of maternal experiences, grandma Gabica is portrayed as so devoted to lovingly raising her granddaughter. This image fractures when Gabica one day fails to show up to Demirgian's house. The readership is left with the only brief explanation that "grandma Gabica grew tired" together with the announcement: "I'm looking for a grandmother for Irina" ("I'm Looking for a Grandmother for Irina," January 28, 2006). One cannot but be puzzled about how this magnificent grandmother, performing her helping role with such boundless joy, suddenly just abandons her mission. There is no sign in previous stories that grandma Gabica grows unsatisfied or tired with the domestic arrangement. We are only left with the abrupt conclusion that she refuses to show up at their house.

By far the biggest rupture in Demirgian's celebratory maternal narrative discourses occurs when she tears apart some wedding pictures, leaves her husband, and takes her daughter to England.

A couple of days ago I threw in the garbage four lives, hundreds of photos from my youth spent close to various protagonists, fragments from unfulfilled destinies in which I invested so much time and hope ... old certificates, and I began divorce papers. ("Partir," January 20, 2007)

The audience is left puzzled at such an abrupt rupture without any narrative antecedents suggesting gradual dissatisfaction of the author with her marriage. On the contrary, the previous descriptions are all idealizations and serene presentations of her maternal and conjugal experiences. The fact that she is leaving her husband and taking her daughter comes, somewhat paradoxically, after having spent together "two beautiful summers" and following his description as the baby's "principal, and favourite protagonist," the one the baby "calls more often and from whose hands eats more dearly." The break is even more contradictory and confusing after such a romanticization of their family relations, where father and daughter harmoniously construct their relationship, and drink tea together, crunch apples, ride cars in the park, look at the shop windows that display tricycles, ride escalators, and "put a finger on each other's nose and say 'ding' in the middle of the night." ("Since Lenuta Left Us," October 27, 2006). Of course, leaving one's marriage is not a sufficient condition for breaking the strong patterns of sacrificial maternity so enforced by the former communist ideology. However, husbands in the postcommunist space are usually portrayed as "big children," and are constructed as equally needy and dependent beings. (Marody and Poleszczuk, 161). There is even general agreement concerning men's transition from their mothers to their wives, with the wives working extra hard in order to precisely duplicate the maternal role.[23] Getting away from a husband might therefore be seen as an empowering way to claim some agency and autonomy from the overall architecture of the maternal sacrifice. In this way, Demirgian's divorce creates some space for a liberatory "mothering" practice, since the need for maternalization among children and husbands in the postsocialist family equation are convergent.

Only through these ruptures (which are mainly left without explanations, but are not hidden or rendered invisible) does Ada Demirgian start "mothering." The former socialist ideology of "motherhood" is still powerful in Romania and is so internalized that, even when mothers start to describe their own subjective maternal experiences, they do it following the same conventional gender roles. However, there are these ruptures (for example, when Grandma Gabica refuses to play the nanny, and when the author herself takes her child, and abandons her marriage) that still trouble readers and can be converted into signs that "mothering" practice might happen. This practice is still at a rudimentary level, but is not so rudimentary as to be unrecognizable as a sign of something irreversibly taking place.

Conclusions

Through a blogging discourse analysis a Romanian woman is presented as defining and describing her maternal experiences within the context of fifty years of censorship and State-imposed ideologies of motherhood. Apparently, the official rhetoric of the socialist state is not different from a subjective experience of maternity: although Ada Demirgian takes the power to write her own discourse, she keeps idealizing the idea of family while justifying maternal self-sacrifice and suffering. Nevertheless, there are certain breaks in her idealized and romanticized family stories. At one point, from her stories we find out that her mother-in-law refuses to take up conventional gendered roles of taking care of her granddaughter. At another, Demirgian refuses to continue with her marriage, divorces her husband, and leaves for England. These actions are even more abrupt after so much romance in the public construction of her family life and marriage. Although the ruptures do not make the author reevaluate the previous idealization of her stories, they leave the audience thinking of the alternative hidden family life stories that might be simultaneously occurring.

Without the ruptures and discontinuities of Demirgian's blog, her family romance stories might be as fictional and inauthentic as the former official State-rhetoric of the party. Ada Demirgian becomes true and authentic when she shares with us the ruptures that are in such radical contradiction with her former celebration of family life. Socialist "motherhood" ideologies are highly internalized to the point that a mother's self-perception of maternity is indistinguishable from former official portraits of motherhood, justifying acts of maternal self-sacrifice and heroism. But Demirgian also presents courageous moments when she leaves her traditional roles, previously so highly celebrated, and starts performing a more empowering "mothering" practice. She has the power to move from her own fantasies of idealised maternity.

It is important to mention that at the moment of completing this article Demirgian returned to her husband, returning to a portrayal of largely traditional, devoted motherhood roles. For example, in one of her latest blog entries, Demirgian teaches her three-year-old daughter how to take care of her adult father in her absence. "Take care of your Daddy, right? … 'How should I take care of him, Mummy? 'Listen to him, caress him, kiss him and tell him not to cry because I arrive quickly" ("Transparent Little Boat," February 24, 2008). As we can observe easily, daughters are socialized and educated into the care politics of male adults at an absurdly young age. However, in a previous narrative we find out that Demigian's partner is left, through some accidental occurrences, in charge of the baby while Demirgian enjoys her individual free time and liberation from traditional maternal roles: "You may think that I suffer a lot (for father-daughter bonding) and that I bite my nails in jealousy. Eh, not at all. I don't know how to be more happy about it" ("The Golden Age," February 4, 2008).

The practices of "motherhood" and "mothering" are not separated in time, and mothers like Demirgian walk back and forth between the two. Mothering and motherhood do not belong to separate categories or oppositional ones: one can begin experiencing maternity in a patriarchal way while gradually switching to a more and more empowered mothering practice. The option of "mothering" is not always a definitive choice; it has many regressive movements to former "motherhood" roles that have already been deeply internalized. Ada Demirgian's blog is an example of this migration.[3]

[1]Note: All translations of Demirgian's blog were done by this author.
[2]The obvious heterosexism in this paradigm is deeply problematic and is a further legacy of the former communist regime.
[3]I would like to thank Professor Rusty Shteir for solidly articulating my arguments and correcting preliminary versions of the paper, as well as Professor Andrea O'Reilly, Shana Calixte, May Friedman and Iris Mendel.

Works Cited

Demirgian, Ada . *The First One Thousand and One Nights*. Trans. Oana Petrica, 2005-2008.

Einhorn, Barbara. *Cinderella Goes to Market: Citizenship, Gender and Women's Movement in East Central Europe*. London: Verso, 1998.

Kligman, Gail. *The Politics of Duplicity: Controlling Reproduction in Ceausescu's Romania*. Berkeley and Los Angeles: University of California Press, 1998.

Magyari-Vincze, Eniko. *Femei si barbati in Clujul multiethnic*. Cluj: Editura Fundatiei Desire, 2001.

Marody and Anna Giza-Poleszczuk. "Changing Images of Identity in Poland: From the Self-Sacrificing to the Self-Investing Woman?" *Reproducing Gender. Politics, Publics, and Everyday Life After Socialism*. Eds. S. Gal and G. Kligman. Princeton: Princeton University Press, 2000.

Miller, Tina. *Making Sense of Motherhood: A Narrative Approach*. London: Oxford University Press, 2006.

Miroiu, Mihaela. "Ana's Land: The Right to Be Sacrificed." *Ana's Land*.

Sisterhood in Eastern Europe. Ed. T. Renne. Boulder, Colorado: Westview Press, 1997

O'Reilly, Andrea. *Mother Outlaws: Theories and Practices of Empowered Mothering*. Toronto: Women's Press, 2004.

Rich, Adrienne. *Of Woman Born: Motherhood as Experience and Institution*. New York: W. W. Norton and Company Inc, 1995.

Roman, Denise. *Fragmented Identities: Popular Culture, Sex, and Everyday Life in Post-Communist Romania*. Lanham: Lexington Books, 2003.

Tismaneanu, Vladimir. *Stalinism for All Seasons: A Political History of Romanian Communism*. Berkeley, Los Angeles, London: University of California Press, 2003.

Verdery, Katherine. *What Was Socialism and What Comes Next?* Princeton, NJ: Princeton University Press, 1996.

Verdery, Katherine. *National Ideology Under Socialism: Identity and Cultural Politics in Ceausescu's Romania*. Berkeley: University of California Press, 1991.

Verdery, Katherine and Ivo Banach. *National Character and National Ideology in Interwar Eastern Europe*. New Haven: Yale Center for International and Area Studies, 1995.

Chapter Twelve

Schadenfreude for Mittelschmerz?

Or, Why I Read Infertility Blogs

MAY FRIEDMAN

I)

When I became a mother I was hungry. Literally hungry from the work of labour, from the endless nursing, but also metaphysically hungry: hungry for community, for companionship and for some verification that the feelings I was feeling weren't madness but somehow made sense within this new realm of motherhood. I struggled to reach out, to reach other mothers and to find sense within other women's experiences. Being shy, however, I struggled with in-person interactions, and thus was drawn quickly into community that required no input on my part, in the guise of the mommyblog.

Mommyblogs, women's life writing about motherhood, have commandeered a tremendous amount of bandwidth. Although estimates vary wildly, there are vast multitudes of women detailing varied experiences of motherhood on the Internet. For every type of mother, for every social location, it would seem, there is a discussion to be had online. So how did it occur that I reached out toward a community that was not my own, that did not share my location, with whom it would seem I had little in common? Specifically, what was the draw of the infertility blog to a new mother like myself?

As my children could attest, I am fertile. Quite fertile, in fact, as evidenced by the fact that both my kids were conceived a little more, ahem, readily than I anticipated. Surrounded by endless mommybloggery, what led me to become such a dedicated reader of infertility blogs? What was provided by these blogs that I felt I couldn't acquire elsewhere in the blogosphere, or in Real Life, for that matter? This paper attempts to use the lens of my own experience, coupled with a therapeutic and critical academic analysis to interrogate the tremendous popularity of infertility blogs in order to understand the ways they may challenge traditional notions of femininity and maternity.

II)

Perhaps it's schadenfreude[1] that draws me in. It is certainly possible that I read infertility blogs for the same reasons that people rubberneck at car accidents—in order to derive some sick pleasure from someone else's misfortune. As a woman with the great good luck of avoiding infertility, perhaps I simply read infertility blogs in order to salivate over other people's suffering. Needless to say, I hope that this isn't my primary motivation and that my interest is rather informed by a more virtuous position. Despite my own fecundity, there is a difficult history of infertility within my immediate family. Like many families, however, the infertility has gone undiscussed despite its obviously painful implications for all. (As an aside, after a dozen years, this particular experience of infertility has drawn to a close with the recent joyous arrival of my niece and nephew.) Reading infertility blogs has allowed me to access the experience of infertility without asking nosy questions, without putting those around me on the spot, without being, in short, insensitive. Furthermore, reading blogs allowed me to exercise that sensitivity when my physical condition most demanded it, when I was the burgeoning pregnant woman in the room, while I was breastfeeding a toddler and potentially unwittingly rubbing salt into the wounds of those around me. I wanted to learn and understand. *Stirrup Queen* responds to this desire, saying, "We can't take you to the edge where we stand—we can only tell you about it. And hearing it is nothing like living it" ("Manifesto," October 15, 2007).

To read these blogs was to confirm that I was infertile women's worst nightmare in many ways—thoughtlessly fertile, I could afford to have the home birth with the midwife, to bitch about mastitis and morning sickness, to overlook, in short, the privilege of my own fertility. In many respects, reading infertility blogs let me see the invisible knapsack of my own privileges as a fertile woman within a society that equates childfulness with femininity. As a woman with children, I was normal; but only by reading about other women's experiences, could I perceive my experience as *normative*, and as performative within a hegemony of maternity that is deeply oppressive to women who, by choice or by misfortune, do not opt into motherhood as a life path.

On a purely educational level, women who experience infertility or undertake alternative reproductive technologies (ART) for other reasons reluctantly access a wealth of knowledge about their bodies that is unavailable to me as a woman who can pursue a more mainstream approach to family planning. Reading infertility blogs provided a fascinating crash course in the intricacies of human conception. I became aware of myriad potential pregnancy symptoms (harbingers of fertility, of course) that I'd never considered, of the surprising number of stages required between the chance meeting of sperm and egg and the presence of an actual, viable pregnancy, and about medical "truths" grounded in fact and fiction (who knew that Robitussin could be so useful![2]). I learned about the vagaries of cervical mucus, temperature changes around ovulation (the thermometer, I learned in my reading, goes in your *mouth*!) and the importance of detecting *mittelschmerz*, the all-too-mistakable *ping* of discomfort that some women associate with ovulation. My reading brought with it a familiarity with my own body and its processes that I never achieved in my eighth grade sex ed. class.

Much more importantly, I learned that when someone loses a baby, my best response is simply to say, and act, sorry for their loss. I learned that, without being told, I could assume that at least some of the women I know have struggled to build a family, that infertility and loss of all sorts—miscarriage, stillbirth, terminations et al.—are often kept deeply closeted. I learned that infertility bears with it a psychic pain that parallels other experiences of oppression, a pain that is not entirely healed even by the eventual presence of children, a pain that, as an outsider, I can't begin to imagine. I can't imagine, but I can read, and in doing so, I hope that my sensitivity has grown.

III)

My noble intentions and lofty educational altruism notwithstanding, I can't let the notion of *schadenfreude* go completely. A cursory examination of the comment patterns of a few "superstar" infertility blogs (for example, *a little pregnant, So Close* and *The Naked Ovary*, among others) shows that readership and comments increase as a blogger is "cycling" or actively taking steps toward trying to conceive. Although I imagine that the majority of readers are simply cheering bloggers toward conception, there is no doubt that infertility blogging, by the nature of the enterprise, lends itself to a type of drama that allows for an impressive narrative arc. Infertility is a theatrical enterprise. In vitro fertilization (IVF), for example, begins with the stockpiling of pharmaceuticals and moves toward the counting of viable follicles, trigger shots, the retrieval of ova, conception, a count of viable embryos, the placing of embryos within a woman's uterus, and finally, the dreaded two week wait to confirm whether any given cycle has been successful. A successful cycle, of course, only creates further hoops to jump through in the interminable eight months between positive pregnancy test and birth. And, as in all stories in which our intrepid protagonist overcomes adversity, the relief of the eventual climax is heightened by the prolonged anxiety of repeated failure. When a blogger fails to conceive, or an adoption falls through, or, heart-wrenchingly, when babies are born still, blogs increase in readership and popularity.

For infertile women, at every stage there are numbers and measurements that can be endlessly pored over. Likewise, bloggers who make the choice to move to adoption are held in the grip of a bureaucracy that provides endless waiting and pining. From a narrative perspective, such tangible markers of success or failure create the suspense and excitement of any good literary experience. So while I'd like to maintain only a pedagogical interest in infertility blogs, I doubt that I am alone in readings such blogs while waiting on tenterhooks for word of some remote woman's home pregnancy test results. Though it pains me to admit it, blogs are, at heart, a unique form of entertainment, and we maintain our addiction to them based on how readily we are entertained. Unsavoury as it may seem, infertility blogs hook us, keep us riveted and driven to read due to their inherent suspense and narrative flow. The overwhelming proof of this can be found in the rather steep dropoff of comments and readership for blogs written by the "formerly" infertile[3]—once such women achieve success in their dreams to bring home baby (in whatever way this is accomplished) readers often disappear.

IV)

As a former therapist, social worker, and social work educator, I am fascinated by the role that infertility blogs have played in providing both community and education to people fertile and infertile alike. Although I have alluded to the education that I have taken from these blogs in terms of informing my own experience, the Internet teems with anecdotal accounts of women who are able to empower themselves to manage their own medical care based on their ability to connect with other women. In this respect, many women's blogs are being used as feminist tools. In the realm of infertility, however, this potential is pronounced in that women who have thus far been viewed as patients (and sometimes as medical objects divorced from actual personhood), are able to pool information in order to challenge their providers and advocate for themselves. In addition, many women write about the shame and isolation of infertility, and the burden of remaining closeted within their families and communities. On the Internet, such women can "come out" and find both community and solace with others like themselves, yet can maintain anonymity within their real lives at home. Karen of *The Naked Ovary* writes that, "...The pages and pages of medical advice that popped up just wouldn't do it for me. I didn't want to read the doctor's cold diagnosis, or the infertility center's prediction.... I needed to hear the personal side of this dark, lonely thing called infertility" (qtd. in *a little pregnant* "Confessions of a baby blogger manqué," March 21, 2004). *Stirrup Queen* states that, "Infertility breeds seclusion, and blogs allow empathy, sympathy, and a good old-fashioned virtual back pat to seep into the caves we build for ourselves" ("Cheers to Infertility (Blogs)," September 16, 2006).

Blogger Julie of *a little pregnant* maintains that another theme is prevalent, suggesting that women who experience only short-term infertility take comfort in online bulletin boards and other rapidly evolving communities. She writes that,

> By the time my two-week wait was over, everyone else in the group had moved on, either to the pregnancy boards or to the next group of cycle buddies—perhaps the Lucky Little Leprechauns or Fuzzy Easter Snuggleducks, whichever was more seasonally appropriate to their plan. There was no one left to celebrate with me when I eventually got my own positive. And there was certainly no one on hand to offer me virtual solace when it became clear the pregnancy would fail.

Julie goes on to say that,

> I'd like to apologize if my mockery has offended anyone who finds special comfort in friendly online groups. Their chief appeal, as I know firsthand, is that they can keep us from feeling alone in a situation that can be profoundly isolating. Their main failing in my eyes is that I experienced them as communities based on coincidence rather than on any real affinity—the kind of affinity I've found only here with my fellow blogging cranks. The effect overall is the same: I feel less alone knowing you're there." ("Cycle Buddies? No, psycho buddies," March 18, 2004)

As Julie articulates, women struggling with long-term infertility may reject the panacea afforded by short-term situationally oriented support groups. Blogging allows women to express more of their own personalities, resulting in communities that are based on shared experience, but that evolve beyond the coincidence of shared suffering to the "affinity" (as Julie states) of true friendship. As such, many infertility bloggers have found community that extends beyond the realm of the computer, becoming friends with voices, bodies and complete lives.

V)

Cycle buddies, due date friend groups and other such cyber-pals that maintain group membership on the basis of somewhat irrelevant shared minutiae have the potential to flatten the complexities of women's lives. Topics are theoretically set by anyone in the group but in practice, it is difficult for community to evolve beyond the coincidence that brings women together within these forums. By contrast, blogging allows people to document their lives within a very rich, evolving format. Although a blog may be largely about a person's journey through infertility, there is nonetheless a much larger emphasis on setting the situational context. From the perspective of creative writing, blogging is unlike online chat forums in that it allows the author editorial control over the product set before the audience. Despite the often well-developed discussion that may be played out within a blog's comments, posts themselves are presented as finite blocks of content given up for audience consideration. In this way, bloggers are able to maintain a complexity of content that is potentially missing from other online contexts. In this respect, blogging may be the fundamental postmodern project, wherein a chorus of voices band together in order to create some rough position on any given topic.

Within the realm of infertility, the postmodern project of creating a wealth of narratives is even more striking, given the relative scarcity of accounts on the topic elsewhere. And although many, many infertility bloggers are both white and socio-economically privileged, the act of blogging has created unexpected allies and provoked discussions that are stretching the boundaries of experience. Specifically, gay and lesbian parents who may use reproductive technologies and/or adoption to build families are often side by side with "traditional" infertility narratives. Bloggers struggle with the implications of transracial adoptions and the implications for families considering donor gametes. As these discussions take place, ideally, no one position is privileged. Rather, a picture of non-traditional families (in both their creation and maintenance) may emerge based on the range of experiences present within the blogging world. Politically, this means that even voices that appear self-contradictory have a space to contribute to the overall picture of family.

Speaking about miscarriage, *Stirrup Queen* writes, "Even though I'm a pro-Choice feminist, I also love my children when they're only embryos" ("Manifesto," October 15, 2007). *Stirrup Queen* links to *Uncommon Misconceptions*, the blog of a religious Republican woman who tragically underwent a late-term abortion due to fetal anomalies. The complexity of women's experiences thus emerges in a way that is tremendously exciting. Patti Lather writes that

> postmodernism offers feminists ways to work within and yet challenge dominant discourses. Within postmodernist feminism, language moves from representational to constitutive; binary logic implode, and debates about "the real" shift from a radical constructivism to a discursively reflexive position which recognizes how our knowledge is mediated by the concepts and categories of our understanding. (39)

Within infertility blogs, then, binaries are shattered by the multitude of experiences at the same time that commonality of suffering breeds community. This is not to say that the blogging world is free of all the inequalities of "real life," however—some connections do not weather transitions well. For example, women may connect based on their experiences of using donor sperm, but women parenting with men may abandon those connections when it is clear that they can "pass" as biological parents, while lesbian mothers may find themselves targeted as "obvious" users of reproductive technologies, by contrast. Parents who adopt inter-racially may find that early connections with other adoptive parents wither away when their issues split around parent and child "matching." Nonetheless, the presence of the Internet has allowed for some different connections—and indeed, different tensions—to emerge.

The implications of infertility blogs as a postmodern project extend beyond the lives of the infertile women who read and write them. As Linda Singer writes, "part of the tradition of critical writing that postmodernism and feminism inherit, albeit in ways that are differentially specified, is a tradition of writing as a form of resistance, writing which works not to confirm cohesion, but rather to disrupt, destabilize, denaturalize" (469). The wealth of infertility narratives literally denaturalize the coupling of motherhood and femininity. In providing a view of human reproduction that emphasizes its mechanistic nature as well as its very real failings, the myth of motherhood as intrinsic to women's experience is exploded. Although many individual women may nonetheless view their infertility as a failure, and eventual motherhood as the only real possibility of "success," as a genre, infertility blogs genuinely destabilize a normative perception of women's life cycles.

Although the Internet has allowed infertile women to connect in heretofore unheard of numbers, there are still limits to the types of communities that may be preserved within infertility blogs, and within the world of treated infertility itself. The choice to undertake alternative reproductive technologies is a notoriously expensive one. Similarly, both domestic and international adoptions are hugely expensive, although there are select circumstances under which this may not be the case. Responding to infertility (in any way other than acceptance and mourning) therefore requires a level of class privilege that automatically limits the diversity of couples in this situation. I say couples, because although single women obviously experience infertility and may choose to use ART, people attempting to achieve pregnancy in this very public way undergo a level of scrutiny that may, tacitly or explicitly, privilege traditional heterosexual two-parent families. For adoptive families, the need to measure up to a societal expectation of "good" parenting (an expectation, no less, that varies wildly from jurisdiction to jurisdiction) is viewed as notoriously unfair, one further indignity that infertility visits upon those who experience it.

Within the blogosphere, a picture of infertility has emerged that is diverse and eclectic, representative of a range of experiences and opinions on infertility, adoption, and ART. This diversity, however, is shut down, however, with respect to social location. Infertility begs questions of sexuality (same-sex couples generally require some type of fertility assistance), race (usually around issues of transracial adoption), biology (regarding families who, through ART or adoption have children who are not biologically related) and class (with respect to the implications for birth mothers and egg donors who might have very different financial choices from the families to whom they contribute). All this experience and analysis, however, is largely undertaken by white, straight women who belong to the middle-class. While infertility blogs are, then, extraordinarily useful tools for unmasking infertility and otherwise challenging normative perceptions of motherhood, they must be viewed with caution. Without this note of hesitation, infertility potentially becomes re-normalized as a white woman's condition, with no discussion of how experiences of infertility are vastly different for those whose options for responding to the condition might be severely curtailed.[4]

VI)

Although some mothers choose to shift from blogging about infertility to blogging about motherhood, others see the transition as awkward or as a potential betrayal of the infertile community. *Stirrup Queen* writes that,

> I don't blog about my kids for the most part because (1) I want this blog to be like a virtual *Cheers* where you can drink heavily after a [Big Fucking Negative] and everyone knows your name and (2) I don't want it to change. I want there to be one blog that is solely about infertility. Infertility-24/7-all-the-time-never-leaving-you-to-go-be-about-mommyhood. There's a need for that, I think, based on the comments. That there's a sadness and envy that also takes place with the congratulations and the happiness. Because their happiness is your loss—one less story about the trenches and one more about pregnancy when you're still back in the war zone. ("Cheers to Infertility (Blogs)," September 16, 2006)

Likewise, the blog *In the Barren Season* gives the following insight: "Infertility humor is a way of triumphing over bitterness, of turning that bitterness inside out, into something that gives solace and strength. Bitter humor about my pregnancy would just be ... what, self-indulgence?" ("Hilarious (Really, really funny!)," February 6, 2006).

So what has become of the baby and the bathwater? Although there are still a huge number of infertility blogs available on the web, the popularity of the genre does seem to have decreased over the last few years. In some respects this may be because the previously mentioned star bloggers have "graduated" into motherhood themselves (or, in the case of a few such bloggers have chosen to live childfree). On the face of it, the decline of these star blogs appears to herald a shift in interest away from infertility. Perhaps instead, however, the quieting of certain key voices only confirms the fundamentally egalitarian nature of the blogosphere, wherein legions of quieter voices are now overtaking the superstars and contributing to a variegated picture of infertility that is potentially richer and more dynamic.

VI)

Susan Winnett suggests that "We have been taught to read in drag and must begin to question seriously the determinants that govern the mechanics of our narratives, the notion of history as a sense-making operation, and the enormous investment the patriarchy has in maintaining them" (qtd. in Kadar 11). I would argue that in discussions about motherhood and mothering we are particularly guilty of "reading in drag." Infertility blogs, and indeed, infertility itself, challenge us to critically examine our perceptions of maternity, biology and normativity. Infertility challenges us to consider variation in family creation and blogs push us to synthesize innumerable perceptions while simultaneously creating, from disparate life experiences, a supple and responsive community. While my own fascination with infertility blogs comes from a variety of experiences both noble and otherwise, the presence of these blogs presents a challenging and exciting contribution to the discussion of motherhood.

[1]Schadenfreude is defined in the *Oxford Paperback Dictionary* as "malicious enjoyment of another's misfortunes" (Pollard 715).

[2]Lore has it that Robitussin encourages the thinning of all kinds of mucus including cervical mucus, thus increasing the potential for conception.

[3]In point of fact, many infertility bloggers discuss whether one ever becomes "formerly infertile" or whether one may simply become an infertile woman with children, retaining all the psychic trauma of the label despite transcending its physical definition.

[4]There is also a need for further discussion regarding women who deliberately make different choices around fertility. For example, the "lavender conception conspiracy"—queer women who dealt with their "infertility" by going out and having sex with random strangers. In addition, we must consider the ways that the term "infertility" is inherently heterosexist, because lesbians become such just by not having access to sperm.

Works Cited

a little pregnant. Retrieved October 4, 2008. <www.alittlepregnant. com>.

In the Barren Season. Retrieved October 20, 2007. <www.inthebarren-season.blogspot.com>.

Julia {Here Be Hippogriffs}. Retrieved January 14, 2008. <www.julia. typepad.com>.

Kadar, Marlene, ed. *Essays on Life Writing: From Genre to Critical Practice*. Toronto: University of Toronto Press, 1992.

Lather, Patti. *Getting Smart: Feminist Research and Pedagogy With/in the Postmodern*. New York: Routledge, 1991.

Naked Ovary, The. <www.thenakedovary.typepad.com>. Retrieved May 8, 2006.

Pollard, Elaine. *Oxford Paperback Dictionary.* Oxford: Oxford University Press, 1994.

Singer, Linda. "Feminism and Postmodernism." *Feminists Theorize the Political.* Eds. J. Butler and J. W. Scott. New York: Routledge, 1992. 464-475.

So Close. Retrieved January 8, 2008. <www.tertia.typepad.com>.

Stirrup Queens and Sperm Palace Jesters. Retrieved January 4, 2008. <http://stirrup-queens.blogspot.com>.

Uncommon Misconception. Retrieved May 9, 2006. <www.uncommon-misconception.typepad.com>.

Chapter Thirteen

"HEY CELEBS! QUIT THAT BEHAVING! DON'T MAKE US COME DOWN THERE!"[1]

Celebrity Moms, Babies, and Blogs

ELIZABETH PODNIEKS

"If you can't get enough of the Tom Kitten, the newest Trump Spawn or bursting-at-the-seams Brangelina, check out babyrazzi.com for the latest commentary and photos of celebrity breeders." This quotation from *MSNBC Newsweek BlogWatch* appears as an epigraph at the top of *babyrazzi*, one of countless blogs with millions of readers devoted to celebrity mothers and children that have come to populate the Internet over the last few years. The term paparazzi entered the lexicon in 1960 when the character "Paparazzo," in Federico Fellini's *La Dolce Vita*, began using invasive measures to capture his photographic subjects (Cashmore 18-19). Several decades later, and with a nod to the traditional familial tripartite of papa, mama, and baby, we now have not only the paparazzi but also *Mamarazzi.org*, *babyrazzi.com*, and a brood of dotcom siblings which stalk the stars and their offspring. Blogs such as these are posted in large part by non-famous mothers who are, by their own admission, obsessed with celebrity mothers and babies, and who chart, admire, and or critique the maternal behaviour of Hollywood women. These blogs are slowly being complemented by those kept by celebrities themselves—such as Tori Spelling, Britney Spears, and Gwyneth Paltrow—who use their web pages in part to document that while they live privileged lives, when it comes to mothering their concerns and aspirations reflect those of their non-famous counterparts.[2] Through a close reading of some of these blogs, I want to show how they testify to the increasing power of celebrities to shape cultural responses to, and practices of, mothering in the twenty-first century; and to the role of new media in fostering maternal communities in which ideologies of motherhood are shared, contested, and or redefined. At the same time, I want to consider how the celebrity mom and baby blogs, tied as they are to the entertainment industry, promote and perpetuate the commodification of maternity in general and celebrity children in particular; and to address the ethical issues concerning privacy and identity that occur when blogging about these children.

Blogs of the maternally famous are created and maintained first and foremost by fans, and before going on to discuss some of these sites in particular I want to position motherhood scholarship alongside studies in celebrity culture. "Fan," according to Ellis Cashmore, is a term that describes "followers, devotees, or admirers of virtually anybody or any-thing in popular culture" (79). Fans look up to celebrities, view them as role models, and "adopt what they see as a celebrity's attributes, includ-ing his or her values and behavior" (83). Accordingly, then, bloggers who self-identify as fans of celebrity mothers regard those mothers as role models, and adopt the specifically maternal "values and behavior" they observe in and associate with those celebrities. Citing the work of Benson Fraser and William Brown, among others, Cashmore asserts that fans and their fandom can be viewed positively: "The fans' attachment [to celebrities] is not the result of desperate innocence, but of enthrall-ment. Not a sign of intellectual bankruptcy, but of emotional liquidity. The fans actually form the relationship, inflating the significance of the celebrity, with a well-meaning intensity that stimulates and inspires." Further, more often than not they simply want to engage in a dialogue about their own tastes and interests with other like-minded fans (85),[3] a point which leads us to the networks of countless bloggers who share their passion for celebrity moms and children.

Associations between blogging, community, and motherhood can be further appreciated by turning to Carol Brooks, whose article "What celebrity worship says about us" is used by Cashmore to reinforce his argument about the benefits of fan culture. Defined by the *Review of General Psychology* as "evaluative talk about a person who is not pres-ent," gossip, once dismissed by psychologists as meaningless, has been gaining recognition as a more serious and necessary phenomenon that should be given its cultural due, especially in light of the fact that today gossip is inflected into two-thirds of all conversations among women and men from all walks of life. As Brooks explains,

> Pointless conversation is one powerfully healthy social elixir. Just by gabbing in the right way, you can expand your social circle, deepen your existing relationships, consolidate your sense of self and feel dramatically less stressed—in mere minutes. Not to mention the benefits to society at large: By using other people's

triumphs and tragedies as fodder for discussion, we collectively define who we are and what we value as a culture.

In celebrity mom and baby blogs, we "collectively define who we are" as mothers, and "what we value" in our child-rearing practices and beliefs. Unlike the past, when we inhabited isolated villages or small communities, at present we live fast-paced and fragmented lives that unfold within a range of spaces such as home, home-pages, school, work, and vacation spots. In this global world where local friends and neighbors have been displaced, celebrities provide a "universal cultural currency" that attracts and links disparate people from across their disparate locations. It is important to qualify that while Brooks suggests gossip forges bonds "between generations and across socioeconomic, religious, gender and cultural divides," celebrity mom and baby blogs appear, based on blogger profiles and reader commentary, to be written by and directed towards a more limited maternal community, one whose members are mainly white, middle-class, and range in age from their 20s-40s.[4] When we talk (or blog) about celebrities, we are in fact talking (or blogging) about ourselves. In the end, our fascination with celebrities should not be interpreted as a facile sign of an uncritical and obsequious reception towards them but rather as indicative of our needs, abilities, and commitments to forming connections with others (Brooks).[5]

Blogs are predicated on this theme of connection. A blog is "a personal diary. A daily pulpit. A collaborative space. A political soapbox. A breaking-news outlet. A collection of links. Your own private thoughts. Memos to the world" ("Blog"). In the context of celebrity culture, Reni Celeste notes that the media joins fan to idol by means of "gossip and exposé." Bloggers of celebrity moms and babies rely for their content on the gossipy images and text circulated in entertainment journalism, which the bloggers post on their sites with commentary, and for which they receive feedback, or reader responses. Such an ongoing dialogue allows for vital bonds to be forged among bloggers, between bloggers and their readers, and between fans and celebrities.

In focusing on maternal connections, I turn to Susan J. Douglas and Meredith W. Michaels who analyze, in *The Mommy Myth*, representations of mothering in the media through what they call the "new momism," defined as "a set of ideals, norms, and practices, most frequently and powerfully represented in the media, that seem on the surface to celebrate motherhood, but which in reality promulgate standards of perfection that are beyond your reach" (5). Of particular relevance here is the authors' critique of the celebrity mom profile, a genre proffered in home and entertainment magazines from the 1980s on, which promotes a "symbolic, fantasy response to the very real deficiencies mothers experienced in everyday life." Specifically, where the majority of real mothers are tired, financially strapped, and work tirelessly at unglamorous jobs, celebrity moms—so the fantasy goes—inhabit a world in which their energy, economic resources, and employment are, respectively, boundless, endless, and exciting (116). While Douglas and Michaels contend that the celebrity mom profile is the dominant disseminator of the tenets of new momism, refining, reinforcing, and romanticizing the myths of supermomdom (113), celebrity mom and baby blogs constitute a new, more complex genre which promotes and sells, while simultaneously questioning and even undermining, ideologies of mothering.

Despite the influence of new momism, as Douglas and Michaels report "we may also be talking back to the maternal mirage before us," and it is precisely this "talking" that drives the practice of blogging. Just as Cashmore identifies the relationships that fans posit in relation to their idols, so Douglas and Michaels categorize the approaches mothers take towards the celebrity profile: "On the one end is the totally accepting uncritical fan, on the other end is the cynical hip mama who don't believe none of it, and in the middle—where most women are—are the negotiators who work and play with what they know to be the blurriness between fact and fantasy" (124). These possibilities are played out on the mom and baby blogs. The "accepting uncritical fans" view celebrities as role models who inspire them to dream of inhabiting the superstar-supermom stratosphere. The "cynical hip mama" fans dismiss the celebrities with responses ranging from the humorous to the derisive; moreover, these fans might also judge celebrities negatively as a means to feeling more positively about their own parenting skills. The middle-ground fans negotiate reality and myth in part by assuming a shared maternal sensibility between celebrities and themselves, a notion popularized in *US* magazine's feature "Stars, They're Just Like Us!" It is this democratizing spirit that marks the fascination of "star spotting" for Celeste, who posits that stars are most interesting when observed "simply eating at a cafe, entering an elevator, or using a lavatory" because here they are moving "the light from screen to world," transforming the everyday into a theatre in which even the non-famous play a part. In this context we can understand why so many women who perform their maternal roles within the theatre of their own lives find blogging about celebrity moms and babies so exciting and rewarding.[6]

The subsequent explosion of the blogosphere since the late 1990s has permitted fans to interact with entertainment sources and resources in unprecedented ways. Celebrity mom and baby blogs have become an active forum where women explore their maternal relationships to each other and to celebrities on a daily, even moment-to-moment, basis. In the next section, I offer a brief survey of some of these blogs before going on to examine more closely three sites which appeal, to varying degrees, to the "uncritical fan," the "cynical hip mama," and the negotiator: the *Celebrity Baby Blog*, Tori Spelling's *MySpace* blog, and *Mamarazzi*.

The *Celebrity Baby Blog*, now in its fifth year, honours itself for launching the phenomenon of celebrity maternity blogs. Creator Danielle Friedland, who lives in New Jersey, tells us that she "stumbled upon the idea for the *Celebrity Baby Blog* while watching the Golden Globes in January 2004. While reeling off facts about who was pregnant with twins (Marcia Gay Harden) or had recently given birth (Mary-Louise Parker), [her husband] Josh suggested she create a blog about the pregnancies and offspring of celebrities. After searching to see if one already existed (none did)," she "grabbed her laptop (with newly installed wi-fi internet connection) and created the first website dedicated to celebrity babies" ("About the *Celebrity Baby Blog*," November 2007). Friedland's idea was clearly a topical one, reflecting the zeitgeist for all things maternal that has been spreading for the past two decades, and so it is not surprising that other similar sites appeared in short order. In addition to the aforementioned *Mamarazzi*, a particularly irreverent blog that makes fun of its subjects, "Because Celebrity Parenting Is So Easy To Snark"[7]; and *babyrazzi*, which we are tantalizingly told is "run by a secret celebrity mom who likes to spy on her peers," there are blogs such as the following: *Celebrity BabyBlog*, "a simple weblog dedicated to celebrity babies and thier parents [sic]"; *Celebrity Baby Watch*, "All About the World's Famous Babies"; *Celebrity Babies Blog*, "Welcoming the little bundles born to be stars"; *Celebrity Babies, Celebrity Baby Pictures & Baby Blog*; *Black Celebrity Kids*, "a one stop portal for information and pictures on black celebrity kids, babies and their parents"; *Celebrity Baby Scoop*: "dishing it out daily"; *FAMEbaby*, "All the bark of celebrity parenting gossip—without the bite"; *Celebrity Pregnancy*; and *FameCrawler*, "Your Daily Baby Celebrity Fix." While this list is not exhaustive, it contains some of the most popular and successful blogs dedicated solely to the topic.

The *Celebrity Baby Blog* offers hundreds of stories as either daily features or accessed via the "Archives" tab, yet the approach to the material remains uniformly respectful because Friedland and her associates are Douglas and Michaels' "totally accepting uncritical fan."[8] The bloggers deliver straightforward reports with accompanying photos depicting celebrities as doting, hands-on mothers. The blog's friendly approach to its subjects is exemplified in a brief look at how it represents actor and mother Angelina Jolie.[9]

In one post titled "Angelina Jolie talks to Marie Claire—and Zahara knows how to work mom over!" *Celebrity Baby Blog* staff editor Sarah provides readers with highlights from the interview with the magazine, such as the following:

> "Zahara works mom over: 'Zahara is the smartass personality. The other day, Z said to me, 'I need a cookie.' I said, 'You need a cookie? You don't need a cookie!' So she says, 'Daddy gonna cry.' I ask, 'Why is Daddy going to cry?' 'Daddy wants me to have a cookie!' She's just that smart'"; "On conceiving Shiloh: 'All the girlfriends around me said, 'It's going to take an average of 6 months.' I said, 'Good, I'll schedule that into my life.' And it happened maybe our first try and there it was!'"; "On pregnancy: 'I loved being pregnant, and fortunately, I was with a man who found it really sexy too. During the weeks leading up to the birth, we would have dinner in the dunes by candlelight.... We would have tents out there. We had the ocean....'"; "On Shiloh's birth: 'Brad has a film of me in the hospital: they were trying to put the IV in me, and I began laughing so hard, with tears rolling down my face. I was out of my mind. But it was lovely. He put on an iPod, and 20 minutes later, they were like, 'OK, we are going to lift her out.' A half-hour later I was breastfeeding'" (June 1, 2007).

The material presented from this interview inscribes the new momist dictates of the celebrity profile: for Jolie, conception was instantaneous, pregnancy was romantic, breastfeeding was a breeze, and mothering is a lark. This glamourised and stress-free version of motherhood is touted as the one we should all be enviously striving for.

The *Celebrity Baby Blog's* endorsement of Jolie's maternal iconicity is both matched and challenged by its readers who, in the 109 responses this post generated, speak as middle-ground fans who negotiate with personal reflection the terrain of celebrity idolatry. The description of Zahara as a "smartass," for instance, led Penny to state that she has "reservations about using the word smartass to describe children. I think in family situations where you are conversing with another adult that you're comfortable with it would be ok. Not in an interview the world will read, it's [sic] sounds a bit trashy." Shea Clarke counters: "In my home ... being a smartass and knowing the proper way to use sarcasm, is highly regarded around here!" On the topic of adoption, Robin urges Jolie:

> I wish she would start a web blog for herself and her fans with updates on the children, their growing up, the lessons she learns from all of them. It would help other parents who are considering adopting children from other countries and what it's like to be such a special part of their lives and this experience.... Angelina, if your [sic] reading this! Come on! Do this for all of us parents, like yourself, struggling, crying, and laughing all the way through motherhood. It's a beautiful thing!

Judy, however, privileges quality time over quantity of children: "I hope she and Brad put off increasing their family by either birth or adoption for at least another year, preferably two ... so that little Pax can be fully integrated into his new culture and comfortable with his new language and country." Lastly, Lauren takes to task one reader whom she accuses of Jolie worship: "I'm sure you adore every celebrity and never say anything negative about any of them, right? If only we could all be as martyr-esque as yourself." She emphasizes: "This is not the Angelina Jolie fanlisting; it is a message board where people of differing opinions can share their thoughts" ("Angelina Jolie talks to Marie Claire—and Zahara knows how to work mom over!" June 1, 2007).

In a post for June 5, 2007, staff editor Sarah returns to the subject with "Angelina Jolie in Esquire; discusses co-sleeping and time for the kids." A portion of the interview is reproduced on the blog: "**Co-sleeping:** *Right now, Pax is sleeping in our bed. It's kind of nice, him immediately knowing and feeling comfortable with us. Mad slept with me until Brad and I got together. They're fun to sleep with. We have family sleep on Sundays. Everybody sleeps together.*" In "Your Comments" the readers engage in a vibrant discussion about co-parenting. Shmoo writes, for instance, "Great to hear about co-sleeping. It's not too private to hear about cribs, so why would it be too private to hear about co-sleeping? It's like home birthing, or breastfeeding. The more we hear about it, from AJ or whoever, the more it makes it into mainstream consciousness." Nicole agrees, "I love that she's speaking out and saying that Pax sleeps with them.... Co-sleeping is a great thing, yet it is looked down upon because so many people feel it's spoiling the child or because it's dangerous. It's only dangerous if you don't know how to do it properly" (June 6, 2007). Later in the year, Friedland herself did a feature on "The year in celebrity attachment parenting" and reposted the Jolie blurb (December

25, 2007). The reader response was overwhelmingly positive, as in this note from Marian: "Great post. I love hearing about AP celeb moms, since they encourage other mothers to try things they might not have considered (breastfeeding, cloth diapering, etc)" ("The year in celebrity attachment parenting," December 25, 2007).

This brief examination of Jolie's appearance on the *Celebrity Baby Blog* show us that on one hand Jolie epitomizes the myths of new momism promoted by the media, and in this light she is respected and adored by some of the blog's readers who aspire to her condition of blessedness while also imagining an affinity with her mothering practices and experiences, so that she is both "above" them and "just like" them. On the other hand, some readers contest what she purports to stand for, using the blog to voice their disdain for her choices and thereby reject her as a role model. Either way, readers use Jolie as the springboard to engage in a dialogue about crucial issues related to mothering, articulating and negotiating through the communal space of the blog their public as well as personal maternal perspectives.

Blogger commentary underscores Brooks' assertion, noted earlier, that when we talk about celebrities we are in fact talking about ourselves. Friedland identifies two reasons for our preoccupation with celebrity mothers: "It's something that's so humanizing.... Being a parent is such a basic sort of thing, and the love that you feel for a child is something that's universal. It's sort of a universal milestone that's always pretty much going to be the same, so people really identify with celebrities (when they become parents). The other thing is it kind of humanizes celebrities" (Matheson). This same philosophy works in the reverse as well. That is, Tori Spelling illustrates the ways that a celebrity delights in presenting herself as "humanized" in light of becoming a mother, while elevating "ordinary" women who are mothers to the status of superstars. Spelling uses her blog to promote herself as an actor (starring with her husband in the Reality TV show "Tori&Dean: Inn Love"); an author (of her memoirs *sTORI Telling* and *Mommywood*); jewelry maker; and peripatetic famous person. Perhaps most significantly, though, since becoming a mother first to son Liam and then to daughter Stella, she has used the blog to promote herself as a mother and to sing the praises of motherhood itself.

For instance, in her entry entitled "Liam's Mommy," she thanks her "MySpace friends" "for all the congratulatory messages on the arrival of Liam. Everyone has been so kind and we loved reading all your messages and comments." Returning home from the hospital, she expands upon "the most amazing week and experience" of her life:

I might be a biased mommy but he is so beautiful. I just stare at him in amazement. I can't believe I have been given this unbeliev- able little gift. I feel like the luckiest girl in the world. He is my little angel baby and I had no idea you could love someone you've only known for 4 days this much. But, my heart is jumping out of my chest with love. Mommihood ROCKS! Well, Liam needs to be fed so momma must go ... love to all of you and especially every mommy out there. I have such a new found respect for you! T xoxo. (March 17, 2007)

Spelling's "new found respect for" "every mommy out there" turns mothers into leading ladies within their own home theatres, a role em- braced by blogging sites like *Mommywood.com*, whose tag line promises to make "every mom a star!" (January 15, 2009).

Spelling's appreciation also allies her with her fans, who gleefully rel- ish her empathy while rushing to accept her into their maternal sphere. "Regina is a Little Cookie," for instance, replies "Congrats, babe. I feel like I've known you my whole life, so it's great to see you enter a new phase with positivity and grace! Happy birthday, Liam!" Katie writes, "welcome to the cool mommy club!!! we're so much hipper then our parents were and we turned out pretty rad, just wait to see what our kids will do!!"; Susie J, too, extends a "Welcome to the 'mom' club!"; and Ang returns the praise with, "For the record, I think there r some mothers out there who have a new found respect for u too. Thank you for coming on here (so soon-omg!) & letting us know how u r. We by no means expect it but we genuinely appreciate it when u do. That must mean we're doing something right..." ("Liam's Mommy," March 17, 2007). These responses signal that the relationship the fans have been imagining with Spelling have become "real" through the bond of moth- erhood and that, in turn, Spelling has garnered appreciation specifically for her "performance" as a mother.

Spelling's blog is the pay-off for and pay-back to her fans, in that she uses it to reach out to them in ways they could only fantasize about prior to the internet and blogging. Addressing her readers with "Hi friends," she offers them such personal nuggets as this note about the season finale of her TV show:

Enter Little Man Liam tomorrow night. Its a very special intimate episode that we wanted to share with all the friends and fans who have gone on this special journey with us. You'll see never before seen personal wedding footage and hear a very private audio tape of Liam's entrance into this world. I promise there won't be a dry eye in the house. Please share it with us and enjoy this final episode that is so near and dear to all 3 of us. From my family to yours.... Please tune in and enjoy!

She closes with "Love, T" (a signature she alternates with the equally affectionate "T xoxo)" ("T&D finale!" May 7, 2007). Soon after, she posts this update titled "Mother's Day," reporting: "So, yesterday was my first official Mother's Day ... And, Liam also turned 2 months old. We had alot to celebrate! It was an amazing feeling waking up knowing that I am somebody's mother. It is the one title that stays with you forever and is the greatest accomplishment anyone can ever achieve. In my opinion at least!" (May 14, 2007). Comments posted by 72 readers indicated that they agreed with her. This note from Heather echoes the general tone: "Being a mommy is truly the greatest blessing in the world. Mother's day is a very special day. It brings a whole new meaning once you become a mother yourself. Glad to hear you had a great day!! I did as well!! Take care!!!!!!" ("Mother's Day," May 14, 2007). Spelling appeals to the "accepting uncritical fan" while herself becoming an "accepting uncritical" celebrity who adores "every mommy out there." At the same time, she occupies a middle ground whereby she negotiates the "fact and fantasy" of her life as a mother and a celebrity.

Of course, not all bloggers hold celebrity mothers in high esteem. The five women who constitute the "Mamas of Razzi"—as the bloggers of *Mamarazzi.org* refer to themselves—epitomize Douglas and Michaels' "cynical hip mamas" in that they dilute with humour and irony the often saccharine taste of the celebrity mothering endorsed by Friedland and Spelling. Indeed, their blog exists solely, as the banner announces, "Because Celebrity Parenting Is So Easy to Snark." The *Urban Dictionary* defines "snark" accordingly: "Combination of 'snide' and 'remark'. Sarcastic comment(s). Use of sarcasm or malice in speech. Commonly found in the LiveJournal community" ("snark"). *Mamarazzi's* stance is made clear in the "Notice" in which we are warned that there is "much finger pointing and snickering associated with this website" (April 2006). To be sure, after a spell in which the bloggers witness seemingly *not* inappropriate behavior in celebrity parenting, they beg the stars to provide them with better fodder for their snarky mandate: "HEY CELEBS! QUIT THAT BEHAVING! DON'T MAKE US COME DOWN THERE!" ("Baby Bust," June 21, 2007).

The "finger pointing" and "snickering" is initiated by the five Razzi bloggers, all of them mothers, who are Jennifer, Kristin, LemonySarah, poppy, and susie. We have seen how the *Celebrity Baby Blog* handled Jolie's *Esquire* cover; a look at how *Mamarrazzi* reported on the same material drives home the differences between the two approaches to both fandom and motherhood. In the piece "Snarky Soup For Your Soul" one Razzi blogs: "Angelina Jolie graces the July cover of *Esquire* magazine ... and inside is one of those interviews that makes you want to throw up." She isolates the key points from the article: "*It wasn't hard for her to get pregnant"; "*Brad found pregnancy 'incredibly sexy' and she LOVED being pregnant"; "*She has a secret tattoo just for Brad ... but won't tell us where (*va-jay-jay anyone?*)." The Razzi then surmises, "Right there are 3 reasons I am guessing Angie doesn't have a lot of close girlfriends," and concludes: "The parenthetical in these types of articles always seems to be ... *we are hotter than you. Our relationship is better than yours ... and children fall from the sky into our waiting plane/uterus.*" In a self-reflexive gesture, she adds: "And so I am grateful for *Mamarazzi* and all the other sites that are dedicated to knocking the culture of celebrity on it's [sic] liposucked ass. Make that secret tattooed ass" (June 5, 2007).

The reader comments are equally sarcastic. Missy: "Stick a fork in her already. She is so done"; Susu: "There is nothing sexy about throwing up for 3 months straight!"; Jennifer: "Don't hate her because she's beautiful. Hate her because she's a husband-stealing ho"; Suzanne: "What Jennifer said"; Lissy: "Definitely, what Jennifer & Suzanne said"; Melanie: "I'm really getting sick of her and her perfect little family and perfect little life and all that. When it was perfect Reese Witherspoon, I applauded her, but Angelina seems so freaking SMUG about everything"; Jenny: "The fact that anyone says 'it was soo easy for me to get pregnant' bleck. And the tats ... WTF? Hello!!! White trash biatch [sic]. I am sick of looking at her. Completely sick of her"; DDM: "ICK! So. Sick. Of. Her. Loved the comments above, lol" ("Snarky Soup For Your Soul" June 5, 2007). This exchange, in which by laughing *at* Jolie they laugh *with* each other, underscores Cashmore's argument that fans "itch to share their enthusiasm with like-minded members of their cohort," and also supports Brooks' point that gossiping can make one feel "dramatically less stressed—in mere minutes." Words such as "SMUG," "soo," "bleck," "WTF," "ICK," and "lol" suggest that the writers are experiencing an emotional release as they yell, swear, and sound off about Jolie's reputation as the ideal mother. The readers thus reject the new momism, asserting to themselves and each other that it is a myth belying the realities of motherhood the bloggers face on a daily basis.

The snide remarks also indicate that the bloggers and readers do not particularly care for the celebrities in question, and are using them only to talk about themselves. Indeed, in addition to running *Mamarazzi. org*, Jennifer, Kristin, LemonySarah, poppy, and susie all keep personal blogs which they link to the site via their personal profiles. These blogs are titled, respectively, *Jen on the Edge*, *It's All Fun & Games*, *Lemon Life*, *The Opiate of the Masses*, and *The Underpaid Kept Woman*. It is apparent from these humorous titles alone that their blogs undercut the myth of new momism, playfully reflecting the irreverent attitudes towards the media's construction of the ideal celebrity mother which makes *Mamarazzi* so fun.

In blogging through the sensibilities of the "accepting uncritical fan," the "cynical hip mama," or the middle-ground negotiator, the bloggers examined here show us that "gossip and exposé" allow women to participate in a community—the "mommy club" noted by Spelling's fan—and use that membership to reflect on and gauge mothering practices and experiences from cultural and personal perspectives. Celebrity mothers provide these bloggers with examples of mothering that whether embraced or rejected are clearly debated, and it is in this dialogue with self and others that we understand how the stars serve as the springboard for the bloggers to articulate, define, and legitimize their own maternal values, assumptions, and prerogatives. Famous mothers, "BEHAVING" or not, inspire their non-famous counterparts to "COME DOWN THERE" to the blogosphere where they meet in symbolic and maternal terms.

Blogs can certainly be appreciated and enjoyed in these contexts discussed above. However, the fact that some bloggers reap financial gains through the running of their sites and earn pop-cultural status while doing so may be problematic. More profoundly, ethical issues challenge readers and bloggers alike to examine their roles in contributing to and endorsing a culture that commodifies, exploits, and potentially harms the children of celebrities.

Friedland, for example, began *Celebrity Baby Blog* as a lighthearted gesture to her favorite pastime—maternity star gazing—but its extraordinary popularity led her to advertisers who enabled her to transform the blog into a business. During her maternity leave from Avon Products—she gave birth to her first child, Anya, on October 14, 2005—she realized the blog was so financially successful that she quit her job and committed herself to the blog full time, employing 16 women (13 of whom are mothers) including a staff editor, senior contributors, writers, and reviewers ("About the *Celebrity Baby Blog*," November 2007). Consequently, the blog has evolved into a marketing machine: a "Shopping Guide" greets readers at the top of the home page, and the blog has recently added the *Celebrity Baby Blog VIP* section, where subscribers may "weigh in on a wide range of topics including the latest celebrity baby news, maternity style, fashion, gear, toys, beauty, shopping, advertising and more" ("Welcome," 2009). Specifically, readers are required to complete surveys while in the VIP space, the answers to which "are used to let our Marketing Department hear what you have to say, help develop new products, and improve advertising for leading brands" ("About Us," 2009). *Mamarazzi*, too, includes the header "shameless advertising" which, ironic self-awareness notwithstanding, establishes the fiscal underpinnings of the blog.

The marketing of maternity goods, services, and lifestyles leads ultimately, of course, to the marketing of the celebrity moms and tots themselves, whose images and identities are tied to brand products and are therefore necessarily commodified in the process of blogging. For instance, *Celebrity Baby Blog*'s ad for Bravado Designs nursing bras informs us that the product is used by "A-listers like Angelina Jolie, Jessica Alba, Cate Blanchett, Julia Roberts, Jennifer Garner, Christina Aguilera, Stella McCartney, and Sarah Jessica Parker" ("Shopping Guide – Bravado Designs," August 15, 2008). And in its report on Barack Obama's inauguration, *Celebrity Baby Blog* focuses on the clothes worn by daughters Malia and Sacha Obama: "Both girls wore wool coats from J. Crew's CrewCuts kids' line that were designed for the First Family and will be available in the Fall 2009 collection." A click on the Crew link takes readers to the store's website where they can place an order ("Our Beaming First Daughters," January 20, 2009).

Friedland has used her blog to track her own pregnancy and to give readers details about her daughter, complete with photo gallery, as in "Anya update: 7 months" (May 24, 2006) and "Happy Birthday Anya!" (October 14, 2006). In the former, she announces: "If you have questions about products or clothes in the photos, post a comment and I'll ad the info below." She then goes on to provide an extensive, itemized list of the brand-name goods Anya uses, such as "Blue dress with cherries (Babies R Us)" and "I Love Mom tee (Old Navy)." Friedland commodifies not only her own maternity/baby but also herself in that she has ironically and perhaps not surprisingly garnered a modicum of celebrity status. Her site won the "Best Celebrity-Obsessed Web Site" category in the 2nd Annual Lizzie Awards (2007) hosted/posted by the *washingtonpost. com* (Kelly) and she has been featured on *E!*, on VH1's "The Fabulous Life of Celebrity Kids," and in *US Weekly* (*Federated*). In a related sense, Spelling's blog, as noted earlier, is a running infomercial for her various media-related projects. Because some of these are directly related to her maternity, like her Reality TV show, and her momoir, *Mommywood*, Spelling conflates the marketing of her career with the selling of both herself and her children. Friedland hit pay-dirt in May, 2008, when she literally sold her site to *People* magazine. Although she continues to run the blog, the *People* logo and accompanying *people.com* links sit atop the *Celebrity Baby Blog* header, and ads for the magazine are spread throughout the blog.

Celebrity Baby Blog's purchase by *People* underscores the more pervasive connection between all celebrity baby blogs and the entertainment or tabloid industry. As mentioned previously, bloggers are dependent on the work of journalists who do the initial reporting, which the bloggers then respond to. In particular, bloggers rely on images obtained by the paparazzi via their notoriously intrusive and increasingly threatening, stalker-like techniques; the images can earn the photographers upwards of thousands, even hundreds of thousands of dollars. When bloggers post or reproduce these pictures on their sites, they participate in the (re)invasion of the stars' privacy and contribute to the fallout that may ensue for the photographed subject, such as being embarrassed, humiliated, or simply "captured" and exposed in an ordinary moment of assumed privacy. Even Friedland's seeming respectful *Celebrity Baby Blog* is predicated on such shots. In short, celebrity mom and baby blogs all are, to varying degrees, implicated in condoning and endorsing the tactics and maneuvers of the tabloid industry.

Blogging is a form of life writing in which the genres of auto/biography intersect as the blogger inscribes details of her own life while also telling the story of other people's lives. In the case of celebrity mom and baby blogs, multiple auto/biographies of mothers and children are recorded. Life writing scholars have of late been especially concerned with the ethical implications of writing about subjects without their knowledge or permission. Paul John Eakin and Janet Malcolm, for instance, question whether we can ever own the stories of our lives, and posit that in our cultural climate of prurient interest in and ability to access information about others, the answer is a resounding "no." G. Thomas Couser refers to those who are unable to speak for themselves or to grant consent to others to speak for them as "vulnerable," and he includes children within this category. While adult celebrities are presumably aware of the consequences related to fame, and knowingly put themselves at risk of media persecution, their children are not and do not, and should not be considered fair game by the press. These ethical issues have become a topic of debate in articles like "Julia Roberts: Leave my kids alone" (*All the Rage*, January 7, 2008) and "In tot pursuit—do the children of celebrities have rights?" (Elder and Byrne), which discuss how famous offspring are now considered big, and exploitable, business. Quoted in both pieces, actor Roberts likely speaks for many of her colleagues when she voices her contempt for the paparazzi: "I think it is inhuman to chase a woman with her children." Would, and should, this indictment apply to bloggers as well?

It is easy to get caught up in the global village or water cooler gossip about celebrities and their children. However, bloggers and their readers must weigh their interests in forming networks and communities, and being entertained and entertaining, with recognition of how celebrity-driven blogs function as an extension of the viral tabloid industry. Blogging about celebrity maternity has implications for how we condone and trivialize the commodification of those "vulnerable" subjects: the children. Within the cultural exchange of the blogging universe, some celebrities do control and even "sell" the facts of their lives, as evidenced by Spelling. More persistently, though, celebrity mothers and children own neither the mediated stories nor the images of their lives, but rather are burgled by the bloggers for the bloggers' own amusement and even profit.[10] In such a light, we can invert the quotation which heads this chapter to reflect the perspectives of celebrity mothers like Roberts: "HEY BLOGGERS! QUIT THAT MISBEHAVING! DON'T MAKE US COME DOWN THERE!"

[1] *Mamarazzi*, "Baby Bust," June 21, 2007.
[2] See respectively *Tori Spelling & Dean McDermott Official Site blog*, <http://blog.myspace.com/index>. Path: blogs; Tori Spelling; <www.britneyspears.com>; <http://goop.com>.
[3] Cashmore draws on studies by Fraser and Brown, "Media, Celebrities, and Social Influence: Identification with Elvis Presley," *Mass Communication and Society*, 1 (2) (May 2002): 183-207; Neil Alperstein, "Imaginary Social Relationships with Celebrities Appearing in Television Commercials," *Journal of Broadcasting and Electronic Media*, 35 (1) (Winter 1991), unnumbered; and Susan Boon and Christine Lomore, "Admirer-Celebrity Relationships Among Young Adults," *Human Communication Research*, 3 (2001): 432-65.
[4] The audience for the *Celebrity Baby Blog*, for instance, breaks down accordingly: 99 percent are female; 95 percent are between the ages of 18-39; 35 percent have an annual income of $75,000 or higher; and 83 percent have one or more children (*Federated Media Publishing*, "Celebrity Baby Blog," June 4, 2008).

[5]See, also, Cashmore (85-88).

[6]Cashmore draws attention to the moment when, in 1962, Elizabeth Taylor (a married mother) was photographed kissing Richard Burton (a married father), leading to a seismic shift in the expectations of fans: "After glimpsing the stars in the raw, so to speak, audiences would never be satisfied with lush, dreamy portraits that had been such staples of show business." As a result, with the paparazzi suddenly on the prowl, "Scarcely credible as it was, onlookers watched the hitherto untouchable stars dissolve into characters who bore a remarkable resemblance to themselves." This resemblance made the stars only more fascinating (22-23).

[7]This quotation, and almost all of the ones which follow in the paragraph, appear in the title headers of the respective blogs. The two exceptions are *babyrazzi* ("About," 2008) and *Black Celebrity Kids* ("About," November 2007).

[8]Friedland calls for strict "ground rules" which contribute to the respectful tone of the blog: "We encourage open dialogue but inevitably things get out of control so we ask that you keep your comments relevant to the post and refrain from making nasty remarks about anyone—the celebrities and their children, the staff of the *Celebrity Baby Blog*, other readers, and anyone, in general. You are free to agree or disagree with each other, but please do so respectfully" (*"Celebrity Baby Blog* ground rules," March, 2005).

[9]Jolie, an actor as well as humanitarian, is perhaps most famous as a mother (to adopted children Maddox, Zahara, and Pax, and biological children Shiloh, Vivienne, and Knox) and partner to actor Brad Pitt.

[10]Malcolm argues that, "The biographer at work, indeed, is like the professional burglar" (8-9).

Works Cited

All the Rage. Retrieved January 10, 2009. <http://latimesblogs.latimes.com/alltherage/2008/01/julia-roberts-l.html>.

Babyrazzi. Retrieved May 2008 to present. <www.babyrazzi.com>.

Black Celebrity Kids. Retrieved January 5, 2009. <www.blackcelebkids.com>.

"Blog." *Blogger.* Retrieved May 10, 2008. <www.blogger.com/tour_start.g>.

Britney Spears. Retrieved January 5, 2009. <www.britneyspears.com>.

Brooks, Carol. "What celebrity worship says about us." *USA Today.* September 13, 2004. Retrieved May 25, 2008. <http://www.usatoday.

com/news/opinion/editorials/2004-09-13-celebrity-edit_x.htm>.

Cashmore, Ellis. *Celebrity/Culture*. Oxford: Routledge, 2006.

Celebrity Babies Blog. Retrieved June 4, 2008. <www.celebritybabies. info>.

Celebrity Babies, Celebrity Baby Pictures & Baby Blog. Retrieved June 4, 2008. <www.celebritybabies.org>.

Celebrity Baby Blog. Retrieved June 2008 to present. <www.celebrity-babies.com>.

Celebrity Baby Blog VIP. Retrieved January 5, 2009. <www.celebrity-babiesvips.com>.

Celebrity BabyBlog. Retrieved June 4, 2008. <www.celebrity.babyblog. com>.

Celebrity Baby Scoop. Retrieved June 4, 2008. <www.celebritybabyscoop. com>.

Celebrity Baby Watch. Retrieved June 4, 2008. <www.celebritybaby-watch.com>.

Celebrity Pregnancy. Retrieved June 4, 2008. <http://celebritypregnancy. com>.

Celeste, Reni. "Screen Idols: The Tragedy of Falling Stars." *Journal of Popular Film & Television* Vol 33: 1 (Spring 2005). Retrieved May 10, 2008. http://O-proquest.umi.com.innopac.lib.ryerson.ca/.

Couser, Thomas G. *Vulnerable Subjects: Ethics and Life Writing*. Ithaca: Cornell UP, 2004.

Douglas, Susan J., and Meredith W. Michaels. *The Mommy Myth*. New York: Free Press, 2004.

Eakin, Paul John, ed. *The Ethics of Life Writing*. Ithaca: Cornell University Press, 2004.

Elder, John, and Megan Byrne. "In tot pursuit – do the children of celebrities have rights?" *The Age*. January 6, 2008. Retrieved January 10, 2009. www.theage.com.au/articles/2008/01/05/1198950131139.html.

FAMEbaby. Retrieved June 4, 2008. <http://blogs.parentcenter.babycenter. com/celebrities>.

Federated Media Publishing. Retrieved May 25, 2008. www.federated-media.net/authors/cbb.

Goop. Retrieved January 5, 2009. <http://goop.com>.

It's All Fun & Games. Retrieved January 5, 2009. <www.kkfast.blogspot. com>.

Jen on the Edge. Retrieved January 5, 2009. <http://jenontheedge. com>.

Kelly, Liz. "2nd Annual Lizzie Awards: Winners." "Celebritology." *Washingtonpost.com*. July 9, 2007. Retrieved June 6, 2008. <http://

blog.washingtonpost.com/celebritology/2007/07/2nd_annual_lizzie_ awards_winne.html>.

Lemon Life. Retrieved January 5, 2009. <www.lemonysarah.blogspot. com>.

Malcolm, Janet. *The Silent Woman: Sylvia Plath and Ted Hughes*. New York: Vintage, 1995.

Mamarazzi. Retrieved May 2008 to present. <www.mamarazzi.org>.

Matheson, Whitney. "A chat with ... Celebrity Baby blogger Danielle Friedland." *USA Today.com*, 11 December 2006. Retrieved June 6, 2008. <http://blogs.usatoday.com/popcandy/2006/12/a_chat_with_cel. html>.

Mommywood. Retrieved January 5, 2009. <www.mommywood.com>.

Opiate of the Masses, The. Retrieved January 5, 2009. <http://poppisima. blogspot.com>.

"Snark." *Urban Dictionary*. May 5, 2008. Retrieved June 2, 2008. <www. urbandictionary.com/define.php?term=snark>.

Tori Spelling & Dean McDermott Official Site blog. Retrieved May 25, 2008. <http://blog.myspace.com/index>. Path: blogs; Tori Spelling.

Underpaid Kept Woman, The. Retrieved January 5, 2009. <http://underpaidkeptwoman.blogspot.com>.

Contributor Notes

Liza Barry-Kessler is the founder and coordinator of the blog aggregator web site <http://www.lesbianfamily.org>. She has been blogging since January 2005, and her personal blog, <http://www.lizawashere.com>, won a 2006 Weblog Award in the "Best of the Rest" category. Liza also blogs with <www.deepsouthmoms.com> (an affiliate of the Silicon Valley Moms Group), and somehow finds time for a day job as an attorney. She and her partner have a toddler son and baby daughter.

Shana L. Calixte is a Ph.D. candidate in the School of Women's Studies at York University and a sessional lecturer in the Department of Women's Studies at Laurentian University. Her current academic work is focused on examining the histories of Caribbean Girl Guide associations, girlhood, sexuality, and HIV/AIDS education. She is also reconnecting with her love of Hip Hop music, and has recently taught a course entitled: "Theorizing Hip Hop Feminisms: Race, Gender and Sexuality." She lives with her partner and son, Dré, in Sudbury.

Catherine Connors (Ph.D./ABD) is a former sessional instructor in the Department of Political Science at the University of Toronto. She blogs as *Her Bad Mother* at <www.badladies.blogspot.com>, is the founding editor of MommyBlogsToronto.com, is a contributing writer and editor at *BlogHer.com, Babble.com*, and *MamaPop.com*, and is currently at work on a book on how parenting and motherhood have been understood in the canon of ancient and modern political philosophy. These, however, are just hobbies: her real job is Chief Household Officer and First Attendant to her little girl and baby boy.

Ann Douglas was part of the passionate and opinionated team who spoke about mothers and blogging at the Motherlode Conference in 2006. She has reported on trends in mother blogging for *Canadian Family* magazine and blogs weekly about parenting issues for ParentCentral.ca. The author of the bestselling *The Mother of All Pregnancy Books* and numerous other books about pregnancy, birth, and mothering, Ann is also the author (with her daughter Julie) of the award-winning pre-teen body image book *Body Talk: The Straight Facts on Fitness, Nutrition, and Feeling Great About Yourself.* She and her husband Neil live in Peterborough, Ontario, with their four kids, ages 11 through 21.

Lisa Ferris earned a Master's in Education from the University of Kansas, specializing in the education of students with severe and multiple disabilities before working as a disability advocate. She worked at Oregon Health and Sciences University as a researcher and disability advocate, and also has worked in the health care field providing direct care to children and adults with disabilities. She currently works as a freelance writer while raising her twin boys in Portland, Oregon. She can be found online at <www.twinklelittlestar.typepad.com>.

Dawn Friedman lives and writes in Columbus, Ohio. Her work has appeared in publications including *Yoga Journal, Brain Child, Utne, Ode* and *Salon.com.* She blogs at <thiswomanswork.com> and is also the founder of OpenAdoptionSupport.com, a site for anyone interested in openness in adoption.

May Friedman lives in downtown Toronto with her partner and delicious kids, Molly and Noah. She is a devoted reader of mommyblogs, a skill she hopes to put to good use in her forthcoming dissertation on the topic. When she's not surfing the web, May can be seen juggling parenthood, academic work and social work while teaching at both York and Ryerson Universities.

Jennifer Gilbert is a childfree manuscript editor whose hobbies are roller derby, writing, and dodging awkward questions at baby showers. She lives in St. Louis with her dear husband and two pet rabbits, all of whom are cute, mischievous, and very spoiled. Before she dies, she wants to finish at least one novel, become enormously wealthy, and finally convince society that the sight of baby booties do not give her maternal urges. (Note: none of these goals may actually be possible.)

Jillian Johnson is a young, radical, queer, mama blogger from Durham, North Carolina. She is a 2003 graduate of Duke University and a sometimes Ph.D. student at the University of North Carolina at Chapel Hill. Her academic work focuses on Palestinian-led nonviolent resistance movements in the West Bank and Gaza Strip and the cultural life of diverse political movements. In working life, she runs a small non-profit organization that promotes progressive politics among young people. Her favorite person and the inspiration for her forays into the blogosphere is her son, who is almost exclusively known as punkin-punkin.

Jen Lawrence is the voice behind the blogs, *MUBAR: Mothered Up Beyond All Recognition*, and *Dwell on These Things*. When not escorting her three-year-old and five-year-old to playdates around Toronto, she is Co-editor, *Reviews at LiteraryMama.com*. Her work has appeared in *The Toronto Star, Literary Mama* and *The Philosophical Mother*, and her essay, "Unhinged," was featured in the anthology *Between Interruptions: 30 Women Tell the Truth About Motherhood*. She is working on her first novel.

Julie Palmer completed her Ph.D. in 2007 at the Centre for Women's Studies, University of York, UK. Her doctoral thesis, titled "The Visible Techno-Foetus: Ultrasound Imagery and its Non-Medical Significances in Everyday Contexts," critically engages with a series of examples of two- and three-dimensional sonograms appearing in popular culture and the cultural and political issues they raise.

Oana Petrica is an international third-year Ph.D. Candidate at the School of Women's Studies, York University, Canada, working on gender and social reproduction in Eastern Europe, mothering practices and popular culture, transnational and postmodern feminism and feminist postcolonial scholarship connected to postsocialist/ postcommunist frames of analysis.

Elizabeth Podnieks is an Associate Professor in the Department of English and the Graduate Program in Communication and Culture at Ryerson University. Her teaching and research interests include life writing, mothering, modernism, and popular /celebrity culture. She is the author of *Daily Modernism: The Literary Diaries of Virginia Woolf, Antonia White, Elizabeth Smart, and Anaïs Nin* (McGill-Queen's University Press, 2000). She is the co-editor of *Hayford Hall: Hangovers, Erotics, and Modernist Aesthetics* (Southern Illinois University Press, 2005). She is the sole editor of two special issues of *a/b: Auto/Biography Studies*: "Private Life, Public Text: Women's Diary Literature" (Summer 2002), and "Contemporary Approaches to Biography" (Fall 2009). Podnieks has recently submitted to the Wilfrid Laurier University Press the manuscript *Textual Mothers, Maternal Texts: Motherhood in Twentieth- and Twenty-First-Century Women's Literatures,* a collection of scholarly essays co-edited with Andrea O'Reilly (York University). She is also preparing the sole-edited collection entitled *Mediated Moms: Mothering in Popular Culture,* for which she is writing a chapter on representations of celebrity mothers in entertainment magazines.

Judith Stadtman Tucker is a writer and activist. She is the founder and editor of the Mothers Movement Online, a web-based independent media project offering resources and reporting on motherhood as a social issue. Prior to founding the MMO, she created and published the proto-blog, Cybermommy.com, a primer on internet technology and locating quality information on the World Wide Web for newly wired women. She has also contributed articles on women, work, family, public policy, and feminist motherhood to numerous print and online publications. She lives in New Hampshire, U.S.A.

Melissa Camara Wilkins lives in Southern California with her husband and four children. Her writing about contemporary motherhood has appeared in print and online publications, including The Mothers Movement Online and Mamazine.com. Melissa blogs at <www.MakingThingsUp. com>.